Study and Listening Guide

For

Concise History of Western Music
Second Edition

And

Norton Anthology of Western Music
Fourth Edition

STUDY AND LISTENING GUIDE

FOR

CONCISE HISTORY OF WESTERN MUSIC
SECOND EDITION
BY BARBARA RUSSANO HANNING

AND

NORTON ANTHOLOGY OF WESTERN MUSIC
FOURTH EDITION
BY CLAUDE V. PALISCA

J. PETER BURKHOLDER

W. W. NORTON & COMPANY
NEW YORK   LONDON

ISBN 0-393-97803-6 (pbk.)

W. W. Norton & Company, Inc.
500 Fifth Avenue, New York, N.Y. 10110
http://www.wwnorton.com

W. W. Norton & Company, Ltd.
Castle House, 75/76 Wells Street, London W1T 3QT

1 2 3 4 5 6 7 8 9 0

CONTENTS

READ THIS SECTION FIRST

The purpose of this *Study and Listening Guide* is to help you learn the material in *Concise History of Western Music,* Second Edition (CHWM), by Barbara Russano Hanning and acquaint yourself with the music in the *Norton Anthology of Western Music,* Fourth Edition (NAWM), by Claude V. Palisca. Each chapter of this *Study and Listening Guide* is coordinated with a chapter of CHWM and several pieces in NAWM.

There is much to know about the history of Western music and much to discover in the music itself. The best way to learn it is to follow some simple rules of successful learning.

1. Know your goals. It is easier to learn and to chart your progress if you know what you are trying to accomplish.
2. Proceed from what you know to what is new or less familiar. We learn best when what we are learning relates to what we already know. Thus it is usually easiest to start with the big picture and proceed from the general to the specific, from the main points to the details; this helps us see quickly how each element relates to the others, and what is most important. But it is also helpful to get to know a single example and discover broader principles by looking at it closely; indeed, broad statements may not be meaningful or clear until we have a concrete example.
3. Do not try to do everything at once. Trying to do too much, too fast makes learning difficult and frustrating. Divide the task into units small enough to grasp at one sitting. Do not cram for tests; study every day.
4. Write down what you learn. You will retain information and concepts much more readily if you write them down for yourself rather than merely read them or hear them or highlight them in a book. The mental act of putting ideas into your own words and the physical act of writing out names, terms, dates, and other information create multiple pathways in your brain for recalling what you have learned.
5. Apply what you know. You learn and retain the skills and knowledge that you use.
6. Review what you know. We learn through repetition.
7. Have fun. You learn better and remember more when you are having fun. This means allowing yourself to enjoy the process of learning, mastering, and applying concepts and skills, whether riding a bike or discovering music history.

This *Study and Listening Guide* is designed to help you do all of these, through the following features.

Chapter Objectives

Each chapter begins with an overview of what you should learn from reading the texts and studying the music. These are the central issues addressed in the chapter. When you read the objectives before studying the material, they will pinpoint what you are trying to achieve. When you reread them after you have read the chapter, studied the music, and worked through the study questions, they can help you to evaluate your achievement. They direct you to the big picture, so you do not miss the forest for the trees.

Chapter Outline

The chapter outline shows how the corresponding chapter in CHWM is divided into sections, summarizes the main points in each section, introduces important terms and names (highlighted in *italics*), and indicates which selections in NAWM relate to each topic. By reading the outline *first,* you begin with an overview of the subject. Then, as you read the chapter, the details presented there will flesh out the general concepts given in the outline. Since you have already read the main ideas in the outline, as you read the text you are beginning to review and reinforce what you have learned, while increasing the depth of your knowledge. When you have finished a section or chapter, reread the outline to make sure you grasp the main points. The outline will also be useful as you review.

Study Questions

The readings are full of information, and it may sometimes be difficult to figure out what is more and less significant. The study questions are designed to help you focus on the most important issues and concepts addressed in each section of each chapter and to apply those concepts to the music in NAWM. Material related to a question may be found in a single place in CHWM or scattered throughout the section. Relevant material may also be found in the analytical discussions of individual pieces in NAWM.

Questions are grouped by topic, and each question focuses on a single issue. This divides each chapter into units of manageable size and allows you to proceed step by step. Questions vary in kind, from fill-in-the-blank questions to short essays that ask you to synthesize material and apply it to the music, or exercises that ask you to sing or play through the music. Tackling the material in small units and doing a variety of things in each section can help to make your work more fun.

Write down your answers. Space is provided to answer the study questions in this book. Writing down what you learn, rather than merely reading or highlighting the text, will help you retain it better. This is particularly helpful for recalling terms, names, and titles in foreign languages, since spelling them out for yourself will make them more familiar. If you have trouble remembering how to spell a foreign or unfamiliar word or name, writing it several times will help you recall it.

The study questions are not review questions, to be filled in after you have finished reading and have closed the book. They are guides to the reading and to the music. After you have read a section of the text, or even while you are reading it, work through the relevant study questions, rereading the text for answers as needed. Always respond to the questions in your own words, rather than copying directly from the text; this will help you to master each concept, making it your own by phrasing it in your own way. If there is anything you do not understand, return to the reading (in CHWM, NAWM, or this *Study and Listening Guide*) to find the missing information, or ask for assistance from your instructor.

Some study questions ask you to define or to use terms that are introduced in the text. There is rote learning in every subject, and in music much of it is of terminology. Each musical repertory has its own specialized vocabulary, often borrowed from Italian, Latin, French, or German. You cannot communicate with others about this music without mastering these terms.

Many questions ask you to apply to the pieces in NAWM concepts and terms that are presented in the text. In this way you will to get to know the music better and will reinforce your grasp of the concepts and terms by applying what you know to the music itself. These study questions on the music are set off in boxes headlined *Music to Study.* Each of these subsections begins with a list of the pieces in NAWM under consideration, indicating the CD number and tracks for each piece on the recordings that accompany NAWM.

You should listen to each piece in NAWM several times, including at least once before reading about it and at least once afterward. The heart of music history is the music itself, and a major part of your study should be listening to and becoming familiar with the music.

Terms and Names to Know

Near the end of each chapter is a list of important terms and names that appear in the texts and are highlighted in italics in the chapter outline. Most of these are covered in the study questions. They are listed separately here to help you review and to test your retention of what you have learned. In addition to these names, you should know the composers and titles of the pieces you studied. Use the lists in reviewing at the end of each chapter and in reviewing for examinations.

Review Questions

Each chapter ends with review questions that ask you to reflect more generally on the material you have learned. Most of them are like essay questions that you might encounter on a test. These may be used as springboards for discussion in class or with your study group, or as essay questions to use for practice as you study for examinations. Others are exercises that ask you to pull together information from several places in the chapter.

How to Proceed

The following procedure is recommended, but any procedure that helps you learn the most effectively and efficiently is the right one for you. You might vary your approach until you find the one that works best.

1. As you start each chapter, **read the chapter objectives** first to see what is expected of you.
2. **Read through the chapter outline.** Notice the topics that are covered, the main points that are made, and the terms that are introduced. Important new terms and names are given in italics.
3. **Read the "Prelude"** at the beginning of the chapter in CHWM **and the "Postlude"** at the end. These summarize the chapter and sometimes provide historical background. (Since the "Postlude" repeats material already given, it is usually not included in the chapter outline unless it introduces new ideas or information.)
4. Now work through the chapter section by section, as marked by roman numerals in the chapter outline and centered headings in CHWM.
5. Start each section by **listening to the pieces in NAWM** that are listed in this section of the outline. Read through the text and translation before listening to vocal pieces, and listen to every piece with the score. (If you have time, you might first listen to each piece without the score, and you might also sing or play through the piece yourself.) This lets you encounter the music first, just as music. Later, you will come back to it and apply the principles you learn in reading the text.
6. Next, **read the section in CHWM,** using the chapter outline as a guide. As the text refers you to pieces in NAWM, look again at the music and read the analytical discussion of each piece.
7. **Work through the study questions** for this section. Refer again to the music when the questions direct you to do so, and study the music or review CHWM and the analytical discussions in NAWM to find the information you need to answer the questions. (Instead of reading first and then working through the study questions, you may find it more convenient to answer the study questions as you read through the text.)
8. When you have answered the study questions, **review the chapter outline** for this section and look over your answers. If there is anything you do not understand, refer back to the text, or make a note of it in the margin and ask your instructor for help.
9. **Listen to the music again,** and check your answers to the relevant study questions. Then congratulate yourself for finishing this section of the chapter. You may move on to the next section, or save it for another day.
10. At the end of the chapter, **reread the "Postlude"** in CHWM for a summary. Then **review** by checking your knowledge of the **terms and names to know,** rereading the chapter outline, and reviewing your answers to the study questions. Read the objectives again to make sure you have accomplished them. **Read the review questions** and write brief answers in outline form, or use them as practice essay questions before examinations.

NOTE TO THE INSTRUCTOR

This *Study and Listening Guide* is designed to walk the student through the material in CHWM and NAWM step by step. Not every teacher will want to include all the content covered in the texts, and each is likely to emphasize different aspects of the music and its history. Each instructor is encouraged to tailor this study guide to the needs of the individual course.

The study questions are designed to be used as guides for the student, as the basis for work in discussion sessions, or as problem sets to be handed in. There are many questions, so that each significant topic can be covered. The instructor is encouraged to select which of the questions students should do on their own, which they may omit, and which should be handed in, if any. The review questions can also be used in several ways: as guides for individual review, as model test questions, or as short writing assignments in or out of class. For courses in which this *Study and Listening Guide* is a required text, permission is granted to use any of the questions on examinations.

ACKNOWLEDGMENTS

Any book is a collaborative effort, and teaching materials are especially so. The first edition of this *Study and Listening Guide* was adapted from a similar guide, published in 1996, for *A History of Western Music,* Fifth Edition, by Donald Jay Grout and Claude V. Palisca, and the *Norton Anthology of Western Music,* Third Edition, edited by Claude V. Palisca. That guide originated in a group of study questions for the first twelve chapters of the Fourth Edition of *A History of Western Music,* which I developed in collaboration with my teaching assistants for Music History and Literature I at Indiana University School of Music in fall 1993, Brian Bourkland, Nicholas Butler, Kirk Ditzler, Gesa Kordes, and Mario Ortiz-Acuña. I am grateful for their cooperation, their suggestions, and the questions of theirs that remain here in some form.

I am grateful also to my teaching assistants in fall 1995, John Anderies, Nicholas Butler, Pablo Corá, David Lieberman, Felicia Miyakawa, and Patrick Warfield, who used the first draft of the study guide for *A History of Western Music* and offered very helpful feedback. My students and my colleagues Austin B. Caswell and Thomas Noblitt provided encouragement and useful comments. Thanks also to the late Claude V. Palisca and to Kristine Forney for advice and suggestions.

In undertaking this revision, I owe a great debt to the many instructors and students who have used the first edition and have shown me how it is helpful and what can be improved. Thanks to the staff at W. W. Norton, particularly to Claire McCabe, Kathy Talalay, Michael Ochs, and Maribeth Anderson Payne, for assistance of all kinds. Thanks finally and as always to Doug McKinney for his support and encouragement.

MUSIC IN ANCIENT GREECE AND EARLY CHRISTIAN ROME

1

CHAPTER OBJECTIVES

After you complete the reading, study of the music, and study questions for this chapter, you should be able to

1. identify several elements of Western music and theory that derive from the music of ancient Greece or Israel;
2. describe in general terms ancient Greek music and ideas about music;
3. explain why the Greeks linked music to numbers, astronomy, and poetry, and how they thought it affected a person's character and behavior; and
4. summarize early Christian attitudes toward music, including the role of music in the church, the place of music among the liberal arts, and the relation of audible music to the mathematical proportions that govern nature and humans, and explain how these views relate to ancient Greek views of music.

CHAPTER OUTLINE

Prelude (CHWM 1–3)

Knowing the history of music can help us understand it. Western culture has roots in ancient Greece and Rome. Although little ancient music has survived, ancient writings about music, particularly music theory, had a strong influence on later centuries. This ancient heritage was passed on in part through the early Christian Church. The continual influence of ancient ideas and practices on music of all later periods makes it appropriate to begin our study with music in the ancient world.

I. Music in Ancient Greek Life and Thought (CHWM 3–8, NAWM 1–2)

In ancient Greece, music was linked to the gods and divine powers.

1. Extant Greek music

About forty pieces or fragments of music survive, most from relatively late periods. Greek music was *monophonic* (in a single melodic line), but was often performed in *heterophony*. It was usually improvised or learned by ear, not read from notation.   **Music: NAWM 1**

Etude: Ancient Greek Instruments: Kithara and Aulos
There were three main instruments, played alone or to accompany singing or recitation:

1. The *lyre,* a plucked string instrument associated with Apollo;
2. The *aulos,* a reed instrument associated with Dionysus and Greek drama (as in NAWM 2);
3. The *kithara,* a larger relative of the lyre.

Music was used in religious ceremonies, and festivals and contests were also important parts of Greek musical life. *Aristotle* and others opposed the rise of professional musicians and the increasing virtuosity and complexity of music, and later Greek music became simplified.   **Music: NAWM 2**

2. Greek theory
Greek music theory had a profound effect on music of the Middle Ages. *Plato* and Aristotle wrote on the nature and uses of music, and music theorists described musical materials and ways of composing.

3. Music and number
Pythagoras (ca. 500 B.C.E.) is credited with having discovered that the basic consonant intervals were produced by simple number ratios of 2:1 for the octave, 3:2 for the fifth, and 4:3 for the fourth.

4. Music and poetry
Music was closely tied to poetry, which was usually sung. The rhythms of a melody followed the rhythms of its text, and the pitch contour often followed the inflections of a speaking voice.

5. The doctrine of *ethos*
The Greeks held that music could directly affect character (*ethos,* related to the English word "ethics") and behavior.

6. Theory of imitation
Aristotle wrote that music represents the *passions* or states of the soul and arouses passions in the listener. He felt that music that stimulates undesirable attitudes should be avoided.

7. Music in education
Plato gave music an important role in education, arguing that the right kind of music disciplined the mind and aroused virtue. Aristotle also endorsed music for entertainment and for its role in drama.

8. Music and politics
Like Plato and Aristotle, the church fathers and modern politicians have opposed certain kinds of music because of the effects attributed to them.

9. The harmonic system
The Greek musical system laid the foundation for later Western systems with such concepts as notes, intervals (including tones, semitones, thirds, fourths, fifths, and octaves), scales, and modes.

10. Tetrachords
Greek scales were constructed from *tetrachords,* groups of four notes spanning a perfect fourth. There were three *genera* (plural of *genus,* meaning type) of tetrachords: *diatonic, chromatic,* and *enharmonic.*

II. The Early Christian Church: Musical Thought (CHWM 8–11)

1. Rome's decline
As the Roman empire declined and collapsed, the Christian Church became the main cultural force in Europe.

2. Church fathers
Christian writers and scholars known as the church fathers saw in music the power to inspire piety and to influence the character of listeners.

3. Dangers of music
Many early church leaders opposed listening to music for pleasure.

4. Transmission of Greek music theory
Greek theory and philosophy were summarized and passed on by early Christian writers, notably Martianus Capella and Boethius.

5. Martianus Capella
Martianus helped to codify the *seven liberal arts:* the three verbal arts called the *trivium* (grammar, dialectic or logic, and rhetoric) and the four mathematical disciplines called the *quadrivium* (geometry, arithmetic, astronomy, and harmonics, or music).

6. Boethius
The heritage of Greek music theory was transmitted to the Middle Ages primarily through *De institutione musica* (The Fundamentals of Music) by *Boethius* (ca. 480–524).

Etude: Boethius's *Fundamentals*
Boethius listed three kinds of music: *musica mundana* (cosmic music), the orderly numerical relations that control the natural world; *musica humana* (human music), which controls the human body and soul; and *musica instrumentalis,* audible music produced by voices or instruments.

III. The Early Christian Church: Musical Practice (CHWM 11–16)

The early Christian Church absorbed musical practices from Greece and other cultures, but its leaders rejected pagan uses of music and excluded instrumental music from church services.

1. The Judaic heritage
Although Christian worship was not based directly on Jewish ceremonies, there are parallels, including a symbolic sacrifice, a ceremonial meal, the reading of Scripture, the singing of *psalms,* and the practice of assigning certain readings and psalms to specific days of the calendar.

2. Christian Mass
In the Christian Mass, worshipers shared wine and bread, representing the blood and body of Christ, as his disciples did at the Last Supper.

3. Psalms and hymns

As Christianity spread, the Church absorbed influences from many areas. Among the most important were psalm singing and *hymns* as used in Syria and later cultivated in Byzantium and Milan.

4. Eastern churches

Each region of the church in the East developed its own *liturgy* (set of texts and rites). *Byzantium,* later called Constantinople, was the capital of the Eastern Roman Empire from 395 to 1453, and its musical practices influenced the West.

5. Western churches

Between the fifth and eighth centuries, each region of the Western church also developed its own liturgy in Latin.

6. Chant dialects

Along with a separate liturgy, each region had its own repertory of liturgical melodies, called *chants.* From the ninth century on, most regional dialects were replaced with a common liturgy and set of melodies authorized by *Rome,* home to the pope (the bishop of Rome).

7. Ambrosian chant

One chant dialect that survived was the Ambrosian, centered in Milan. It is named for St. Ambrose, who introduced *responsorial psalmody* to the West.

8. Responsorial psalmody

In responsorial psalmody, a soloist sings the first half of a psalm verse and the congregation responds by singing the rest.

9. Rome's musical dominance

At first, chant melodies were passed down orally; starting in the ninth century, they began to be written down. Rome was the dominant influence because several popes worked to standardize and preserve the melodies through a papal choir and the Schola cantorum, a group of teachers who trained church singers.

10. Gregorian chant

Gregorian chant is the standard repertory of liturgical chants from the ninth to the sixteenth centuries. It was named for Pope Gregory I or II.

Etude: The Restoration of Gregorian Chant

Modern editions of Gregorian chant were prepared in the late nineteenth and early twentieth centuries by monks at the Benedictine *Abbey of Solesmes* in France. Today, Latin is seldom used in Catholic services, and the chants are seldom heard.

Window: Sounding and Silent Harmony: Music and Astronomy (CHWM 14–15)

The ancient Greeks linked music and astronomy, since both depended on numerical proportions. This is embodied in Plato's notion of "the music of the spheres." These ideas persisted through the Middle Ages and Renaissance.

STUDY QUESTIONS

Music in Ancient Greek Life and Thought (CHWM 3–8, NAWM 1–2)

1. What were the three main instruments used by the ancient Greeks? For each one, how was it played, and on what occasions was it used? Which instrument was associated with Apollo, and which with Dionysus?

    a. _____

    b. _____

    c. _____

2. When did Pythagoras live? According to legend, what did he discover?

3. In Greek musical life, how was music related to or dependent upon poetry?

4. According to Plato and Aristotle, how could music affect a person's character and behavior? Why was it important that certain kinds of music be promoted and other kinds suppressed? What is the relevance of this debate for our own time?

5. What are some of the concepts in the Greek harmonic system that are part of later Western systems of music?

6. What is a *tetrachord*?

What are the three *genera* of tetrachord?

_____   _____   _____

Music to Study

NAWM 1: *Epitaph of Seikilos,* song (ca. first century C.E.)
  CD 1.1 (Concise 1.1)
NAWM 2: Euripides, *Orestes,* tragedy, excerpt: Stasimon chorus (either 408 B.C.E., the date of Euripides' play, or by third century B.C.E., the date of the papyrus on which the music is preserved)
  CD 1.2

7. How do the *Epitaph of Seikilos* (NAWM 1) and the stasimon chorus from Euripides' *Orestes* (NAWM 2) exemplify the characteristics typical of Greek music as described in CHWM, pp. 3–8 and the summary on p. 16? (Note: One way they are not typical is in being notated, rather than improvised or transmitted orally.)

The Early Christian Church: Musical Thought (CHWM 8–11)

8. What attitudes toward music were held by the leaders of the early Christian Church? How do these views compare to the views of Plato and Aristotle?

9. How does music fit into the seven liberal arts? Why is music (or harmonics) grouped with the mathematical arts, rather than with the verbal arts?

10. Why was Boethius important for music in the Middle Ages?

11. In Boethius's view, what was *musica instrumentalis,* and how did it relate to *musica mundana* and *musica humana*? How does this view compare to ancient Greek ideas about music?

The Early Christian Church: Musical Practice (CHWM 11–16)

12. What parallels do you notice between Jewish religious practices and the liturgy and music of early Christian worship?

13. How far back does hymn singing go in Christian worship?

14. When did chant melodies begin to be written down? _____

    How were they transmitted before notation was developed?

15. What is *Gregorian chant,* and what did it replace? Why is it seldom heard in Catholic churches today?

16. What is the significance of the Abbey of Solesmes for Gregorian chant?

Window: Sounding and Silent Harmony: Music and Astronomy (CHWM 14–15)

17. In the Greek conception, what were the links between music, numbers, and astronomy? How did these concepts influence European thinkers in the Middle Ages and Renaissance?

TERMS TO KNOW

Terms Related to Ancient Greek Music

lyre
aulos
kithara
monophony, heterophony

doctrine of ethos
tetrachord
genus (pl. genera): diatonic,
    chromatic, enharmonic

Terms Related to Music in the Early Christian Church

liberal arts
trivium, quadrivium
musica mundana, musica humana,
    musica instrumentalis
psalms

hymns
liturgy
chant
responsorial psalmody
Gregorian chant

NAMES TO KNOW

Pythagoras
Plato
Aristotle
Boethius

De institutione musica
Byzantium
Rome
Abbey of Solesmes

REVIEW QUESTIONS

1. According to the summary in the "Postlude" (CHWM, pp. 16–17) and other parts of the chapter, what are some basic characteristics of ancient Greek music? Which of these are shared with other ancient musical traditions?

2. What does ancient Greek music have in common with our music (including classical music of the eighteenth and nineteenth centuries and popular music of the twentieth century)? What are some similarities between Greek music and ours? What are some similarities between Greek music theory and common-practice music theory?

3. What are some Greek ideas about the power of music and its role in society that are still relevant today?

4. How did early Christian writers, including St. Augustine and Boethius, view music? How do their attitudes compare to those of the ancient Greeks, including Plato and Aristotle?

5. What are some of the sources of Gregorian chant, the repertory of melodies used in the Western church? What were the contributions of the Judaic tradition, Syria, Byzantium, and Europe? How did Gregorian chant come to be standardized?

CHANT AND SECULAR SONG IN THE MIDDLE AGES, 400–1450

2

CHAPTER OBJECTIVES

After you complete the reading, study of the music, and study questions for this chapter, you should be able to

1. describe in general terms the liturgical context for plainchant in the Roman Church, including the main outlines of the Office and the Mass;
2. read a melody in plainchant notation;
3. describe several varieties of Gregorian chant and explain how the shape and manner of performance of some chants relate to their liturgical function;
4. characterize the eight church modes by their final, tenor, and range, and identify the mode of a given chant or song;
5. name some of the kinds of secular musicians active during the Middle Ages and the regions and social classes from which they came;
6. describe some examples of medieval secular song by troubadours, trouvères, *Minnesinger,* and *Meistersinger*; and
7. name and briefly identify a few of the people who contributed to the repertory of medieval monophonic music.

CHAPTER OUTLINE

Prelude (CHWM 18–19)

Two large repertories of song survive from the Middle Ages: the chant of the church, or *plainchant,* and secular songs, including those of the *troubadours, trobairitz,* and *trouvères,* poet-composers of the twelfth and thirteenth centuries. Both repertories are mostly monophonic and were at first passed down by memory, before the development of musical notation.

I. Roman Chant and Liturgy (CHWM 19–23, NAWM 3–4)

Chant was created for religious services in the Roman Church. It reflects medieval values and faith and includes some of the oldest extant melodies.

It is also appealing in its own right and was incorporated into countless works by later composers. The shape of each chant is determined by its role in the service.

1. Liturgy

There are two main types of service in the Roman liturgy, the Office and the Mass.

2. The Office

The *Office* or *Canonical Hours* evolved from group prayer and psalm-singing. Eight services are celebrated at specified times each day, of which Matins, Lauds, and especially *Vespers* are musically the most important. Office services feature the singing of psalms and *canticles* (songs of praise from the Bible, such as the *Magnificat* at Vespers), each with an associated chant called an *antiphon*. They also include the singing of hymns and the chanting of lessons (passages from Scripture) with musical responses called *responsories*.   **Music: NAWM 4**

3. The Mass

The *Mass* is the most important service. It opens with introductory prayers and chants, continues with Bible readings, responses, and the creed, and culminates in a symbolic reenactment of the Last Supper of Jesus and his disciples. The texts for certain parts of the Mass, called the *Proper of the Mass,* change from day to day (they are "proper" to a certain day). The texts of other portions, called the *Ordinary of the Mass,* are the same each time, although the melodies may vary. (For this reason, the Proper chants are called by their function, such as Introit or Communion, while the Ordinary chants are named by their first words, such as Kyrie or Credo.) **Music: NAWM 3**

4. The notation of chant

Notation helped to standardize chant melodies and promote uniformity. (It also reduced the need for memorization and made chant easier to learn than it had been when it was passed down orally.)

Etude: Modern Chant Books and Notation

Music for the Office is in a book called the *Antiphonale,* while music for the Mass in the *Graduale.* The *Liber usualis* contains music for both. Plainchant notation uses a four-line staff, two movable clefs, and various note-shapes called *neumes,* which may indicate one or more notes.

II. Classes, Forms, and Types of Chant (CHWM 24–33, NAWM 3–7)

Chants can be classified in several ways:
  1. by the type of text (biblical or nonbiblical, prose or poetical);
  2. by the manner of performance (*antiphonal,* alternating between choirs; *responsorial,* alternating between soloist and choir; or *direct,* sung without alternation); or
  3. by the number of notes per syllable (*syllabic,* mainly one note per syllable; *neumatic,* 1–5 notes; or *melismatic,* with many syllables having many notes).

1. Text setting

   Chant melodies often reflect the inflection and rhythm of the words as well as their role in the liturgy.

2. Melodic structure

   Each melody divides into phrases and periods, following divisions in the text. Phrases tend to be archlike, rising, sustaining, then falling.

3. Chant forms

   There are three main types of form for chant: two balanced phrases, as in a psalm verse; strophic form, as in hymns; and free form.

A. *Chants of the Office*

1. Psalm tones

   Psalm tones are formulas for singing the psalms in the Office. There is one psalm tone for each of the eight church modes (plus one "wandering tone"). Most of the formula consists of recitation on the *tenor* or *reciting tone* of the mode, with an initial figure at the beginning of the first verse and cadential figures to mark the middle and end of each psalm verse.

2. Doxology

   The *Lesser Doxology,* praising the Trinity, is sung at the end of each psalm, using the same psalm tone.   **Music: NAWM 4c, 4e, 4g, and 4i**

3. Antiphonal psalmody

   In performing psalms in the Office, the half-verses alternate between two halves of the choir, a practice called *antiphonal psalmody.*

4. Antiphons

   Each psalm is paired with an antiphon (a term derived from antiphonal singing), sung before and after the psalm. There are also independent antiphons used on other occasions.   **Music: NAWM 4b, 4d, 4f, and 4h**

B. *Chants of the Mass*

1. Introit

   In the Mass, the *Introit* and *Communion* were once full psalms with antiphons (more elaborate than Office antiphons). The Introit now has only one verse plus the Doxology, and the Communion has none.   **Music: NAWM 3a and 3j**

2. Gradual and Alleluia: Responsorial performance

   The *Gradual* and *Alleluia* are responsorial, alternating between soloist (or solo group) and choir. Both are highly melismatic (note the correlation between solo performance and melismatic style), with a single verse framed by a *respond.* The respond for the Alleluia is always the word "Alleluia," ending with a long melisma called a *jubilus.* The *Tract* (a series of psalm verses in melismatic style), originally a solo song, substitutes for the Alleluia in periods of penitence. The *Offertory* was originally an antiphon with psalm, but it lost its verses and is performed responsorially. (Those chants that originated as antiphonal psalms originally accompanied actions; those performed by soloists were associated with the reading of lessons from the Bible.)   **Music: NAWM 3d, 3e, and 3g**

3. Chants of the Ordinary

The chants of the Ordinary began as syllabic melodies sung by the congregation. Now they are sung by the choir. The *Gloria* and *Credo,* with their long texts, remain mostly syllabic, while the others are more elaborate. Because of their texts, the *Kyrie, Sanctus,* and *Agnus Dei* have three-part sectional arrangements.   **Music: NAWM 3b, 3h, and 3i**

C. *Later Developments of the Chant*

Because of the rise of new cultural centers in western and central Europe and the rise of Muslim influence in the south, most important developments in European music from the ninth century to near the end of the Middle Ages took place north of the Alps.

1. Tropes

Tropes are newly composed additions to existing chants, especially Introits, Kyries, and Glorias. There are three types: adding text to existing melismas; adding music only; or adding both text and music. Tropes flourished in the tenth and eleventh centuries; later few were composed, and they were banned in the sixteenth century.   **Music: NAWM 7**

2. Sequences

Sequences were newly composed chants, usually sung after the Alleluia in the Mass. Like tropes, all but a few sequences were eliminated from the liturgy by the Council of Trent (1545–63).   **Music: NAWM 5**

Etude: Structure of the Sequence

The form of the sequence usually consists of a series of musical phrases, of which all but the first and last are repeated to new phrases of text.

3. Liturgical drama

Liturgical dramas were short dialogues set to chant and performed just prior to the Mass. Other sacred musical plays were performed outside the liturgy.   **Music: NAWM 7**

4. Hildegard of Bingen

Hildegard of Bingen (1098–1179), a famous abbess and mystic, wrote both words and music for several sequences and for the sacred music drama *Ordo virtutum* (The Virtues, ca. 1151).   **Music: NAWM 6**

III. Medieval Music Theory and Practice (CHWM 33–36)

Treatises from the eighth century through the late Middle Ages tend to focus on practical issues such as performance, notation, and the modes.

1. The church modes

Medieval theorists recognized eight *modes,* diatonic collections defined by the arrangement of whole and half steps in relation to their *final* (Latin, *finalis,* usually the last note in a melody) and their *range. Authentic modes* have a range that runs up an octave from the final; *plagal modes* run from a fourth below to a fifth above the final. There is one plagal and one authentic mode on each of four finals: D, E, F, and G. Each chant is assigned to a mode, though some early chants do not fit the theory exactly.

Etude: More about the Medieval Church Modes
Each mode also has a *tenor* or *reciting tone*. The note B was sometimes flatted, making the modes on D and F resemble modern minor and major. Some medieval theorists applied Greek names to the church modes, which were more commonly identified by number.

2. Solmization
Guido of Arezzo (ca. 991–after 1033) devised *solmization* syllables to help singers recall where whole tones and semitones occur. With some alterations, these syllables are still used.

3. The Guidonian hand
The *Guidonian hand* assigned a note to each joint of the left hand as a tool to teach notes and intervals.

4. The staff
The musical staff (which evolved from earlier systems of using lines to indicate relative pitch) allowed precise notation of relative pitch. This made it possible to learn a melody directly from the written page.

IV. Nonliturgical and Secular Monody (CHWM 36–43, NAWM 8–11)

1. Goliard songs
Early forms of secular music (from the eleventh and twelfth centuries) include *Goliard songs,* songs with Latin texts celebrating the vagabond life of students and wandering clerics called Goliards. The music that survives is too imprecise in its notation to be transcribed.

2. Conductus
Conductus is a term used for any serious, nonliturgical Latin song, sacred or secular, with a metrical text and a newly composed melody.

3. *Chansons de geste*
The *chanson de geste* was an epic narrative poem sung to melodic formulas. An example is the *Song of Roland,* the French national epic.

4. Jongleurs
Jongleurs, or *ménestrals* (minstrels), made a living as traveling musicians and performers, on the margins of society.

5. Troubadours and trouvères
Troubadours (feminine: *trobairitz*) were poet-composers active in southern France in the eleventh and twelfth centuries. They wrote in the language of the region, called *Provençal* (or *langue d'oc* or *Occitan*), and were from or associated with the aristocracy. Their counterparts in northern France, called *trouvères,* wrote in the *langue d'oïl,* the ancestor of modern French, and remained active through the thirteenth century.

6. Types of songs
The songs of both troubadours and trouvères are varied in structure and topic. Some songs may have accompanied mime or dance. Many trouvère songs include a *refrain,* a segment of text that returns in each stanza with the same melody.

7. *Robin et Marion*

Some songs were used in musical plays, such as *Jeu de Robin et de Marion* (ca. 1284) by *Adam de la Halle* (ca. 1237–ca. 1287).   **Music: NAWM 8**

8. Provençal lyrics

Many of the troubadour and trouvère songs were about love. They often depicted a kind of love—called *courtly love*—in which a discreet, unattainable woman was adored from a distance.

9. Bernart de Ventadorn

Bernart de Ventadorn (ca. 1150–ca. 1180), one of the most popular poets of his day, rose from low status to consort with aristocrats. His *canso* (song) *Can vei la lauzeta mover* is well known.   **Music: NAWM 9**

10. Typical song structure

Troubadour and trouvère poems are strophic. The melodies are mostly syllabic with a range of an octave or less. The rhythm of troubadour melodies is uncertain in the notation, but later trouvère melodies have clear rhythms. Various patterns of repetition are used, along with free composition.

11. Beatriz de Dia

Beatriz de Dia (d. ca. 1212) was a countess and trobairitz. Her canso *A chantar* shows the woman's perspective on courtly love. Each stanza has a musical form of a b a b c d b.   **Music: NAWM 10**

12. Minnesinger

The *Minnesinger* were knightly poet-composers in German lands from the twelfth through the fourteenth centuries. They sang of an idealized love (*Minne*), and their melodies are formed of phrases that repeat in orderly patterns. A common form is *Bar form*: a a b.

13. Meistersinger

The *Meistersinger* were German poet-composers of the fourteenth through sixteenth centuries, drawn from the urban middle class rather than the aristocracy. Their music was governed by rigid rules.   **Music: NAWM 11**

Window: Eleanor of Aquitaine and Her Courts of Love (CHWM 42–43)

Eleanor of Aquitaine (1122?–1204) was a member of an aristocratic family, granddaughter of a troubadour, wife and mother of kings, and a patron of troubadours and trouvères.

STUDY QUESTIONS

Roman Chant and Liturgy (CHWM 19–23)

1. What are the *Offices* or *Canonical Hours*? From what earlier practice do they derive?

2. What does the *Mass* commemorate?

3. What are the three sections of the Mass liturgy? What is the main focus of each one?

    a.

    b.

    c.

4. What is the *Ordinary of the Mass,* and what is the *Proper of the Mass*?

5. Example 2.1 in CHWM (p. 25) is a transcription in modern notation of the chant on the facing page. The plainchant notation uses a four-line staff. As in the modern five-line staff, each line stands for a pitch a third lower than the line above it, and the spaces stand for the pitches in between. The first symbol in each line is a clef; here it is a C-clef on the top line, indicating that the top line stands for middle C. What pitch does each of the following lines and spaces stand for?

    the second line from the top _____   the bottom line   _____

    the space below it   _____   the space below it _____

    In plainchant notation, what does a dot after a note signify? (Note: This is a sign added by modern editors and does not appear in medieval manuscripts.)

Musical exercise in reading chant notation (**CHWM 24–25**)

You do not have to know the names of the different note-shapes. But with a little practice you should be able to read the chant notation. Practice in the following way:

Reading the modern notation in Example 2.1, sing or play on an instrument the first phrase of the chant (the top line of the example). You may omit the words if it is easier for you to do so.

Then sing (or play) the same phrase, using the plainchant notation. Go back and forth between the two ways to notate the phrase until you understand how the plainchant notation indicates the same pitches and rhythms as the modern notation. If you have trouble reading any of the note-shapes, check the explanation in the text on p. 23 of CHWM or p. 7 of NAWM.

Go through the same process for each phrase in turn: sing (or play) it first from the modern notation, then from the plainchant notation.

When you are finished, sing (or play) through the whole chant from the plainchant notation. If you get stuck, refer to the modern transcription.

Classes, Forms, and Types of Chant (CHWM 24–33, NAWM 3–7)

6. What manner of performance does each of the following terms describe?

   antiphonal

   responsorial

   direct

   Which type is most often associated with melismatic chants? _____

7. Which of the following chants are from the Mass Ordinary, and which are from the Proper?

Introit	_____	Credo	_____
Kyrie	_____	Offertory	_____
Gloria	_____	Sanctus	_____
Gradual	_____	Agnus Dei	_____
Alleluia	_____	Communion	_____

Music to Study

NAWM 3: Mass for Christmas Day, in Gregorian chant

3a: Introit: *Puer natus est nobis*	CD 1.3
3b: Kyrie	CD 1.4 (Concise 1.2)
3c: Gloria	CD 1.5
3d: Gradual: *Viderunt omnes*	CD 1.6–7
3e: Alleluia *Dies sanctificatus*	CD 1.8
3f: Credo	CD 1.9
3g: Offertory: *Tui sunt caeli*	CD 1.10
3h: Sanctus	CD 1.11
3i: Agnus Dei	CD 1.12 (Concise 1.3)
3j: Communion: *Viderunt omnes*	CD 1.13
3k: Ite, missa est	(Not on recording)

NAWM 4: Office of Second Vespers, Nativity of Our Lord (evening service on Christmas Day), in Gregorian chant

4b: Antiphon for first psalm	CD 1.14 (Concise 1.4)
4c: First psalm	CD 1.15 (Concise 1.5)
4j: Short Responsory: *Verbum caro*	CD 1.16
(other sections not on recording)	

8. Look at the chants of the Mass and Office in NAWM 3 and 4. Find and list two examples of primarily *syllabic* chants, two *melismatic* chants, and two that are *neumatic,* frequently using more than two notes per syllable but rarely using long melismas.

    syllabic   neumatic   melismatic

    _____   _____   _____

    _____   _____   _____

9. What are some ways that the music of chant reflects the accentuation and phrasing of the text? For each way you mention, find an example among the chants of the Mass and Office in NAWM 3 and 4.

10. What are *psalm tones*? Where are they used?

11. How are psalm tones shaped, and how do they adjust to suit the many different texts they are used with? Give an example from NAWM 4.

12. What is an *antiphon*? Diagram the way an antiphon and psalm would be performed in the Vespers in NAWM 4, using A for antiphon, V for each psalm verse, and D for the Lesser Doxology.

13. The Introit, Offertory, and Communion were all once antiphons with psalms. What is the structure of each now? (Use the same symbols as in question 12 above.)

   Introit _____   Communion _____

   Offertory _____

14. How is the Alleluia in NAWM 3e shaped by musical repetition?

   Which parts are sung by the soloist(s)? _____

   Which parts are sung by the choir? _____

   What is the *jubilus*? _____

15. What is the pattern of musical repetition in the Kyrie in NAWM 3b (as it is performed)? How does this relate to the pattern of repetition in the text?

16. What is a *trope*? What are the three types of trope?

17. Why are there no tropes and so few sequences in the modern liturgy?

Music to Study

> **NAWM 5:** Wipo, *Victimae paschali laudes,* sequence for Mass on Easter
> Day (first half of the eleventh century)
> CD 1.17 (Concise 1.6)
> **NAWM 6:** Hildegard of Bingen, *Ordo virtutum* (The Virtues), sacred music
> drama (ca. 1151), excerpt: closing chorus, *In principio omnes*
> CD 1.18–19 (Concise 1.7–8)
> **NAWM 7:** *Quem quaeritis in praesepe,* trope (liturgical drama) at Mass on
> Christmas Day (tenth century)
> CD 1.20

18. Diagram the form of the sequence *Victimae paschali laudes* (NAWM 5). Use
a new letter for each new melodic segment (a for the first line of text, b for
the second, and so on), and repeat that letter when a segment of melody
repeats with a new text.

In addition to the repetition of complete phrases for successive verses, where
else does melodic repetition appear in this sequence?

19. How is melodic repetition used in Hildegard of Bingen's *In principio omnes*
(NAWM 6)? How does this song differ from liturgical chant in function and
in style?

---

20. In what sense is *Quem quaeritis in praesepe* (NAWM 7) a trope? Where does it fit in the Mass to which it is attached?

21. What makes *Quem quaeritis in praesepe* a *liturgical drama*? (In what sense is it liturgical? In what sense is it a drama?)

Medieval Music Theory and Practice (CHWM 33–36)

22. The eight church modes are labeled by number and name. Each is defined by (1) its *finalis* or *final,* (2) its *tenor* or *reciting tone,* and (3) its *range.* Give the name, final, tenor, and range for each of the church modes.

Number	Name	Final	Tenor	Range
1				
2				
3				
4				
5				
6				
7				
8				

23. Which modes are *authentic* (indicate by number)? _____

Which are *plagal*? _____

What is does a plagal mode share with its corresponding authentic mode?

How does it differ?

24. Using the criteria of final and range, identify by number the mode of each of the following chants:

   Quem quaeritis in praesepe (NAWM 7)   _____

   Alleluia Pascha nostrum (NAWM 15a)   _____

   Conditor alme siderum (NAWM 28, verse 1)   _____

25. What is *solmization*? Why was it useful? When was it invented, and by whom? How is modern solmization similar to medieval practice? How does it differ?

Nonliturgical and Secular Monody (CHWM 36–43, NAWM 8–11)

26. Who were the *Goliards*? Who were the *jongleurs* or *minstrels*? What kinds of music did each perform, and when and where did they perform it?

27. What is a *conductus*? How does it differ from a liturgical chant?

28. What is a *troubadour*? A *trobairitz*? A *trouvère*? When were they active, and what languages did they use? From what social classes did they come?

29. What is *courtly love*?

30. Who were the *Minnesinger*? When and where were they active? How are their songs like troubadour and trouvère songs, and how do they differ?

31. Who were the *Meistersinger*? When and where were they active?

Music to Study

> **NAWM 8:** Adam de la Halle, *Robins m'aime,* rondeau or trouvère song, from *Jeu de Robin et de Marion* (ca. 1284)
>> CD 1.21
>
> **NAWM 9:** Bernart de Ventadorn, *Can vei la lauzeta mover,* troubadour song (ca. 1170–80)
>> CD 1.22 (Concise 1.9)
>
> **NAWM 10:** Beatriz de Dia, *A chantar,* canso or troubadour song (second half of twelfth century)
>> CD 1.23
>
> **NAWM 11:** Hans Sachs, *Nachdem David war redlich,* Meisterlied (ca. 1520–76)
>> CD 1.24

32. Describe the melodic characteristics of troubadour songs, using Bernart de Ventadorn's *Can vei* (NAWM 9) and Comtessa Beatriz de Dia's *A chantar* (NAWM 10) as examples.

How many notes are set to each syllable? _____

How large a range does the melody typically cover? _____

Does the notation indicate the rhythm? _____

How else would you describe the melodic style?

33. How is the trouvère song *Robins m'aime* (NAWM 8) by Adam de la Halle different in style from the troubadour songs (NAWM 9–10)?

   How is it similar?

34. How do *Can vei, A chantar,* and *Robins m'aime* use melodic repetition? Chart the form of each (for the first two, chart the form of a single strophe; for the third, use capital letters for repetitions of music *and* text, and lower-case letters for repetitions of music with new words).

   Can vei   _____

   A chantar   _____

   Robins m'aime _____

35. What is the mode of each of these songs? (Use the mode number.)

   Can vei   _____

   A chantar   _____

   Robins m'aime _____

36. What is *Bar form*? How is it used in Hans Sachs's Meisterlied *Nachdem David war redlich* (NAWM 12)?

TERMS TO KNOW

In part because the Middle Ages are so long ago and the culture so distant from our own, there are many unfamiliar terms that relate to the music of this period. They are listed below in three groups. The terms related to liturgy will be useful for church music of later periods as well, since the liturgy has shaped church music of every period down to our own time.

Terms Related to Liturgy

Office or Canonical Hours
Vespers
canticle
Magnificat
Mass
Proper of the Mass: Introit, Gradual, Alleluia or Tract, Offertory, Communion

Ordinary of the Mass: Kyrie, Gloria, Credo, Sanctus, Agnus Dei, Ite, missa est or Benedicamus Domino
Lesser Doxology (Gloria Patri)

Terms Related to Chant

plainchant
antiphon
responsory
neume
antiphonal, responsorial, or direct performance
syllabic, neumatic, melismatic
psalm tone
tenor or reciting tone
antiphonal psalmody

respond
jubilus
trope
sequence
liturgical drama
mode: the eight church modes
final (finalis), range
authentic mode, plagal mode
solmization
Guidonian hand

Terms Related to Other Monophonic Music

Goliard song
conductus
chanson de geste
jongleur or ménestral (minstrel)
troubadour, trobairitz
Provençal (langue d'oc)
trouvère

langue d'oïl
refrain
courtly love
canso
Minnesinger
Bar form
Meistersinger

NAMES TO KNOW

Liber usualis
Hildegard of Bingen
Guido of Arezzo
Song of Roland

Adam de la Halle
Bernart de Ventadorn
Beatriz de Dia
Eleanor of Aquitaine

REVIEW QUESTIONS

1. Make a time-line from 800 to 1600 and locate on it the pieces in NAWM 5–11, their composers, and the Council of Trent and Guido of Arezzo. (The chants in NAWM 3–4 come from many centuries and most cannot be dated accurately, so they cannot be fixed on your time-line.)

2. Why was notation devised, and how was it useful? How would your life as a musician be different if there was no notation?

3. How has the music of chant been shaped by its role in the ceremonies and liturgy of the Roman Church, by the texts, and by the manner in which it has been performed? Use as examples at least two individual chants of varying types, and show in what ways the musical characteristics of each are appropriate for its liturgical role, its text, and its manner of performance.

4. Describe at least three practical contributions to the theory and performance of monophonic music that were made between the seventh and the twelfth centuries.

5. Trace the history of monophonic secular song from the Goliards to the Meistersinger. For each group of poet-composers, note their region, language, place in society, and time of activity, and briefly describe their music, using the examples in NAWM 8–11 as appropriate.

POLYPHONIC MUSIC FROM ITS BEGINNINGS THROUGH THE THIRTEENTH CENTURY

CHAPTER OBJECTIVES

After you complete the reading, study of the music, and study questions for this chapter, you should be able to

1. name the new trends in eleventh-century music that became distinguishing characteristics of Western music;
2. describe the varieties of polyphony practiced between the ninth and thirteenth centuries and trace their historical development;
3. define important terms and identify the people, works, and schools of composition that played a major role in the development of medieval polyphony; and
4. describe the origins and early evolution of the motet.

CHAPTER OUTLINE

Prelude (CHWM 45–46)

The eleventh and twelfth centuries brought prosperity and cultural revival, including in scholarship and the arts, to much of western Europe.

1. Polyphony
Polyphony, music of two or more independent voices, arose in church music and set the stage for the later evolution of Western music.

2. Composition
The development of precise notation allowed composers for the first time to fix a work in definitive form and transmit it accurately to others. As a result, written composition began to replace improvisation as a way to create new works. The main types of polyphony in the Middle Ages were *organum, conductus,* and *motet.*

I. Early Organum (CHWM 47–51, NAWM 13–14)

Polyphony was probably improvised before it was written down. It was first described in the ninth-century treatise *Musica enchiriadis*. In the early polyphony described there, called *organum,* an added voice (*organal voice* or *vox organalis*) appears below a chant melody (*principal voice* or *vox principalis*), moving either in parallel motion at the interval of a fourth or fifth (*parallel organum*) or in a mixture of parallel and oblique motion (*organum with oblique motion*). In *eleventh-century organum* (also called *note-against-note organum*), the added voice is usually above the chant (although the voices may cross), moving most often in contrary motion to the chant and forming consonant intervals with it (unison, fourth, fifth, and octave).

1. Winchester Troper
The oldest collection of pieces in this style is the *Winchester Troper* (eleventh century). Instructions on how to compose or improvise organum of this type are preserved in the treatise *Ad organum faciendum* (To Make Organum, ca. 1100). Only those portions of chant that were sung by soloists were set polyphonically, so that in performance sections of polyphony alternate with sections of chant sung by the choir.   **Music: NAWM 13**

2. Florid organum
New types of polyphony, called *Aquitanian polyphony,* appeared early in the twelfth century in Aquitaine, a region now in southwestern France. In *florid organum,* the chant is sustained in long notes in the lower voice (called the *tenor*), while the upper voice sings from one to many notes above each tenor note.

3. Organum purum
This texture came to be known as *organum, organum duplum* (double organum), or *organum purum* (pure organum). *Organum* (pl. *organa*) was also used to refer to a piece that used this style.   **Music: NAWM 14**

4. Discant
A style in which voices move mainly note-against-note was called *discant.*

5. Notation of organum
Manuscripts for these types of polyphony use *score notation* (one part above the other, with notes that sound together aligned vertically), but do not indicate rhythm or duration.

II. Notre Dame Organum (CHWM 51–57, NAWM 15a–c, 15e, 16)

1. Léonin
Léonin (ca. 1135–ca. 1201) and *Pérotin* (fl. 1180–ca. 1207) worked in Paris at Notre Dame Cathedral, the center for a style of music known today as *Notre Dame polyphony.* (We know their names because a treatise known as *Anonymous IV* describes their music and names some of their works.) Léonin wrote or compiled the *Magnus liber organi* (Great Book of Organum), a cycle of organa for the solo portions of the Graduals, Alleluias, and Office Responsories for major feasts for the entire church year.

Etude: A Summary of the Rhythmic Modes

A notation to indicate patterns of long and short notes was developed during the twelfth and early thirteenth centuries. By about 1250, these patterns were codified as the six *rhythmic modes*. The modes were based on divisions of a three-fold unit called a *perfection*. Each mode was indicated by a different succession of note groupings or *ligatures*.

2. *Alleluia Pascha nostrum*

The Easter chant *Alleluia Pascha nostrum* (NAWM 15) shows several layers of elaboration. The first is Léonin's addition of organa for the solo portions. His organa are in two voices and alternate sections of organum, in which the upper voice may be in free rhythm, with sections in discant style, in which both voices use the rhythmic modes (the slow fifth mode in the tenor, a faster mode in the upper voice). **Music: NAWM 15a–c**

3. Clausula

A section in discant is called a *clausula* (pl. *clausulae*). Clausulae are used where there are melismas in the original chant.

4. Pérotin

Pérotin and his contemporaries revised Léonin's *Magnus liber,* writing discant clausulae to replace sections of organum.

5. Substitute clausulae

They also replaced older discant clausulae with new ones, which today are called *substitute clausulae*. The tenors in Pérotin's clausulae often repeat rhythmic patterns and segments of melody. **Music: NAWM 15c**

6. Triple and quadruple organum

Pérotin also wrote organa in three and four voices, called *organum triplum* and *organum quadruplum* respectively, in which the upper parts are in the rhythmic modes over sustained notes in the tenor. The second voice (reading up from the bottom) was called the *duplum,* the third the *triplum,* and the fourth the *quadruplum*. **Music: NAWM 16**

III. Polyphonic Conductus (CHWM 57–58, NAWM 17)

The *polyphonic conductus* is a setting of a metrical Latin poem, like the earlier monophonic conductus, and can be sacred or secular. The tenor is newly written, not based on chant. The two, three, or four voices move in similar rhythm and declaim the text together, in an almost homorhythmic and syllabic texture known as *conductus style*. Some conductus feature long melismas called *caudae* (tails), especially at the beginning or the end. As in organa and discant clausulae, vertical consonances of the fifth and octave are prominent throughout and required at cadences, and the music is written in score notation. Both organum and conductus fell out of favor after 1250. **Music: NAWM 18**

IV. The Motet (CHWM 58–62, NAWM 15d, 15f–g, 18)

Starting in the early thirteenth century, words were often added to the upper voice or voices of a discant clausula. This produced a new genre, the *motet* (from the French *mot,* for "word"). The duplum of a motet is called the *motetus.*

1. Cantus firmus

   The tenor of a motet, like that of a clausula, consisted of a borrowed chant melody or *cantus firmus.* Composers created motets by reworking existing clausulae or composing new lines over a given melody. The borrowed tenor lost its connection to the liturgy and became musical raw material. A typical thirteenth-century motet has three voices. Each of the top two voices has its own text, and the tenor could be played or sung. The texts could be in Latin or French, sacred or secular, and were usually on related subjects. A motet is known by a compound title with the first word(s) of each text, including the tenor.   **Music: NAWM 15d, 15f, and 15g**

2. Franconian Motet

   In many motets from the second half of the thirteenth century, the upper voice moves more quickly and has a longer text than the middle voice, while the tenor moves more slowly. This type is called the *Franconian motet,* after the composer and theorist *Franco of Cologne* (fl. ca. 1250–1280). The phrases of the upper voices often overlap each other, and the texts can be on sacred or secular topics.   **Music: NAWM 18**

Etude: Thirteenth-Century Notation

   Notation for the rhythmic modes used patterns of ligatures, but the syllabic text-setting of motets made ligatures impossible. This required a notation that indicated the duration of each note. *Franconian notation,* codified by Franco of Cologne in *Ars cantus mensurabilis* (The Art of Measurable Music, ca. 1280), solved this problem by using different note-shapes for different relative values. This same principle underlies modern notation. With this more exact notation, polyphonic works no longer had to be written in score. They were notated instead in *choirbook format,* in which the voices appear on the same or facing pages but are not vertically aligned.

Window: The Motet as Gothic Cathedral (CHWM 62–63)

The voices in a thirteenth-century motet are rhythmically independent yet coordinated, the higher voices moving faster than the lower ones. This has parallels in the architecture of the Gothic cathedrals of the time.

Postlude (CHWM 62–64)

The development of polyphony paralleled in many ways that of chant, as it moved from improvisation to composition, added new melodies or texts to existing music, and reworked existing works into new ones.

STUDY QUESTIONS

Prelude (CHWM 45–46)

1. What important new developments in European music were under way in the eleventh century? Which of the trends that were new then were still typical of Western music in the eighteenth through twentieth centuries?

Early Organum (CHWM 47–51, NAWM 13–14)

2. In what treatise was polyphony first described? _____

   About when was this treatise written? _____

3. State the rules that govern the composition of Example 3.1 in CHWM, p. 47 (parallel organum in two voices, with a modified cadence).

4. In Example 3.3 in CHWM, p. 47, why can the chant (the upper line, marked *vox principalis*) *not* be accompanied by a voice a parallel fourth lower? What adjustments have been made to solve this problem?

Music to Study
>   **NAWM 13:** *Alleluia Justus ut palma,* organum from *Ad organum faciendum*
>   (ca. 1100)
>   CD 1.30 (Concise 1.10)

5. In the eleventh-century organum *Alleluia Justus ut palma* (NAWM 13), some
   sections are not set in polyphony. Why not?

6. In the sections in two-voice polyphony, which part is the original chant, and
   which is the added voice? Which of the two is more disjunct (fewer steps,
   more skips)? Why?

7. If you had to write down the rules for composing organum like this, what
   would they be? Include mention of the harmonic intervals normally used.

8. In florid organum, which voice has the chant? _____

   What is this voice called? _____

   Why did it receive this name?

9. Describe the relationship between the parts in florid organum. What is each voice like?

Music to Study
   NAWM 14: *Jubilemus, exultemus,* florid organum (twelfth century)
      CD 1.31

10. How does the florid organum *Jubilemus, exultemus* (NAWM 14) differ from the eleventh-century organum *Alleluia Justus ut palma* (NAWM 13)?

   How are the two similar?

Notre Dame Organum (CHWM 51–57, NAWM 15a–c, 15e, 16)

11. For which chants of the Mass and Office did Léonin write organa?

    Of these chants, which portions did he set in polyphony?

    What was his collection of organa called? _____

12. Show the rhythmic pattern for each of the six rhythmic modes:

    Mode I   _____

    Mode II _____

    Mode III_____

    Mode IV_____

    Mode V _____

    Mode VI_____

13. According to the treatise called Anonymous IV, what was Léonin best at?

    What was Pérotin noted for?

14. What is a *clausula*?

    What is a *substitute clausula*?

Music to Study
> **NAWM 15a–c and e:** *Alleluia Pascha nostrum,* plainchant and Léonin's
> setting (late twelfth century), with later anonymous substitutions
> 15a: Plainchant   (Not on recording)
> 15b: Léonin, organum duplum (pp. 54–55, 57, 59–60)
>   CD 1.32–34, 1.36, 1.38–40
> 15c: Anonymous discant clausula on "nostrum" (pp. 55–56)
>   (Not on recording)
> 15e: Anonymous substitute clausula on "-la-" (pp. 57–58)
>   (Not on recording)

> (NAWM 15 can be confusing to follow. See the explanation in NAWM.)

15. The setting of *Alleluia Pascha nostrum* in NAWM 15b, c, and e includes sections in both organum duplum and discant style. What are the main features of each style?

    organum duplum

    discant style

16. Which sections of *Alleluia Pascha nostrum* use organum style?

    Which sections use discant style? Why is discant used in these passages?

17. Which sections of NAWM 15b use no polyphony? Why are these sections not sung polyphonically?

18. In the discant clausula on the word "nostrum" (NAWM 15c), which rhythmic mode predominates in the upper voice? In the lower voice?

   upper voice _____   lower voice _____

   Besides the rhythmic mode itself, what repeated rhythmic pattern is used in the lower voice?

19. In NAWM 15c, how does the lower part compare to the chant melody on "nostrum" in NAWM 15a (other than being a fifth lower)? What happens in the lower voice at m. 19, where the editor has added a double bar and a Roman numeral II?

20. In NAWM 15c, how many times does each of the following vertical sonorities appear on the downbeats?

   octave _____   perfect fifth _____   third _____   unison _____   other _____

21. Using questions 18–19 above as guides, describe the use of rhythmic modes and rhythmic and melodic repetition in the discant clausula on "-lu-" in NAWM 15b (p. 60, CD 1.40).

22. What are the names for the various voices in an organum?

   bottom voice   _____

   second voice from the bottom   _____

   third voice from the bottom (if any)   _____

   fourth voice from the bottom (if any)   _____

   Which voice carries the chant?   _____

Music to Study
   NAWM 16: Pérotin, *Sederunt,* organum quadruplum (late twelfth or early
        thirteenth century), respond only
      CD 1.42–44 (Concise 1.11–13)

23. Compare the organum of Léonin in NAWM 15b with that of Pérotin in
    NAWM 16, an organum quadruplum on *Sederunt.* How is Pérotin's style like
    Léonin's, and how is it different?

24. Which rhythmic mode predominates in each of the following passages of
    Sederunt?

    the top three voices, mm. 2–10   _____

    the top voice, mm. 13–23   _____

    the top voice, mm. 35–40   _____

25. What vertical sonority is used most often at the cadences in *Sederunt?*

Polyphonic Conductus (CHWM 57–58, NAWM 17)

26. How is a polyphonic conductus like a monophonic conductus?

Music to Study
> **NAWM 17:** *Ave virgo virginum,* conductus (thirteenth century)
>   CD 1.45

27. In what ways is *Ave virgo virginum* (NAWM 17) typical of the polyphonic conductus, as described in CHWM?

  How is it different from organum and from discant?

The Motet (CHWM 58–62, NAWM 15d, 15f–g, 18)

28. How did the motet originate, and how did it acquire its name?

29. What is a *cantus firmus,* and what is its role in a motet?

30. What does the title of a motet indicate?

Music to Study

NAWM 15d: *Gaudeat devotio fidelium,* motet (thirteenth century)
CD 1.35
NAWM 15f: *Ave Maria, Fons letitie / Latus,* motet (thirteenth century)
CD 1.37
NAWM 15g: *Salve, salus hominum / O radians stella / Nostrum,* bitextual motet (thirteenth century)
CD 1.41
NAWM 18: *Amours mi font / En mai / Flos Filius eius,* motet in Franconian style (late thirteenth century)
CD 1.46 (Concise 1.14)

31. How are the motets in NAWM 15d, 15f, and 15g related to the discant clausulae on *nostrum* and *-latus* in NAWM 15c and 15e? What has been added, deleted, or changed in creating these new works? What has stayed the same?

32. What makes *Amours mi font / En mai / Flos Filius eius* (NAWM 18) a *Franconian motet,* and how does it differ from earlier motets?

33. When were Franconian motets written? _____

    After whom were they named? _____

    About when was this person active? _____

---

34. What new notational system was devised to indicate rhythm in motets? How
    was it different from the notation for the rhythmic modes? Why was this
    change necessary, and what results did it have?

35. In what major treatise was this notational system codified?

    Who wrote it, and when? _____   _____

TERMS TO KNOW

Terms Related to Early Polphony

polyphony
organum
principal voice (vox principalis),
  organal voice (vox organalis)
parallel organum
organum with oblique motion
eleventh-century organum (or
  note-against-note organum)

Aquitanian polyphony
florid organum
tenor (in florid organum, discant,
  and motet)
organum duplum, organum purum
discant
score notation

Terms Related to Notre Dame Polyphony

Notre Dame polyphony
rhythmic modes
perfection (in Notre Dame
  notation)
ligatures
clausula (pl. clausulae)
substitute clausula

organum triplum, organum
  quadruplum
duplum, triplum, quadruplum
polyphonic conductus
conductus style
cauda (pl. caudae)

Terms Related to the Thirteenth-Century Motet

motet
motetus
cantus firmus

Franconian motet
Franconian notation
choirbook format

NAMES TO KNOW

Musica enchiriadis
Winchester Troper
Ad organum faciendum
Léonin
Pérotin

Anonymous IV
Magnus liber organi
Franco of Cologne
Ars cantus mensurabilis

REVIEW QUESTIONS

1. Take the time-line you made in Chapter 2 and add the pieces in NAWM 13–14, 15b–g, and 16–18, their composers (when known), Franco of Cologne, and *Ars cantus mensurabilis*.

2. What different forms of polyphony can be found between the ninth century and the first half of the twelfth century? Describe an example of each type.

3. Describe the music of Notre Dame polyphony. Include in your discussion the major composers, the genres they cultivated, the rhythmic and harmonic style of their music, and the way new pieces used, embellished, or substituted for existing music.

4. Trace the development of the motet from its origins through the end of the thirteenth century, using NAWM 15d, 15g, and 18 as examples of three stages in that development.

5. In your view, looking back over Chapters 2 and 3, what developments during the period 900–1300 were most significant for the later evolution of music? What styles, practices, techniques, attitudes, or approaches that were new in this time have continued to affect Western music in the last seven hundred years? In your opinion, which of these have most distinguished music in the Western European tradition from music of other cultures?

FRENCH AND ITALIAN MUSIC IN THE FOURTEENTH CENTURY

4

CHAPTER OBJECTIVES

After you complete the reading, study of the music, and study questions for this chapter, you should be able to

1. explain the increased prominence of secular literature and music in the fourteenth century;
2. describe some of the rhythmic and other stylistic features that characterize the music of the *ars nova, trecento,* and late-fourteenth-century *ars subtilior*;
3. describe isorhythm and its use in fourteenth-century motets and Mass movements;
4. name and describe the forms of secular song practiced in France and Italy during the fourteenth century; and
5. identify some of the major figures, works, and terms associated with music in the fourteenth century.

CHAPTER OUTLINE

Prelude (CHWM 65–67)

The fourteenth century was an unstable and secular age. Church authority was undermined by the move of the papacy to Avignon (1305–78) and a schism between rival popes (1378–1417). Human reason became an authority in its own sphere, independent of church control, and human concerns became more important in literature, education, and art. Great literary works by Dante, Boccaccio, and Chaucer appeared in vernacular languages, and interest in Greek and Latin writings was renewed.

1. Philippe de Vitry

Most music of the fourteenth century was secular. The reigning musical style in France was the *Ars nova* ("new art"), named after a treatise attributed to *Philippe de Vitry* (1291–1361) that introduced innovations in rhythm and notation such as duple divisions of the beat. In Italy, the fourteenth century is known as the *trecento* (from "mille trecento," Italian for 1300).

I. The *ars nova* in France (CHWM 67–74, NAWM 19–21)

1. Motet

By the late thirteenth century motet texts were usually secular and often referred to contemporary events.

2. *Roman de Fauvel*

The *Roman de Fauvel* (1310–14) is a satirical poem with interpolated music, including thirty-four motets and numerous monophonic songs.

3. The isorhythmic motet

At least five motets in the *Roman de Fauvel* are by Vitry, and they are early examples of *isorhythm* ("same rhythm"). In an *isorhythmic motet,* the tenor is composed of a repeating series of pitches, called the *color,* and a repeating rhythmic pattern, called the *talea.* One may be longer than the other, and their endings may coincide or overlap. Upper voices may also be isorhythmic in whole or part, if they feature repeating rhythmic patterns coordinated with repetitions in the tenor. **Music: NAWM 19**

A. *Guillaume de Machaut*

Guillaume de Machaut (ca. 1300–1377) was the leading poet and composer of fourteenth-century France.

1. Motets

Machaut's isorhythmic motets are longer and more complex than Vitry's. The upper voices are often partly isorhythmic.

2. Hocket

Machaut frequently used *hocket,* in which a melodic line is interrupted by brief rests, usually filled in by notes interjected by another voice.

3. Mass

Machaut's *Messe de Notre Dame* (Mass of Our Lady, ca. 1364) is one of the first polyphonic settings of the whole Mass Ordinary. The Gloria and Credo are syllabic, with all four voices declaiming the text together, and end with isorhythmic Amens. The other movements are isorhythmic, often including isorhythm in all or most voices, and their tenors are drawn from plainchant melodies for the same texts from the Ordinary of the Mass. **Music: NAWM 21**

4. Love songs

Machaut wrote many secular songs (chansons), including monophonic *lais* and *virelais* and polyphonic *virelais, rondeaux,* and *ballades.*

5. *Ars nova* traits

The virelai, rondeau, and ballade are called *formes fixes* (fixed forms); each features a particular pattern of rhymes and repeating lines of poetry called *refrains,* and the rhymes and refrains coordinate with repeating segments of music. The chansons do not use isorhythm but do use duple divisions and syncopations, both typical of the *ars nova.*

6. The ballade and ballade style

In the polyphonic secular songs the *cantus,* or top part, is the principal line and was written first. The lower parts are usually played rather than sung. This treble-dominated style of voice and instrumental accompaniment is called *ballade style* or *cantilena style.*

7. Rondeau

The rondeau often includes long melismas at the beginning or middle of lines of poetry.   **Music: NAWM 20**

Etude: Standard Forms of Fourteenth-Century Chansons

Each fourteenth-century song form has two sections of music and a refrain but arranges these elements in a distinctive way. The virelai has the form A b b a A, in which A is the refrain and both A and a use the same music. The ballade has the form a a b C and usually has three or four stanzas, each ending with the same line of text (C, the refrain). Musically, the endings of the a section and the C section may be similar or identical. The rondeau has the form A B a A a b A B, with a refrain in two parts (A and B), the first repeating in the middle of the stanza. The stanza uses the same two sections of music as the refrain, a and b, but with different words.

II. Italian *trecento* Music (CHWM 74–79, NAWM 22–24)

Most fourteenth-century Italian music was monophonic and unwritten, and most sacred polyphony was improvised. Secular polyphony was cultivated among the elite in certain cities in northern Italy, especially Florence.

1. Squarcialupi Codex

The most important manuscript of trecento music, the *Squarcialupi Codex,* contains secular pieces of three types: *madrigale, caccia,* and *ballata.*

2. Madrigale

The fourteenth-century *madrigale* or *madrigal* (not to be confused with the sixteenth-century madrigal) is for two voices without instruments. **Music: NAWM 22**

3. Caccia

The *caccia* features two voices in canon at the unison over a free instrumental part. The texts are often about hunting or other action scenes, with appropriate sounds imitated in the music.

4. Ballata

The *ballata* (from "ballare," to dance) evolved from monophonic dance songs with choral refrains. The polyphonic ballata of the late fourteenth century was a lyrical piece whose form resembles the French virelai.

5. Francesco Landini

Francesco Landini (ca. 1325–1397) was the leading Italian composer of the fourteenth century. He is best known for his ballate and wrote no sacred works.   **Music: NAWM 23**

6. Landini cadences

Landini has lent his name to the *Landini cadence,* in which the usual cadence of a sixth expanding to an octave is decorated by the upper voice descending a step before resolving to the octave.

Etude: Standard Forms of *trecento* Song

The madrigale has two or three three-line stanzas, all set to the same music, with a closing couplet called the *ritornello,* set to new music in a different meter. The caccia has no set form, but may have a ritornello. In a ballata, a three-line *ripresa* or refrain (A) precedes and follows a seven-line stanza. The stanza's first two pairs of lines, called *piedi,* present a new phrase (b), and the last three lines, the *volta,* use the music of the refrain (a), for an overall form of A b b a A.

7. French influence

In the late fourteenth century, Italian composers began to absorb aspects of the French style, and northern composers began to settle in Italy.

8. Later fourteenth century

Composers at Avignon and other courts in southern France developed a style that was complex in rhythm and notation.   **Music: NAWM 24**

Window: The Subtler Art (CHWM 80–81)

The complex late-fourteenth-century style has been called the *ars subtilior* ("the subtler art") because of its intricate rhythms and notation.

III. Theory and Practice in Fourteenth-Century Music (CHWM 82–84)

1. Musica ficta

Performers often altered notes chromatically, a practice known as *musica ficta.* In cadences in which a minor sixth expanded to an octave, the top note was often raised to make a major sixth, so that the top line resolved upward by half step, like a leading tone. A three-voice cadence in which both octave and fifth are approached from a half step below is called a *double leading-tone cadence.*

2. Accidentals

Other chromatic alterations were made to avoid tritones or to create smooth lines. Composers and scribes tended not to notate these changes, leaving it to performers to judge where they were needed. Modern editors often suggest where changes should be made by indicating accidentals above or below the affected notes.

Etude: Fourteenth-Century Notation

In fourteenth-century French notation, the long, breve, and semibreve could each be divided into either two or three of the next smaller note value. These divisions were called *mode, time,* and *prolation* respectively; triple divisions were *perfect* and duple *imperfect* (*major* and *minor* respectively for prolation). Combining time and prolation produced four possible meters, equivalent to 9/8, 6/8, 3/4, and 2/4. The *minim* and *semiminim* were introduced for notes smaller than a semibreve. About 1425, note-heads began to be left open instead of being filled in. The resulting note-shapes evolved into modern notation (whole note, half note, and so on).

IV. Instruments (CHWM 84–85)

Music manuscripts of the fourteenth century do not specify which parts are vocal and which are instrumental, for each piece could be performed in a variety of ways. Polyphonic music was probably most often performed with one voice or instrument on a part.

1. Loud and soft instruments

Instruments were classified as either loud (*haut* or "high") or soft (*bas* or "low"). Loud instruments such as *shawms, cornetts,* slide trumpets, and *sackbuts* were often used outdoors; soft instruments such as the harp, vielle, lute, psaltery, transverse flute, and recorder were used indoors, and percussion was used in both environments.

2. Keyboard instruments

Portative organs and chamber organs were often used for secular music. Larger organs were used in churches.

STUDY QUESTIONS

Prelude (CHWM 65–67)

1. What currents in religion, philosophy, and literature helped to make the fourteenth century a secular age?

2. With what nation and what century is each of the following styles associated?

   ars nova _____ _____

   trecento _____ _____

   What does the phrase "ars nova" mean? _____

   From what does the term "trecento" derive?

The *ars nova* in France (CHWM 67–74, NAWM 19–21)

3. What is the *Roman de Fauvel*? When was it written? What music does it contain?

4. How is the tenor of an isorhythmic motet constructed? What are the names of the elements that repeat?

Music to Study
  NAWM 19: Philippe de Vitry, *In arboris / Tuba sacre fidei / Virgo sum,*
      motet (ca. 1320)
  CD 1.47–48

5. What is Vitry's motet *In arboris / Tuba sacre fidei / Virgo sum* (NAWM 19)
   about? What does each text say, and how do the texts relate to each other?

6. Write out the color of this motet as a series of note names (*C G A* etc.).

   How many notes does the color contain? _____

   How many times is the color stated in the motet? _____

7. Write out the first statement of the talea as a series of durations. Include the
   rests. To make it easier to follow the rhythm, reduce the value of each note or
   rest to a third of its value, so that a dotted whole note becomes a half note, a
   dotted half note becomes a quarter note, and so on. In this notation, the first
   note would be a whole note, the second a half note, and so on.

   How many notes does the talea contain? _____

   How many times is the talea stated in the motet? _____

   How is the talea altered after the midpoint of the motet?

   In this motet, how are the talea and color coordinated?

8. Briefly describe Guillaume de Machaut's career. Where did he live, whom did he serve, and what did he do?

Music to Study
   NAWM 21: Guillaume de Machaut, *Messe de Notre Dame* (Mass of Our
      Lady, ca. 1364), excerpt: Agnus Dei
      CD 2.4–6 (Concise 1.18–20)

9. What is the *Messe de Notre Dame*? What is special about it?

   Which movements are isorhythmic? _____

   What other style is used, and in what movements? Why is it appropriate for these movements?

10. In the Agnus Dei, the isorhythm begins with the words "qui tollis" after each "Agnus Dei." Each time, the color is stated only once, the talea more than once. The last note of each section follows the last statement of the talea.
       (Note that in certain cases, some repetitions of an isorhythmic pattern will subdivide a few notes. For example, compare mm. 15–17 in all four voices with mm. 8–10. For each voice, the rhythm is virtually the same in both passages, but in the top three voices there is a half note in one passage that is divided into smaller note values in the other. This kind of small difference varies, but does not negate, the basic isorhythmic structure.)

   Write out the talea for the first "qui tollis." _____

   How many measures long (in this modern transcription) is this talea? _____

   How many times is it stated? _____

   To what extent are the other three voices isorhythmic?

11. Diagram the form of the three *formes fixes,* using letters to indicate musical repetitions and capital letters to show the refrains.

   virelai   _____

   ballade   _____

   rondeau   _____

Music to Study
   NAWM 20: Guillaume de Machaut, *Rose, liz, printemps, verdure,* rondeau
       (mid-fourteenth century)
   CD 2.1–3 (Concise 1.15–17)

12. Note the rondeau form in your answer to question 11. Which measures in the music of *Rose, liz, printemps, verdure* (NAWM 20) correspond to each letter of your diagram?

   How do the rhymes in the poetry coordinate with this form?

   How do cadences help delineate the form?

13. In this rondeau, what relation does the music in mm. 32–37 have to music heard previously? How does this help to delineate the form?

---

14. Describe the melodic and rhythmic style of the two upper parts of this ron-
    deau—the triplum and the cantus. How do these compare to the upper parts
    of the motets in NAWM 18–19 and to the thirteenth-century monophonic
    rondeau in NAWM 8? Describe what is distinctive about Machaut's style, as
    compared with melodies of the late thirteenth and early fourteenth centuries.

Italian *trecento* Music (CHWM 74–79, NAWM 22–24)

15. Define and describe the fourteenth-century *caccia*.

Music to Study
    NAWM 22: Jacopo da Bologna, *Fenice fù,* madrigal (mid-1300s)
        CD 2.7

16. What is a fourteenth-century madrigal? Describe the type of poetry used, the
    poetic form, the form of the piece, and the melodic style, and show how
    Jacopo da Bologna's *Fenice fù* (NAWM 22) exemplifies these traits.

Music to Study
   NAWM 23: Francesco Landini, *Non avrà ma' pietà,* ballata (second half of
          fourteenth century)
       CD 2.8–10 (Concise 1.21–23)

17. In a ballata, what is the *ripresa*? What measures of Landini's *Non avrà ma'
    pietà* (NAWM 23) correspond to this part of the form?

    What are the *piedi* and *volta*? Where do these appear in Landini's ballata?

    How does the form of a ballata resemble that of a virelai? How is it different?

18. What is a "Landini cadence"? Where in Landini's ballata do Landini caden-
    ces appear?

19. Compare the melodic, rhythmic, and harmonic style of Landini's ballata to
    that of Machaut's rondeau (NAWM 20). Where do melismas occur in each
    piece, and how are the composers similar or different in their placement of
    melismas? What other similarities and differences do you observe?

Music to Study
> **NAWM 24:** Baude Cordier, *Belle, bonne, sage,* rondeau (early 1400s)
>   CD 2.11

20. How does Baude Cordier's rondeau *Belle, bonne, sage* (NAWM 24) resemble Machaut's rondeau (NAWM 20), and how is it different in style? What aspects of the Cordier link it to the *ars subtilior*?

21. In what shape is Cordier's rondeau presented in the manuscript, and why?

Theory and Practice in Fourteenth-Century Music (CHWM 82–84)

22. What is *musica ficta*? Under what circumstances is it used, and why?

23. Briefly describe fourteenth-century French notation. What are the divisions of the long, breve, and semibreve called? What are the four prolations, and how do they correspond to modern meters?

Instruments (CHWM 84–85)

24. What types of instruments were in use during the fourteenth century? What are *haut* ("high") and *bas* ("low") instruments? How were instruments used in vocal music?

TERMS TO KNOW

Terms Related to Ars Nova Music

ars nova
isorhythm
isorhythmic motet
color
talea
hocket
lai

virelai
rondeau
ballade
formes fixes
refrain
cantus
ballade style or cantilena style

Terms Related to Trecento and Late-Fourteenth-Century French Music

trecento
madrigale or madrigal
  (fourteenth-century)
caccia
ballata

ritornello (in fourteenth-century
  madrigal)
ripresa, piedi, volta
ars subtilior

Terms Related to Music Theory and Instruments

Landini cadence
musica ficta
double leading-tone cadence
mode, time, prolation
perfect and imperfect time
major and minor prolation

minim, semiminim
haut and bas instruments
shawm
cornett
sackbut

NAMES TO KNOW

Ars nova
Philippe de Vitry
Roman de Fauvel
Guillaume de Machaut

Messe de Notre Dame
Squarcialupi Codex
Francesco Landini

REVIEW QUESTIONS

1. Make a time-line for the pieces, composers, and treatises discussed in this chapter (or add them to the time-line you made in Chapter 2).

2. What is new about the *ars nova*? How does it compare to thirteenth-century music? How does late-fourteenth-century French music (the *ars subtilior*) extend the ideas of the *ars nova*?

3. Describe isorhythm as practiced in Vitry's motets and Machaut's Mass.

4. Name and describe the forms of secular song practiced in France and Italy during the fourteenth century. How are French and Italian music similar? How do they differ?

5. Describe the melodic, rhythmic, and harmonic style of Machaut. How do the works of Vitry, Jacopo da Bologna, Landini, and Cordier resemble or differ from those of Machaut in melodic, rhythmic, and harmonic style? What features do they all share?

ENGLAND AND THE BURGUNDIAN LANDS IN THE FIFTEENTH CENTURY: THE BEGINNINGS OF AN INTERNATIONAL STYLE

5

CHAPTER OBJECTIVES

After you complete the reading, study of the music, and study questions for this chapter, you should be able to

1. describe the traits of English music that distinguished it from French and Italian styles and influenced music on the Continent in the fifteenth century;
2. describe fauxbourdon, chant paraphrase, and cantus firmus techniques;
3. explain how an international musical style developed in the mid-fifteenth century and the historical circumstances that placed Burgundian composers at the center of these developments;
4. describe the music of Burgundian composers, particularly Du Fay, and explain the differences between their musical practices and those of the fourteenth century; and
5. describe the cantus firmus Mass.

CHAPTER OUTLINE

Prelude (CHWM 86–89)

English music made important contributions to the development of an international style in the first half of the fifteenth century. The influence of English style on Continental composers was celebrated around 1440 in a poem that praised the *"contenance angloise"* (English guise) of "lively consonance." The new style, which blended French, Italian, and English traits, was nurtured especially by composers from the duchy of *Burgundy,* where the dukes maintained a large *chapel* of singers and composers and employed numerous instrumentalists. Due to the dukes' lavish patronage, most of the leading composers of the fifteenth and early sixteenth centuries came from Burgundian lands, mainly from modern-day Belgium and northeastern France. Musicians traveled with their patrons or moved to new posts in other regions, and their interactions with musicians from all over Europe aided the development of an international style.

I. English Music and Its Influence (CHWM 89–93, NAWM 25–26, 28)

English music favored the major mode, homophony, use of imperfect consonances, and fullness of sound. A frequent occurrence in English music is parallel motion in thirds and sixths, often in combination (that is, parallel sixths between the outer voices and parallel thirds between the bottom and middle voices, resolving to an octave and fifth respectively at cadences). A distinctive English form is the *carol*.   **Music: NAWM 26**

1. Fauxbourdon
The parallel sixths and thirds of English music may have inspired the Continental technique of *fauxbourdon* about 1420. This led around 1450 to a new style in which the voices move in similar rhythms and are almost equally important and the music is suffused with imperfect consonances.

Etude: A Closer Look at Fauxbourdon
In fauxbourdon, two notated voices (usually a paraphrased chant in the cantus and a tenor below it) move mostly in parallel sixths, resolving to an octave at cadences, and a third unwritten part is sung a fourth below the cantus, producing parallel thirds with the tenor.   **Music: NAWM 28**

2. Dunstable
John Dunstable (ca. 1390–1453) was the leading English composer of the first half of the fifteenth century. He served for a time in the English possessions in France, which helped bring his music to the Continent. He wrote in all the prevailing genres and styles of polyphony.

3. Dunstable's motets
Dunstable is best known for his three-voice sacred works. They use a variety of techniques, including an ornamented chant melody in the top voice, a cantus firmus in the tenor, and free counterpoint not based on chant. In the fifteenth century, the isorhythmic motet waned in popularity, and the term *motet* came to be applied to any polyphonic setting of a Latin text other than part of the Mass Ordinary.   **Music: NAWM 25**

II. Music in the Burgundian Lands (CHWM 94–97, NAWM 27–30)

1. Guillaume Du Fay
Guillaume Du Fay (c. 1400–1474) was educated at Cambrai in the duchy of Burgundy, served several patrons in Italy and Savoy in the 1420s and 1430s, returned to Cambrai, went back to Savoy in the 1450s, and finished his career at Cambrai, making him a truly international composer.

2. Gilles Binchois
Gilles Binchois (c. 1400–1460) spent most of his career at the Burgundian court chapel. He was best known for his chansons.   **Music: NAWM 30**

3. Genres and style
The main genres of the period were Masses, Magnificats, motets, and French secular chansons. The chansons continued the three-voice treble-

dominated texture of the fourteenth century, but the melodic style was smoother and the harmony more consonant.

4. Cadences

The traditional sixth-to-octave cadence or Landini cadence between tenor and cantus were sometimes harmonized with a contratenor that leapt up an octave from a fifth below the tenor to a fifth above the tenor's note of resolution, creating a sound similar to a modern dominant-tonic cadence.

5. Burgundian chansons

In the fifteenth century, *chanson* (song) was the term for any polyphonic setting of a French secular text. Most chansons were in the form of a rondeau or (less often) a ballade.   **Music: NAWM 27 and 30**

6. Burgundian motets

Motets in this period were often written in the style of the chanson, with the main melody (often paraphrased from chant) in the treble, supported by the tenor, with a contratenor to fill out the harmony.   **Music: NAWM 28**

7. Isorhythmic motets

Isorhythmic motets were still sometimes composed for special occasions.

8. Masses

After about 1420, composers regularly set the Mass Ordinary as a unified cycle, creating the genre of the *polyphonic Mass cycle.* Some Masses were unified simply by musical style or liturgical association, others by opening each movement with the same material, called a *head motive* or *motto.*

9. Tenor Mass

The most important form was the *cantus firmus Mass* or *tenor Mass,* which used the same cantus firmus in every movement. This form was developed by English composers and became predominant throughout Europe by 1450. The cantus firmus was usually placed in the tenor in long notes and treated in isorhythmic fashion. Below it was a *contratenor bassus* (low contratenor) or *bassus* (bass) to provide a harmonic foundation; above it was the *contratenor altus* (high contratenor) or *altus* (alto); the top part was called *cantus* (melody), *discantus* (discant), or *superius* (highest part). The cantus firmus could be taken from a chant, a secular song, or the tenor of a chanson, and the Mass was named after the borrowed tune.

10. *Missa Se la face ay pale*

Du Fay's *Missa Se la face ay pale* uses the tenor of his own ballade in the tenor in all movements of the Mass, usually using doubled or tripled durations in a technique that resembles isorhythm.   **Music: NAWM 29**

11. Layered texture in Du Fay's Masses

In this and other Du Fay Masses, the bottom two voices provide harmonic foundation, while the top two are smoother and more lively with some use of imitation.

12. Consonance and dissonance in Du Fay's Masses

Du Fay's style features an emphasis on consonance and careful control of dissonance, including *suspensions* and passing tones.

STUDY QUESTIONS

Prelude (CHWM 86–89)

1. What political factors facilitated the development of an international musical style in the fifteenth century? Why were Burgundian composers at the center of these developments?

English Music and Its Influence (CHWM 89–93, NAWM 25–26, 28)

2. What characteristics of English music in the thirteenth through early fifteenth centuries set it apart from music on the Continent? How did the Continental style change as it absorbed the influence of English music in the first half of the fifteenth century?

3. Describe the relationship between the Dunstable melody and the plainchant melody it paraphrases in Example 5.2 on p. 92 of CHWM. How does Dunstable embellish the chant?

Music to Study
> **NAWM 25:** John Dunstable, *Quam pulchra es,* motet (first half, fifteenth century)
>> CD 2.12 (Concise 1.24)
> **NAWM 26:** *Salve, sancta parens,* carol (fifteenth century)
>> CD 2.13
> **NAWM 28:** Guillaume Du Fay, *Conditor alme siderum,* motet (hymn paraphrase) in alternation with chant (middle third of fifteenth century)
>> CD 2.17–18

4. In what sense is *Quam pulchra es* (NAWM 25) a motet? Which part, if any, has the chant? How are the parts related to each other? How had the definition of "motet" changed by the early fifteenth century to include a piece such as this?

5. How does Dunstable shape the music of *Quam pulchra es* to reflect the divisions of the text and the rhythms of the words?

6. Where are there passages in *Quam pulchra es* that feature parallel thirds, sixths, or tenths? (Note that the middle voice is to be performed an octave lower than written, so that all three parts begin on middle C.)

About how often during the work are imperfect consonances sounding?

7. How often in *Quam pulchra es* do harmonic dissonances appear? How often do parallel unisons, fifths, or octaves occur? How does this compare with the thirteenth-century conductus *Ave virgo virginum* (NAWM 17) and with Machaut's fourteenth-century Agnus Dei (NAWM 21)?

8. Compare the melodic style of the top voice in Dunstable's motet to that of the top lines in Machaut's *Rose, liz, printemps, verdure* (NAWM 20) and Landini's *Non avrà ma' pietà* (NAWM 23). What are the main differences between the English style of the first half of the fifteenth century and these fourteenth-century styles?

9. Now do the same for the melodic style of the tenors, and for the relationship between the top part and the tenor.

10. Where are there parallel sixths, thirds, or tenths between the outer voices in the carol *Salve, sancta parens* (NAWM 26)? In the three-voice Burden II, where is there a texture in which the outer voices move in parallel sixths and the bottom two voices in parallel thirds? (Note: Sometimes the rhythm of the parts is slightly different, while the voices still essentially move in parallel.)

11. Where are there Landini cadences in the following works?

    Salve, sancta parens (NAWM 26) _____

    Dunstable, *Quam pulchra es* (NAWM 25) _____

12. In Du Fay's polyphonic setting of the even-numbered verses of the chant hymn *Conditor alme siderum* (NAWM 28), how is the plainchant melody embellished? Where in the phrase do embellishments occur? (Note that the chant melody itself is notated here in longs and breves, producing a pattern like the first rhythmic mode.)

13. How does this piece fit the description of *fauxbourdon* in CHWM, p. 91?

    How does this compare to the use of parallel sixth-third sonorities in the English carol *Salve, sancta parens* (NAWM 26)? Which piece is more varied in its texture?

Music in the Burgundian Lands (CHWM 94–101, NAWM 27–30)

14. Briefly summarize Du Fay's career. How was it typical of musicians at the time? How did such a career facilitate the creation of an international style?

15. How does the fifteenth-century cadence formula described on p. 95 of CHWM resemble fourteenth-century cadences, and how is it like cadences in common-practice tonality?

Music to Study
> **NAWM 27:** Guillaume Du Fay, *Resvellies vous et faites chiere lye,* ballade (1423)
> CD 2.14–16
> **NAWM 30:** Gilles Binchois, *De plus en plus,* rondeau (ca. 1425)
> CD 2.26–27 (Concise 1.32–33)

16. In Du Fay's *Resvellies vous et faites chiere lye* (NAWM 27), which parts of the upper line seem to suggest instrumental performance? Why?

17. *Resvellies vous* was composed in 1423 when Du Fay was working in Italy, and it shows a strong influence from fourteenth-century French and Italian music. Which elements in this piece resemble Machaut's rondeau *Rose, liz, printemps, verdure* (NAWM 20)? Which suggest the rhythmically complex late-fourteenth-century *ars subtilior* style? How does the melodic line in the texted portions suggest Italian rather than French influence?

18. How does the musical and poetic form of Binchois's *De plus en plus* (NAWM 30) compare to that of Machaut's *Rose, liz* (NAWM 20)?

19. Compare the melodic style of the top voice in Binchois's *De plus en plus* to those of the vocal line of Machaut's *Rose, liz* and of the top voice of Dunstable's *Quam pulchra es* (NAWM 25). (See question 8 above for your comparison of the latter two.) What traits does Binchois share with his English contemporary that differ from Machaut's style?

20. How do the Machaut, Dunstable, and Binchois pieces compare in harmonic style? For each piece, what cadence formulas are characteristic? What vertical sonorities are common? Where do parallel fifths and octaves occur, if at all? Where do successions of parallel sixths and thirds appear? Again, what traits does Binchois share with Dunstable that differ from Machaut?

21. What is a *cantus firmus Mass* or *tenor Mass*?

22. What kinds of borrowed melodies were used in cantus firmus Masses?

    In which voice of the four-part texture does the cantus firmus usually occur?

Music to Study
NAWM 29a: Guillaume Du Fay, *Se la face ay pale,* ballade (1430s)
    CD 2.19 (Concise 1.25)
NAWM 29b: Guillaume Du Fay, *Missa Se la face ay pale,* Mass (ca. 1450s),
    excerpt: Gloria
    CD 2.20–25 (Concise 1.26–31)

23. How does Du Fay use the tenor of his chanson *Se la face ay pale* (NAWM 29a) in the tenor of the Gloria from his *Missa Se la face ay pale* (NAWM 29b)? How is this like isorhythm? How does it provide a form for the Gloria movement?

24. Where in the Gloria does Du Fay borrow material from the other two voices of his chanson? What purpose might this borrowing serve?

25. How do the four voices of the Gloria differ from each other in function and style?

26. Examine the upper voices in the Gloria. How often do two successive measures have the same rhythm? How often do the top two voices move in the same rhythm at the same time? What does this suggest about Du Fay's use of rhythm?

27. In the isorhythmic works of Vitry and Machaut, we can find parallel fifths and octaves and double leading-tone cadences. Can any of these be found in Du Fay's Mass movement? How would you describe the harmony?

TERMS TO KNOW

"contenance angloise"
chapel
carol
fauxbourdon
motet (fifteenth-century and later)
chanson

polyphonic Mass cycle
head motive or motto
cantus firmus Mass or tenor Mass
bassus (contratenor bassus)
altus (contratenor altus)
cantus, discantus, superius
suspension

NAMES TO KNOW

Burgundy
John Dunstable
Guillaume Du Fay

Gilles Binchois
Missa Se la face ay pale

REVIEW QUESTIONS

1. Make a time-line for the pieces and composers discussed in this chapter. Include dates for the poem that mentions the "contenance angloise"; dates for the end of the duchy of Burgundy and the reigns of Philip the Good and Charles the Bold; the dates and places of Du Fay's birth, death, and employment; and dates for any historical events listed on p. 98 of CHWM with which you are familiar, to help orient you to the fifteenth century.

2. What new ways of using and reworking Gregorian chant developed during the fifteenth century?

3. What special role did the duchy of Burgundy and Burgundian composers play in the development of music during the fifteenth century?

4. Describe the music of Du Fay and explain how he synthesizes elements from France, Italy, and England in a cosmopolitan style.

5. Describe the cantus firmus Mass as composed in the fifteenth century, and compare Du Fay's *Missa Se la face ay pale* (a cantus firmus Mass) to Machaut's *Messe de Notre Dame*.

The Age of the Renaissance: Music of the Low Countries

6

Chapter Objectives

After you complete the reading, study of the music, and study questions for this chapter, you should be able to

1. describe some aspects of the influence of humanism on the culture and music of the fifteenth and sixteenth centuries;
2. name some of the most significant theorists and treatises of the time;
3. describe the beginnings of music printing and its effects on musical life; and
4. describe the music and briefly describe the careers of some of the major composers active at the end of the fifteenth century and the beginning of the sixteenth century.

Chapter Outline

Prelude (CHWM 102–3)

The *Renaissance* was not a musical style, but a period of history marked by the renewed influence of ancient Greek and Roman culture. Although no ancient music was known, ancient writings on music became available during the fifteenth century. Greek and Roman writers' descriptions of the emotional effects of music caused some in the Renaissance to criticize the lack of such effects in the music of their own time. Most prominent composers in the period 1450–1550 came from France, Flanders, or the Netherlands, and they served at courts in Italy and across western Europe. The greatest composer of the era was *Josquin des Prez* (ca. 1450s–1521).

I. The Musical Culture of the Renaissance (CHWM 104–7)

1. Humanism

Humanism, the recovery of ancient culture, was an influence on music as on the other arts. During the fifteenth century, all the major Greek writings on music were translated into Latin.

2. Gaffurio

Franchino Gaffurio (1451–1522) incorporated ancient Greek theory into his treatises, the most influential of his time.

3. Power of the ancient modes

Renaissance musicians were intrigued by the claims of Greek writers that the choice of mode could affect listeners' emotions.

4. Glareanus

In his *Dodekachordon* (The Twelve-String Lyre, 1547), *Heinrich Glareanus* (1488–1563) added four new modes (authentic and plagal modes on A and C, akin to later minor and major modes) to the eight earlier modes.

5. Tuning

New tuning systems were introduced that allowed imperfect consonances to sound well, and triads began to appear at cadences.

6. Consonance and dissonance

Strict rules for controlling dissonance were followed by composers and codified in treatises on *counterpoint*.

7. Tinctoris

The most significant fifteenth-century counterpoint treatise was *Liber de arte contrapuncti* (A Book on the Art of Counterpoint, 1477) by *Johannes Tinctoris* (ca. 1435–ca. 1511). Counterpoint rules were codified in the sixteenth century by Gioseffo Zarlino in *Le istitutioni harmoniche* (The Harmonic Foundations, 1558).

8. Music and words

Humanism encouraged composers to pay increasing attention to the meaning, sound, form, and rhythm of the texts they set. Whereas text underlay had often been left to the singers, sixteenth-century composers sought to fix it precisely, for good accentuation.

9. Music printing

Printing allowed wider distribution of writings on music and of music itself at lower cost, with greater accuracy and less time spent recopying by hand.

10. Petrucci

Ottaviano de' Petrucci (1466–1539) of Venice was the first to print polyphonic music from movable type in 1501.

11. Why Italy?

Humanism and the arts thrived particularly in Italy, where rulers of small city-states and principalities sought to outdo each other in their patronage of literature and the arts. Many of the composers they employed were from France, Flanders, and the Netherlands, especially from the formerly Burgundian lands.

II. Northern Composers and Their Music (CHWM 107–14, NAWM 31)

1. Ockeghem

Johannes Ockeghem (ca. 1420–1497) was born in northern Europe and spent most of his career in the service of the kings of France. He was famous as a composer and as a teacher of many of the leading composers of the next generation. He wrote thirteen Masses, ten motets, and about twenty chansons. He extended the range of the bassus down to low F, giving a fuller and darker sound, and all four voices tend to be equally active.

2. Masses

Some of Ockeghem's Masses are cantus firmus Masses. He often creates contrasts of light and dark by varying the texture, setting some passages for only two or three voices.   **Music: NAWM 31**

3. Naming Masses

Masses without a cantus were sometimes named for their mode or for a structural feature.

4. Canon

Ockeghem seldom uses *imitation* (echoing a motive or phrase in another voice, often at a different pitch level), but does use *canon,* which at this time meant a procedure for deriving more than one voice from a notated voice.

5. Mensuration canons

One type of canon was the *mensuration canon,* in which one notated line generates two voices through a different mensuration sign.

Etude: Mensuration Canons in an Ockeghem Mass

Each movement of Ockeghem's *Missa prolationum* uses two simultaneous mensuration canons, creating a challenging puzzle for performers.

6. Ockeghem's chansons

Ockeghem's chansons continue to follow the formes fixes, especially the rondeau, but feature smoother lines and more use of imitation. Chansons of the period were freely altered, arranged, and transcribed for instruments, and some became very popular.

Window: The "Gutenberg Bible" of Music Printing (CHWM 110–11)

Petrucci used three impressions (for the staff lines, for the notes, and for the text) to print beautiful and clear collections of chansons, motets, or Masses. Most works were published as *partbooks,* one book for each voice or instrumental part. Printing made music widely available and created the first real market for music as a commodity.

III. Josquin and His Contemporaries (CHWM 114–21, NAWM 32–33)

1. Ockeghem's pupils

Many composers of the generation born near the middle of the fifteenth century were taught or influenced by Ockeghem. The three greatest were *Jacob Obrecht* (1457 or 1458–1505), *Heinrich Isaac* (ca. 1450–1517), and Josquin des Prez (ca. 1450s–1521). All were trained in the Low Countries and worked in Italy and elsewhere, and their music blends northern polyphony, intricacy, and subtly flowing rhythms with the Italian preferences for homophony, simplicity, and clearly articulated phrases.

2. *Odhecaton*

The first volume of polyphony printed from movable type was Petrucci's *Harmonice musices odhecaton A* (1501), an anthology of chansons from around 1470 to about 1500 in both older and newer styles.

3. Chansons

The newer style favored four voices instead of three; greater equality between the voices; more imitation; and a clearer harmonic structure.

4. Josquin's chansons

Josquin and others of his generation abandoned the *formes fixes* for more varied poetic and musical forms. The voices are no longer independent layers, but are all equal in a flexible texture that includes imitation and dialogue between voices. Many chansons set a popular tune, treating it like a cantus firmus or in paraphrase.

A. *Josquin des Prez*

1. Career

Josquin des Prez was considered the best composer of his time and is one of the greatest of all time. He was born in northern France and served patrons in Italy and France. His works, which include about eighteen Masses, one hundred motets, and seventy secular vocal works, were published and recopied more widely than any other composer of his day.

2. Motets

The large number of motets by Josquin reflects the interest composers had in setting a variety of texts and exploring word-music relationships.

3. Text and music

The influence of humanism led Josquin and others to match the music more carefully to the meaning and accentuation of the words. (Josquin's music may be the first or among the first to be expressive of the emotions suggested by its text.)   **Music: NAWM 33**

4. Fugal imitation

In a Josquin motet, each phrase of text receives its own musical figure, usually treated in a point of imitation. The full four-voice texture is often reserved until the drive to the cadence at the end of a musical sentence.

5. Masses

Most of Josquin's Masses use a secular tune as a cantus firmus. One Mass honors his patron, the duke of Ferrara, by using a theme derived from his name as rendered in solmization syllables.

6. Imitation Mass

An *imitation Mass* (also called *parody Mass*) borrows, not a single line, but the entire multivoice texture of a polyphonic work, and reworks it to create something new in each movement of the Mass.

7. *Missa Pange lingua*

Josquin's *Missa Pange lingua* is based on a chant hymn. Instead of placing the chant in a single voice, he paraphrased it in all voices (a procedure called a *paraphrase Mass*).   **Music: NAWM 32**

STUDY QUESTIONS

The Musical Culture of the Renaissance (CHWM 104–7)

1. What is *humanism*? What was its role in Renaissance intellectual life? What aspects of music did it influence?

2. Name three important theorists of the late fifteenth and sixteenth centuries and briefly describe their contributions.

3. How did humanism influence the relation between music and text in vocal pieces? How did the new understanding of text setting relate to ancient Greek ideas?

4. When did printing of polyphonic music from movable type begin? _____

   Who was the first printer to use this technique, and where was he active?

   _____   _____

5. What impact did printing have on the dissemination of musical works?

6. Why did Italy provide an ideal ground for Renaissance humanism as a movement and for the development of the international musical styles of the late fifteenth and sixteenth centuries?

Northern Composers and Their Music (CHWM 107–14, NAWM 31)

7. Summarize Ockeghem's career and reputation.

Music to Study
>   **NAWM 31:** Johannes Ockeghem, *Missa De plus en plus,* Mass (second half of the fifteenth century), excerpts: Kyrie and Agnus Dei
>   31a: Kyrie   CD 2.28–30
>   31b: Agnus Dei   CD 2.31–32

8. In his *Missa De plus en plus* (NAWM 31), what does Ockeghem borrow from Binchois's rondeau *De plus en plus* (NAWM 30)? How does he use the borrowed material? How does he alter it?

9. How does Ockeghem's treatment of borrowed material here compare to that of Du Fay in the Gloria from *Missa Se la face ay pale* (NAWM 29b)?

10. How do the ranges of the four voice parts in the Ockeghem Mass compare to the ranges in Du Fay's Mass?

11. How does Ockeghem use changes of texture, especially in the number of simultaneous parts? How does this compare to the Du Fay Mass?

12. What is a *mensuration canon,* and how does it work in Ockeghem's *Missa prolationum*?

Josquin and His Contemporaries (CHWM 114–21, NAWM 32–33)

13. What is *Harmonice musices odhecaton A*? Who published it, and where? What kind of music did it contain? Briefly describe the styles represented in it.

14. How were chansons reworked and reused by composers and performers?

15. Where and when did Josquin live and work? Briefly summarize his career. In what genres did he compose? How was he regarded by his contemporaries?

Music to Study
> **NAWM 32:** Josquin des Prez, *Missa Pange lingua,* Mass (ca. 1515–20), excerpts: Kyrie and portion of Credo
> 32a: Kyrie   CD 2.33–35 (Concise 1.34–36)
> 32b: Credo, excerpt: *Et incarnatus est*   CD 2.36–38
> **NAWM 33:** Josquin des Prez, *De profundis clamavi ad te,* motet (first or second decade of the sixteenth century)
> CD 2.39–42 (Concise 1.37–40)

16. How are the opening two phrases of the chant hymn *Pange lingua gloriosi* used and varied in the first Kyrie of Josquin's *Missa Pange lingua* (NAWM 32a)? Describe how each of the four voices treats the chant. How does this compare to the way borrowed material is used in Du Fay's *Missa Se la face ay pale* (NAWM 29b) and Ockeghem's *Missa De plus en plus* (NAWM 31)?

17. How does Josquin vary the texture in his Mass, especially in the number of simultaneous parts? How does this compare to the Du Fay and Ockeghem Masses?

18. How does Josquin use imitation between the voices in his Mass? What different arrangements of voices does he use for his points of imitation? How does his use of imitation compare to the Du Fay and Ockeghem Masses?

19. How does Josquin's music reflect the meaning of the opening words of *De profundis clamavi ad te* (NAWM 33)?

    How does the music reflect the natural accentuation of the words elsewhere in the motet?

20. Where do cadences occur in Josquin's motet *De profundis clamavi ad te*? How does the location of cadences relate to the structure of the text?

21. A motet of Josquin's generation is made up of a series of phrases. Each segment of the text is given its own musical phrase, which is usually treated in a point of imitation or is presented homophonically. Most phrases are marked off with cadences, although some points of imitation overlap. One of Josquin's trademarks is his alternation of voices in pairs with each other and with the full four-voice texture. These changes of texture, along with the frequent cadences, help to make the structure clear.

   In Josquin's motet *De profundis clamavi ad te,* where do phrases begin with a point of imitation? List each instance, including the measure number it begins, the first words of the phrase of text, and the number of voices that participate in the point of imitation.

Postlude (CHWM 121)

22. Describe the musical style current in Europe around 1500–20. How does it differ from the style of Du Fay?

TERMS TO KNOW

Renaissance
humanism
counterpoint
imitation
canon

mensuration canon
partbooks
imitation Mass (or parody Mass)
paraphrase Mass

NAMES TO KNOW

Josquin des Prez
Franchino Gaffurio
Dodekachordon, by Heinrich
    Glareanus
Liber de arte contrapuncti, by
    Johannes Tinctoris
Le istitutioni harmoniche, by
    Gioseffo Zarlino

Ottaviano de' Petrucci
Johannes Ockeghem
Missa prolationum
Jacob Obrecht
Heinrich Isaac
Harmonice musices odhecaton A
Missa Pange lingua

REVIEW QUESTIONS

1. Make a time-line for the pieces, composers, treatises, and theorists discussed in this chapter.

2. Define humanism as a movement in the Renaissance, and explain how it was reflected in the culture and music of the time.

3. Trace the development of the motet in the fifteenth and early sixteenth centuries from Dunstable to Josquin, using the motets in NAWM as examples.

4. What are the major changes in the style of secular vocal music from Ockeghem's generation to that of Josquin?

5. Describe Ottaviano de' Petrucci's method of music printing and the effects music printing had on musical life.

6. Compare the careers and music of any two of the following composers: Machaut, Du Fay, Ockeghem, Josquin.

THE AGE OF THE RENAISSANCE: NEW CURRENTS IN THE SIXTEENTH CENTURY

CHAPTER OBJECTIVES

After you complete the reading, study of the music, and study questions for this chapter, you should be able to

1. describe the principal styles and genres of sixteenth-century secular vocal music and instrumental music;
2. describe the relation of music and words in sixteenth-century vocal music and contrast it with earlier practices of setting texts;
3. identify some of the major composers of sixteenth-century music; and
4. identify the characteristics of national schools of composition in the sixteenth century.

CHAPTER OUTLINE

Prelude (CHWM 122–23)

The years 1520–50 saw a growing diversity of styles, genres, and forms, including the growth of national styles, the madrigal, the emergence of Italy as the musical center of Europe, and the rise of instrumental music.

I. The Generation after Josquin (1520–50) (CHWM 123–26)

Church composers after Josquin used a similar smooth polyphonic style but increasingly wrote for five or six voices rather than four. Chants were often paraphrased in all voices rather than set apart as a cantus firmus.

A. Adrian Willaert

Adrian Willaert (ca. 1490–1562) was among the most important composers of his generation. Director of music at St. Mark's Church in Venice for the second half of his life, he exercised a great influence through his teaching and his compositions.

1. Attention to text

   Willaert composed music to fit the structure and meaning of the words. He specified which syllable was to be sung to each note and sought to ensure that the text was correctly accented and punctuated.

2. Cadences

   Willaert marked major breaks in the text with full cadences and lesser ones with weak or evaded cadences.

3. Use of chant

   In Willaert's pieces based on chant, often all voices paraphrase the chant, each in a different way, in very free imitative counterpoint.

4. Adherence to mode

   Sixteenth-century composers valued the modes as a link to Christian tradition and to the emotional effects of ancient music. Willaert's melodic lines and cadences convey the mode by emphasizing the final and other important notes in the mode.

II. The Rise of National Styles: Italy (CHWM 126–27, NAWM 35)

1. Frottola and lauda

   The *frottola,* an Italian genre common in the late fifteenth and early sixteenth centuries, was a strophic secular song with an amorous or satirical text set in a simple, homophonic, diatonic, syllabic style. The polyphonic *lauda* was a religious song, not used in the liturgy.   **Music: NAWM 35**

2. Villanella

   Later Italian composers used other light genres of secular vocal music. The *villanella* was a strophic and homophonic piece for three voices.

3. Canzonetta and balletto

   The *canzonetta* was a short secular song, and the *balletto* was a dance song often featuring nonsense syllables such as "fa-la-la."

4. Petrarchan movement

   The rise of the madrigal was closely connected to renewed interest in the poetry and ideals of fourteenth-century Italian poet *Francesco Petrarch* (1304–1374), whose poems reflect the mood or imagery of the words in the sound of the language itself. Early madrigalists often set his poetry, especially his sonnets.

III. The Italian Madrigal (CHWM 127–36, NAWM 36–40)

Unlike the frottola or fourteenth-century madrigal, the sixteenth-century *madrigal* did not use a refrain or set form, but was a through-composed work that sought to capture the ideas and feelings in the words through a series of changing musical textures and images. The poems used were serious or artful and were often by a major poet

1. Social setting

   Madrigals were sung in courtly gatherings and academies, usually by amateurs for their own enjoyment. After about 1570 some patrons employed professional singers to perform madrigals, which led some composers to write more difficult music for them to perform.

2. Concerto delle donne
The most famous of the professional madrigal ensembles was the *concerto delle donne* (women's ensemble) at Ferrara. Madrigals were also sung in plays and theatrical productions. Madrigals were perhaps the first commercial popular music, with over 2,000 collections published and sold by 1600.

3. Voices
Madrigals of 1520–50 are usually for four voices and later ones for five or more, with one singer to a part, sometimes doubled or replaced by an instrument.

4. Arcadelt
Jacob Arcadelt (ca. 1505–ca. 1568) and Willaert, northerners skilled in composing church music, brought into the madrigal the techniques and expressivity of the motet. Arcadelt's style was simpler than Willaert's and closer to the homophony of the frottola.   **Music: NAWM 36–37**

5. Rore
Cipriano de Rore (1516–1565), a student of Willaert's, was the leading madrigalist of his generation. His music was famed for its vivid expression of the feelings in the text. Zarlino described the musical means for representing certain contrasting moods in his treatise *Le istitutioni harmoniche*.
Music: NAWM 38

6. Other northerners
Among the important madrigalists of the later sixteenth century were several northern composers working in or outside Italy.

7. Marenzio
Late in the century, the leading madrigalists were native Italians. *Luca Marenzio* (1553–1599) was the most prolific, renowned for his depiction of feelings and imagery.   **Music: NAWM 39**

8. Vicentino
In his writings and music, *Nicola Vicentino* (1511–ca. 1576) explored chromaticism to an unprecedented degree, inspired by the ancient Greek chromatic and enharmonic genera.

9. Luzzaschi
Luzzasco Luzzaschi (1545–1607) continued Vicentino's interest in chromaticism and in turn influenced Gesualdo.

10. Gesualdo
Carlo Gesualdo (ca. 1561–1613) is known for adventurous chromaticism. While his vertical sonorities are mostly consonant, the motion through successive sonorities can be quite unpredictable. He used contrasts between chromatic and diatonic sections to convey the changing moods of the text.
Music: NAWM 40

11. Monteverdi

Claudio Monteverdi (1567–1643) was the most important Italian composer of the late sixteenth and early seventeenth centuries. He was born in Cremona, worked in Mantua, and was choirmaster at St. Mark's in Venice for the last thirty years of his life. His madrigals show a variety of techniques, including increased use of unprepared dissonance, declamatory passages, and other methods of conveying the feeling of the text.

Window: The Lute Player (CHWM 129)

Caravaggio's picture of a musician playing the lute and singing a madrigal by Arcadelt can reveal much about musical culture in the 1590s.

IV. The Rise of National Styles: Secular Song outside Italy (CHWM 136–41, NAWM 41–44)

1. French chanson

Composers centered in Paris in the first half of the sixteenth century cultivated a new type of chanson called the *Parisian chanson.*

2. Attaingnant

The first French music printer was *Pierre Attaingnant* (ca. 1494–ca. 1551), who published more than fifty collections of chansons.

3. Parisian chanson

Parisian chansons were strophic songs in a light, fast style, mostly syllabic and homophonic, with the melody in the upper voice, occasional brief points of imitation, and short repeated sections.

4. Sermisy

Claudin de Sermisy (ca. 1490–1562) was one of the principal composers in Attaingnant's collections.   **Music: NAWM 41**

5. Janequin

Another was *Clément Janequin* (ca. 1485–ca. 1560), who was renowned for his descriptive chansons.

6. Franco-Flemish chanson

Outside of Paris, Franco-Flemish composers continued the older, more contrapuntal chanson tradition. Late in the century, poets wrote French verse that imitated the long and short syllables of ancient Greek poetry, and *Claude Le Jeune* (1528–1600) and other composers set these to music.)   **Music: NAWM 42**

7. English madrigal

Nicholas Yonge's publication in 1588 of *Musica transalpina,* a collection of Italian madrigals in English translation, launched a fashion for madrigal singing and composition in England. The leading composers included *Thomas Morley* (1557–1602) and *Thomas Weelkes* (ca. 1575–1623).

8. Morley

Morley was particularly skilled in lighter forms such as the ballett and canzonet (related to the Italian balletto and canzonetta).

9. Weelkes

Weelkes's madrigals often feature intense harmony, shapely melodies, and compelling expression of the text.   **Music: NAWM 43**

10. *The Triumphes of Oriana*

Morley's collection *The Triumphes of Oriana* contained madrigals by twenty-five English composers in honor of Queen Elizabeth I. Madrigals were aimed at amateurs and often sung at social gatherings.

11. English lute songs

Solo songs with lute accompaniment, known as *lute songs,* became popular in England after about 1600. The songs, or *airs,* of *John Dowland* (1562–1626) feature less text-painting than the madrigal but carefully follow the natural declamation and overall mood of the text.   **Music: NAWM 44**

12. German lied

Secular polyphony came late to Germany, where the monophony of the Meistersinger continued through the sixteenth century. The polyphonic *lied* wove Franco-Flemish counterpoint around a familiar German tune. Later lieder were influenced by the Italian madrigal, as are the lieder of *Orlando di Lasso* (1532–1594), who also wrote madrigals and chansons.

V. The Rise of Instrumental Music (CHWM 142–44)

The period 1450–1550 saw an increase in instrumental music and the beginnings of independent styles and forms of writing for instruments. Two main trends can be seen: (1) the use of styles and genres idiomatic to instruments and independent of vocal music, and (2) instrumental music adapted from vocal music or inspired by vocal genres.

Etude: Instruments Used during the Renaissance

Renaissance instruments were built in *families,* with each type of instrument built in different sizes and registers from bass to soprano. A complete set of a single type of instrument was called a *chest* or *consort.*

    1. Wind instruments included recorders, shawms, capped-reed instruments, transverse flutes, cornetts, trumpets, and sackbuts.

    2. The main type of bowed string instrument was the *viol,* which had frets, six strings, and a delicate tone.

    3. The *lute* was the most popular household instrument. Its music was notated in *tablature,* which showed not the pitches to play but which string to pluck and where to stop the string to produce the correct pitch. (For examples of tablature, see CHWM, pp. 140 and 205, and NAWM 44 and 63a.)

    4. Keyboard instruments included the organ, the *clavichord,* and the *harpsichord.*

VI. Categories of Instrumental Music (CHWM 145–51, NAWM 45–46)

There are five main categories of Renaissance instrumental music, which continue into the seventeenth century: (1) dance, (2) improvisatory pieces,

(3) contrapuntal works, (4) canzona and sonata, and (5) variation. These categories became more distinct over time.

A. *Dance Music*

1. Social dancing

Social dancing was important to Renaissance society, and thus much of the instrumental music of the time was written for dancing or based on dance forms. In stylized dance pieces, an instrumental style independent of vocal models could develop.   **Music: NAWM 45**

2. Ballet

An important theatrical dance form was the *ballet.*

3. Dance medleys

Dances were often grouped in pairs or in threes, usually a slow dance in duple meter followed by a fast one in triple meter.

B. *Improvisatory Pieces*

Renaissance musicians were trained in improvisation, both in embellishing a given line and in adding contrapuntal lines to a given melody.

1. Basse danse

The fifteenth-century *basse danse* was improvised over a borrowed tenor, but later basses danses were written out with the melody on top. The *branle gay* was a type of basse danse in triple meter.   **Music: NAWM 45**

2. Other improvisatory genres

Players of keyboards and lutes improvised polyphonic pieces, and works in the same general style were written down under names such as *prelude, fantasia,* and *ricercare.* Preludes and fantasias often served to establish the mode for a following vocal piece.

3. Toccata

The chief keyboard genre in improvisatory style in the second half of the sixteenth century was the *toccata* (from the Italian word for "touched").

C. *Contrapuntal Genres*

1. Ricercare

The *ricercare* or *ricercar* evolved from an early improvisatory form into a work for ensemble or solo instrument based on a series of subjects treated in imitation, like an instrumental relative of the motet.

D. *Canzona and Sonata*

1. Canzona

The Italian instrumental *canzona* originated as a work in the same style as a Parisian chanson, with a typical opening figure of a note followed by two notes of half its value (e.g., a half note and two quarter notes). The early canzonas were for organ. Ensemble canzonas were written after 1580 and evolved into the seventeenth-century sonata da chiesa. Canzonas were often based on a series of different figures, most of them treated in imitation. The result was a piece in a series of sections.

2. Sonata

Sonata is a term with many different meanings throughout music history. It was first used for a piece of purely instrumental music. The Venetian sonata of the late sixteenth century was more serious than the canzona. Among the most important Venetian composers of sonatas and canzonas was *Giovanni Gabrieli* (ca. 1557–1612). His *Sonata pian' e forte,* for two instrumental choirs, was among the first instrumental ensemble pieces to designate specific instruments and dynamic markings.

E. *Variations*

Written sets of *variations* first appear in the early sixteenth century. There are both variations on tunes presented in the treble and variations over *ostinatos* in the bass.

1. English virginalists

In the late sixteenth and early seventeenth centuries, *the English virginalists*—composers of music for virginals, or harpsichord—wrote many variations and other keyboard works. The most prominent of these composers was *William Byrd* (1543–1623), and the most important manuscript collection is the *Fitzwilliam Virginal Book.*

2. Themes

The themes chosen for variations were simple and songlike, often familiar tunes. Variations preserved the phrasing and harmony while changing the figuration. **Music: NAWM 46**

Study Questions

The Generation after Josquin (1520–50) (CHWM 123–26)

1. What principles did Willaert follow in setting words to music?

2. In his motet *O crux, splendidior cunctis astris* (excerpted in CHWM, pp. 124–25), how does Willaert project the transposed Dorian mode?

The Rise of National Styles: Italy (CHWM 126–27, NAWM 35)

Music to Study
   NAWM 35: Marco Cara, *Io non compro più speranza,* frottola (ca. 1500)
      CD 2.44–50

3. What is a *frottola*? Where and when was it popular? What traits of the genre are exemplified in Cara's *Io non compro più speranza* (NAWM 35)?

---

4. Who was Francesco Petrarch? When did he live? What was his importance for the sixteenth-century madrigal?

The Italian Madrigal (CHWM 127–36, NAWM 36–40)

5. How does the sixteenth-century *madrigal* differ from the fourteenth-century madrigal? How does it differ from the frottola?

6. In what circumstances were madrigals performed, and by whom?

Music to Study
    NAWM 36: Jacob Arcadelt, *Il bianco e dolce cigno,* madrigal (ca. 1538)
        CD 2.51–52 (Concise 1.41–42)
    NAWM 37: Adrian Willaert, *Aspro core e selvaggio,* madrigal (ca. 1540s)
        CD 2.53–57
    NAWM 38: Cipriano de Rore, *Da le belle contrade d'oriente,* madrigal (1566)
        CD 2.58–60 (Concise 1.43–45)
    NAWM 39: Luca Marenzio, *Solo e pensoso,* madrigal (published 1599)
        CD 3.1–5
    NAWM 40: Carlo Gesualdo, *"Io parto" e non più dissi,* madrigal (1590s?)
        CD 3.6–8

7. In what ways does Arcadelt's madrigal *Il bianco e dolce cigno* (NAWM 36) resemble a frottola, such as Cara's *Io non compro più speranza* (NAWM 35)?

In what ways is it different from a frottola?

8. In the sixteenth century, sexual climax was known as "the little death," and poets often used this image in erotic poetry. How does your interpretation of this poem change, once you know this fact? What is the speaker saying?

9. In what ways does Arcadelt reflect in his music the feelings or the imagery of the text?

10. In what ways is Willaert's madrigal *Aspro core e selvaggio* (NAWM 37) like a sixteenth-century motet, such as Josquin's *De profundis clamavi ad te* (NAWM 33)?

11. What suggestions for setting a text does Zarlino (who was Willaert's student) make in the passage on p. 134 of CHWM? How is this advice reflected in the opening passage of Willaert's *Aspro core*?

12. In Rore's *Da le belle contrade d'oriente* (NAWM 38), how does the music reflect the presence of two speakers in the poem?

    How does the music reflect the meaning and mood of the words?

    How does the music reflect the accentuation and rhythm of the words?

13. Both Rore's *Da le belle contrade d'oriente* and Marenzio's *Solo e pensoso* (NAWM 39) set sonnets, fourteen-line poems divided into an octave of eight lines and a sestet of six lines. How does each composer set off the sestet from the octave? In what other ways does each setting reflect the structure of the text?

14. How does Marenzio's music suggest the poetic imagery of *Solo e pensoso*?

15. How does Gesualdo use chromaticism, contrasting diatonic sections, melodic motion, and rhythm to reflect the emotional sense of the words in *"Io parto" e non più dissi* (NAWM 40)?

16. Briefly outline Monteverdi's career, including his date and place of birth, his early training, and his employment, including place, position, and dates of service.

The Rise of National Styles: Secular Song outside Italy (CHWM 136–41, NAWM 41–44)

17. Who was the major publisher of Parisian chansons in the early sixteenth century?

Who were the principal composers of these chansons?

What evidence is there for the popularity of this type of chanson?

Music to Study

NAWM 41: Claudin de Sermisy, *Tant que vivray,* chanson (second quarter of the sixteenth century)
CD 3.9–10 (Concise 1.46–47)
NAWM 42: Claude Le Jeune, *Revecy venir du printans,* chanson (late sixteenth century)
CD 3.11–19

18. How does the Parisian chanson, exemplified by Sermisy's *Tant que vivray* (NAWM 41), compare to the Italian frottola, such as Cara's *Io non compro più speranza* (NAWM 35), and the early madrigal, such as Arcadelt's *Il bianco e dolce cigno* (NAWM 36)? How is it similar, and how is it different?

19. How does Le Jeune's *Revecy venir du printans* (NAWM 42) reflect the rhythm of the text?

---

20. What was *Musica transalpina,* and when did it appear? What effect did it have on the development of the English madrigal?

Music to Study

NAWM 43: Thomas Weelkes, *O Care, thou wilt despatch me*, madrigal (ca. 1600)

 CD 3.20–23 (Concise 1.48–51)

NAWM 44: John Dowland, *Flow, my tears*, air (ca. 1600)

 CD 3.24–26 (Concise 1.52–54)

21. In Weelkes's madrigal *O Care, thou wilt despatch me* (NAWM 43), how are the images and feelings in the text conveyed in the music?

22. Locate where the following unusual vertical sonorities occur in Weelkes's madrigal. (Some occur more than once.)

 a diminished seventh _____

 an augmented triad _____

 a diminished octave _____

What purposes do these dissonances serve? How can you explain their presence?

23. Comparing Weelkes's madrigal to the madrigals in NAWM 36–40, what similarities and what differences do you notice between English and Italian madrigals?

24. What are the characteristics of an English lute song from around 1600, as exemplified by Dowland's *Flow, my tears* (NAWM 44)? How is it like a madrigal, and how is it different?

The Rise of Instrumental Music (CHWM 142–44)

25. Why do we have so little instrumental music from before 1450? How and why did this change after about 1450? What evidence is there for a rising interest in instrumental music during the Renaissance?

26. What is an *instrument family*? Why is it significant that instruments were built in families?

27. Which were the principal instrument families in the sixteenth century? How do they relate to their medieval ancestors, and how do they relate to their modern relatives?

28. What is *tablature*? What does it convey to the performer?

Categories of Instrumental Music (CHWM 145–51, NAWM 45–46)

29. What were the main kinds of instrumental pieces in the sixteenth century?

Music to Study
> **NAWM 45:** Pierre Attaingnant (editor, compiler, and printer), *Danseries a 4 Parties, Second Livre* (Dances in Four Parts, Second Book, published 1547), excerpts
>
> 45a: Basse danse   CD 3.27 (Concise 1.55)
> 45b: Branle gay   CD 3.28 (Concise 1.56)

30. How do the Basse danse and Branle gay from Pierre Attaingnant's *Danseries a 4 Parties, Second Livre* (NAWM 45) exemplify the characteristics of Renaissance dance music?

---

31. What role did improvisation play in sixteenth-century music performance and education?

32. What is a *toccata*? On which instruments was it performed? What are its main musical characteristics, and how are they exemplified in the toccata by Claudio Merulo excerpted on p. 147 of CHWM?

33. What was a *ricercare* (or *ricercar*) in the sixteenth century? What were its main characteristics? What vocal genre did the late-sixteenth-century ricercare resemble?

34. What is an instrumental *canzona*? What vocal form was it related to, and what did it develop into?

35. What did the term *sonata* mean in the sixteenth century?

36. What is special about Giovanni Gabrieli's *Sonata pian' e forte*?

37. What types of variations were written in the sixteenth century? In the music of the English virginalists, what kinds of tunes were used as themes for variations, and how were they treated in the variations?

Music to Study
> **NAWM 46:** William Byrd, *Pavana Lachrymae,* keyboard variations on
> NAWM 44, Dowland's *Flow, my tears* (early seventeenth century)
> CD 3.29–31 (Concise 2.1–3)

38. How is Dowland's *Flow, my tears* (NAWM 44) treated in Byrd's *Pavana Lachrymae* (NAWM 46)?

TERMS TO KNOW

Terms Related to Sixteenth-Century Vocal Music

frottola

lauda (polyphonic)

villanella, canzonetta, balletto

madrigal (sixteenth-century)

the concerto delle donne

Parisian chanson

lute song

air

lied (polyphonic)

Terms Related to Sixteenth-Century Instrumental Music

instrument family

chest or consort

viol

lute

tablature

clavichord

harpsichord

ballet

basse danse

branle gay

prelude

fantasia

ricercare

toccata

canzona

sonata (sixteenth-century)

variations

ostinato

the English virginalists

NAMES TO KNOW

Adrian Willaert

Francesco Petrarch

Jacob Arcadelt

Cipriano de Rore

Luca Marenzio

Nicola Vicentino

Luzzasco Luzzaschi

Carlo Gesualdo

Claudio Monteverdi

Pierre Attaingnant

Claudin de Sermisy

Clément Janequin

Claude Le Jeune

Musica transalpina

Thomas Morley

Thomas Weelkes

The Triumphes of Oriana

John Dowland

Orlando di Lasso

Giovanni Gabrieli

Sonata pian' e forte

William Byrd

The Fitzwilliam Virginal Book

REVIEW QUESTIONS

1. Make a time-line for the sixteenth century and place on it the pieces, composers, and treatises discussed in this chapter. (You will add to this time-line in the next chapter.)

2. Trace the development of secular vocal music in Italy from the frottola to the madrigals of Gesualdo and Monteverdi. In what ways did humanism and the revival of ancient Greek ideas about music influence this development?

3. Describe the varieties of secular vocal music practiced in France, England, and Germany during the sixteenth century. Which of these forms were influenced by the Italian madrigal, and in what ways?

4. Describe the relation of music and words in the various forms of sixteenth-century vocal music and contrast it with earlier practices of setting texts.

5. In what ways can you compare the madrigal in England (or Italy, or both) to popular music of the present or recent past? Try to come up with as many examples as you can of parallels between the madrigal, the popular music of the sixteenth century, and top-40 pop music, rock, rap, country, or any other type of popular music current today. What are some important differences?

6. Name and describe the various types of notated instrumental music in the sixteenth century. Which ones were related to vocal models, to dancing, or to improvisation?

Church Music of the Late Renaissance and Reformation

8

Chapter Objectives

After you complete the reading, study of the music, and study questions for this chapter, you should be able to

1. describe attitudes toward and uses of music in Protestant churches in the sixteenth century and the genres they used;
2. recount the effect of the Counter-Reformation on sixteenth-century Catholic music and describe the styles of Palestrina, Victoria, and Lasso; and
3. identify some of the most important composers and terms associated with these trends.

Chapter Outline

Prelude (CHWM 153–54)

The *Reformation* brought new Protestant sects with their own liturgies and music, particularly in northern Europe. In reaction, the Catholic Church undertook its own internal program of reform, the *Counter-Reformation,* which likewise had important effects on church music.

I. The Music of the Reformation in Germany (CHWM 154–56)

1. Lutheran church music
Martin Luther (1483–1546), the leader of the Reformation in Germany, loved music and gave it a central position in the Lutheran Church, including congregational singing. Congregations varied in liturgy and music.

2. German Mass
Some congregations kept much of the Latin liturgy. Luther's *Deudsche Messe* (German Mass, 1526) followed the main outlines of the Mass liturgy translated into German but with many changes. The music used included plainsong, Latin polyphony, and German chorales.

3. The Lutheran chorale

The *chorale* was a strophic hymn sung by the congregation in unison. Luther wrote many chorale texts and perhaps some of the tunes. Besides newly written melodies, chorale tunes were often adapted from Gregorian chant or German sacred or secular songs.

4. Contrafacta

Many chorales were adapted from secular songs by revising the text to give it a spiritual meaning or by replacing it with a new sacred text. The new works that resulted are called *contrafacta.*

5. Polyphonic chorale settings

Composers soon began to arrange the monophonic chorales in polyphonic settings for choirs to perform, using a variety of styles from cantus firmus style or imitative motet style to simple chordal style. By the late sixteenth century, Protestant composers began to write *chorale motets,* free polyphonic elaborations of a chorale.

II. Reformation Church Music outside Germany (CHWM 157–60, NAWM 50)

1. Calvinism

Reformation movements in France, the Low Countries, and Switzerland, led by *Jean Calvin* (1509–1564) and others, rejected the Catholic liturgy in favor of rhymed translations of the Psalms. These were published in *Psalters* and sung in unison to simple melodies.

2. French Psalter

The main French Psalter (1562) used tunes composed or adapted by *Loys Bourgeois* (ca. 1510–ca. 1561). His melodies were often borrowed by churches in other lands, including in the New England colonies. Psalm tunes were sometimes set polyphonically or in simple chordal style.

3. England

English composers were relatively isolated in the late fifteenth and early sixteenth centuries and only gradually adopted the newer style of imitative counterpoint. Most English polyphonic music was sacred, with full textures and long melismas.

4. Taverner

The greatest English composer of this period was *John Taverner* (ca. 1490–1545), renowned for his Masses and Magnificats.

5. Tallis

The leading mid-century English composer was *Thomas Tallis* (ca. 1505–1585), known for his music for both the Catholic and Anglican liturgies.

Etude: More about Anglican Church Music

The Church of England separated from the Roman Catholic Church in 1534, largely for political reasons (Henry VIII wanted an annulment of his marriage, and the pope refused to grant it). A new liturgy in English was printed in *The Book of Common Prayer* (1549), and composers wrote church music in English. The two main genres were the *service* and the *anthem.*

1. A *service* consisted of music for Morning and Evening Prayer and for Holy Communion, and could be either a *Great Service* (contrapuntal and melismatic) or a *Short Service* (chordal and syllabic).
2. An *anthem* was equivalent to a motet. There were two types: the *full anthem,* sung by choir throughout, and the *verse anthem,* for solo voice or voices with organ or viol accompaniment, with brief passages for chorus.

Among the most important composers of Anglican music was William Byrd (mentioned in Chapter 7), a Catholic who also wrote Latin motets and Masses.   **Music: NAWM 50**

Window: Music as a Symbol for Human Frailty (CHWM 158–59)

In a Dutch painting on the transience of life, a violin and bow represent the impermanence of music and the tenuous pleasures it offers.

III. The Counter-Reformation (CHWM 160–71, NAWM 47–49)

1. Council of Trent
The *Council of Trent* met intermittently between 1545 and 1563 to reform the Catholic Church. Music was only one factor that was considered. The Council urged very general reforms designed to ensure that the words of the liturgy were clear and the music religious in tone.

A. *Palestrina*

There is a legend, apparently untrue, that *Giovanni Pierluigi da Palestrina* (1525 or 1526–1594) convinced the Council not to abolish polyphony by writing the *Pope Marcellus Mass.*

1. Career
Palestrina spent his entire career in Rome as a church musician, often working for the pope.

2. Editing of chant books
Palestrina supervised the revision of Gregorian chant to conform to the edicts of the Council of Trent. His own compositions were polyphonic and mostly sacred, including 104 Masses and about 250 motets.

3. Style
Palestrina's style became a model for later composers of church music.

4. Masses
Palestrina's Masses use techniques ranging from cantus firmus to imitation Masses and from paraphrase to canon.

5. *Pope Marcellus* Mass
Palestrina's vocal lines move mostly by step in a smooth, flexible arch. Leaps are filled in with stepwise motion in the opposite direction, and chromaticism is avoided.   **Music: NAWM 47**

6. Form

In a Palestrina Mass movement, each phrase of text has its own motive, and phrases overlap. Unity is created by repeating motives and cadencing on important notes in the mode.

7. Text comprehension

In Palestrina's Masses the text is declaimed very clearly, and changes of texture lend variety and illustrate the words.

Etude: Palestrina's Counterpoint

Palestrina's counterpoint is smooth and mostly consonant, with dissonance restricted to suspensions, passing notes, and *cambiatas*. The voices move independently within a regular harmonic rhythm. He uses different spacings to create variety in sonority.

B. *Palestrina's contemporaries*

Other composers of the late sixteenth century share many stylistic traits with Palestrina, yet have distinctive characteristics.

1. Victoria

Tomás Luis de Victoria (1548–1611) was a Spanish composer active in Rome and in Spain whose music is more intense than Palestrina's in text expression and use of accidentals.   **Music: NAWM 48a and 48b**

2. Lasso

Orlando di Lasso (mentioned in Chapter 7) is as important for his motets as Palestrina is for Masses. His motets often use pictorial, rhetorical, and dra-matic devices and are written in a variety of styles. One of the most inter-national of composers, he synthesized aspects of most significant national styles of the time.   **Music: NAWM 49**

3. Byrd

William Byrd (mentioned in Chapter 7 and above) wrote three Masses and numerous Latin motets, in addition to secular music and music for the Anglican church.

Postlude (CHWM 171)

The year 1600 is only an approximate date for the end of the Renaissance. Some Renaissance traits continued into the seventeenth century, and what became known as the *stile antico* or old style continued to be revered.

STUDY QUESTIONS

The Music of the Reformation in Germany (CHWM 154–56)

1. What is a *chorale*? How were they sung, and by whom?

2. What are the chief sources of tunes for chorales? What are *contrafacta*?

3. In what ways did chorales receive polyphonic treatment in the sixteenth and early seventeenth centuries? How were these polyphonic settings performed?

Reformation Church Music outside Germany (CHWM 157–60, NAWM 50)

4. How was music used in the Calvinist churches outside Germany? How does this differ from the Lutheran Church?

5. What is a *Psalter,* and what does it contain?

6. What are the principal forms of Anglican church music? How does a *full anthem* differ from a *verse anthem*? How does a *Great Service* differ from a *Short Service*?

Music to Study
> **NAWM 50:** William Byrd, *Sing joyfully unto God,* full anthem (late sixteenth century)
> CD 3.47–50 (Concise 2.9–12)

7. How does Byrd illustrate the text in *Sing joyfully unto God* (NAWM 50)? How does he highlight the accentuation and phrasing of the text?

The Counter-Reformation (CHWM 160–71, NAWM 47–49)

8. What was the Council of Trent? When was it held, and what was its purpose? What matters relating to music were discussed, and what actions relating to music did the Council take?

9. Briefly summarize Palestrina's career. Why was his music important for later composers?

10. How many Masses did Palestrina write? _____

What compositional techniques did he use in his Masses?

Music to Study
   NAWM 47: Giovanni da Palestrina, *Pope Marcellus Mass,* excerpts (1562–
      63)
   47a: Credo   CD 3.32–36
   47b: Agnus Dei I   CD 3.37 (Concise 2.4)

11. Describe Palestrina's style in terms of melody, harmony, counterpoint and
    dissonance treatment, sonority, and rhythm, using examples from the Credo
    and first Agnus Dei of the *Pope Marcellus Mass* (NAWM 47a and 47b).

    melody:

    harmony:

    counterpoint and dissonance treatment:

    sonority:

    rhythm:

Music to Study
> **NAWM 48a:** Tomás Luis de Victoria, *O magnum mysterium,* motet (published 1572)
> CD 3.38–40
> **NAWM 48b:** Tomás Luis de Victoria, *Missa O magnum mysterium,* Mass (published 1592), excerpt: Kyrie
> CD 3.41–42

12. How is each phrase of text treated in Victoria's motet *O magnum mysterium* (NAWM 48a)? How does the placement of cadences help to give shape to the piece and make clear the divisions of the text?

13. Compare the Kyrie of Victoria's *Missa O magnum mysterium* (NAWM 48b) to the motet on which it is based (NAWM 48a). What has Victoria borrowed from his earlier motet, and how has he varied it?

14. What is an *imitation Mass* or *parody Mass* (see the definition in CHWM, p. 120)? How does Victoria's *Missa O magnum mysterium* exemplify this kind of Mass?

15. How do Orlando di Lasso's career, music, and musical output contrast with those of Palestrina? (Note: There is additional information on Lasso in Chapter 7 of CHWM.)

Music to Study
NAWM 49: Orlando di Lasso, *Tristis est anima mea,* motet (published 1565)
    CD 3.43–46 (Concise 2.5–8)

16. How does Lasso use pictorial, rhetorical, or dramatic devices to convey the meaning of the words in his motet *Tristis est anima mea* (NAWM 49)?

---

17. Briefly recount William Byrd's career. What kinds of music did he write? How did the situation of religion in England affect his career and compositional output? (You may wish to refer back to parts of Chapter 7 of CHWM in answering this question.)

TERMS TO KNOW

Reformation
Counter-Reformation
chorale
contrafacta
chorale motet

Psalter
service: Great Service, Short Service
anthem: full anthem, verse anthem
cambiata

NAMES TO KNOW

Martin Luther
Deudsche Messe
Jean Calvin
Loys Bourgeois
John Taverner
Thomas Tallis

The Book of Common Prayer
the Council of Trent
Giovanni Pierluigi da Palestrina
Pope Marcellus Mass
Tomás Luis de Victoria

REVIEW QUESTIONS

1. Add to the time-line you made for the sixteenth century in Chapter 7 the pieces, composers, and events discussed in this chapter.

2. How was music regarded, how was it used, and what musical genres were cultivated in the Lutheran church and in Calvinist churches during the sixteenth century?

3. How did the Counter-Reformation affect music for the Catholic church?

4. Describe Palestrina's style in his Masses.

5. How did composers of church music in the late sixteenth century treat the words they set? What are some of the approaches to setting or expressing a text, as exemplified by the pieces treated in this chapter?

MUSIC OF THE EARLY BAROQUE PERIOD

CHAPTER OBJECTIVES

After you complete the reading, study of the music, and study questions for this chapter, you should be able to

1. describe the characteristics that distinguish Baroque music from music of earlier periods;
2. relate music of the Baroque period to the culture and art of the time;
3. describe the various styles of music that flourished and competed in the first half of the seventeenth century;
4. trace the evolution of opera in Italy from its forerunners through the middle of the seventeenth century;
5. describe the genres and styles of secular and sacred vocal music practiced in the early seventeenth century;
6. explain what is distinctive about Venice and Venetian music in the late sixteenth and early seventeenth centuries; and
7. name and briefly describe the most important genres and styles of instrumental music in the early Baroque period.

CHAPTER OUTLINE

Prelude (CHWM 172–74)

The *Baroque period* of about 1600 to 1750 embraced a variety of musical styles that shared broad conventions and ideals, notably the belief that music should move the listener's emotions. Many rulers supported music, as did churches, cities, and independent academies. Italy remained the most influential region, with centers at Florence, Rome, Venice, Naples, and Bologna. New vocal genres developed, from opera to cantata, sacred concerto, and oratorio, and for the first time instrumental music became as important as vocal music. Literature and art flourished throughout Europe, from the poetry of Milton to the paintings of Rembrandt. Developments in philosophy and science were particularly spectacular, as Bacon, Descartes, Leibniz,

Galileo, Kepler, Newton, and others helped lay the foundations of modern thought. Musicians around 1600 sought to give expression to a wider range of emotions and ideas than before. Their search for new methods led to the codification of a new musical language by mid-century.

I. General Characteristics of Baroque Music (CHWM 174–79, NAWM 53)

1. Two practices

Writing in 1605, Monteverdi contrasted the *prima pratica* (first practice), in which a composer follows the rules of dissonance treatment codified by Zarlino, with the *seconda pratica* (second practice), in which those rules could be violated in order to express better the feelings in the text.

Etude: Monteverdi and the *Seconda Pratica*

When theorist *Giovanni Maria Artusi* attacked Monteverdi's madrigals for incorrect treatment of dissonance, the composer defended his approach by claiming the right to break the rules of counterpoint in order to represent the feelings in the text.   **Music: NAWM 53**

2. Idiomatic writing

The growing importance of soloists led seventeenth-century composers to write with a specific medium in mind. As a result, distinctive idiomatic styles developed for the voice and various instruments.

3. The affections

Baroque composers sought to write music that was expressive of *the affections,* or states of the soul. These are not the composer's own emotions but generalized states of feeling.

4. Rhythm

Music before the seventeenth century was conceived primarily in terms of durations, but Baroque and later composers thought in terms of strong and weak beats grouped in *measures.* On the other hand, free and irregular rhythms were used in vocal recitative and instrumental preludes and toccatas. Some standard forms paired a relatively free section with a strictly metered section, such as a recitative and aria or a toccata and fugue.

5. Basso continuo

Renaissance polyphony used a texture of equal voices, but in Baroque music the melody and bass were the two essential lines. In the system called *thorough bass* or *basso continuo,* the accompaniment was not fully written out; instead, *continuo instruments* like harpsichord, organ, or lute would play the notated bass line and fill in the appropriate chords above it, while often a sustaining instrument like viola da gamba or bassoon would reinforce the bass. Accidentals, nonchord tones, and chords other than root-position triads could be indicated by numbers and other figures; a part notated this way is a *figured bass.* A basso continuo part can be *realized* by performers in various ways, from plain chords to elaborate improvisations.

6. The new counterpoint

A new kind of counterpoint evolved in which the lines had to fit the chords of the basso continuo, so that the counterpoint was governed by harmony.

7. Dissonance

The new importance of harmony led by the mid-seventeenth century to a conception of dissonance as a note outside a chord, rather than an interval between two voices, and to an increased role for dissonance in defining the tonal direction of a piece.

8. Chromaticism

Chromaticism was used in the early seventeenth century for expression of extreme emotions or to give harmonic interest to improvisations. Later in the century, it also gained a role in defining tonal direction.

9. Major-minor tonalities

These and other developments led, by the last third of the seventeenth century, to *tonality,* the system of major and minor keys organized around a tonic triad, which replaced the older system of modes.

II. Early Opera (CHWM 179–90, NAWM 51–52 and 54–56)

1. Forerunners

An *opera* is a staged drama set to continuous (or nearly continuous) music. The first operas were written around 1600, but many earlier forms of theater used music, including Greek tragedies, medieval liturgical dramas, religious plays, Renaissance theater, and *intermedi* or *intermezzi,* theatrical interludes between acts of a play.

2. Pastoral

A *pastoral* was a poem, sometimes staged as a drama, about rustic youths and maidens in an idealized setting, and it became one source for opera.

3. Greek tragedy as a model

The ancient Greek tragedies were a model for Renaissance theater. Some felt that only the choruses of Greek tragedy were sung, but *Girolamo Mei* (1519–1594) argued that the tragedies were sung throughout.

4. Florentine Camerata

Mei's theory that the Greeks achieved powerful emotional effects through melody that followed the inflections and rhythms of the human voice was a strong influence on the *Florentine Camerata,* an informal group that met at the house of *Giovanni Bardi* (1534–1612) in Florence during the 1570s and 1580s.

5. Vincenzo Galilei

Following Mei, *Vincenzo Galilei* (d. 1591) attacked counterpoint as ineffective in conveying emotions.

6. Monody

Galilei argued that only *monody,* a solo vocal melody with instrumental accompaniment, could express the feelings of poetry.

7. Earliest operas

The first surviving opera was *Euridice* (Florence, 1600) by poet *Ottaviano Rinuccini* (1562–1621) and singer-composer *Jacopo Peri* (1561–1633). That same year, *Giulio Caccini* (1551–1618) also set Rinuccini's *Euridice.*

Both composers wrote monody and sought a style between speech and song that conveyed the text clearly, expressively, and naturally.

8. Caccini

Caccini aimed for a tuneful style that supported the meaning of the text.

9. *Le nuove musiche*

Caccini's song collection *Le nuove musiche* (The New Music, 1602) contains strophic *airs* and through-composed *solo madrigals,* with vocal ornaments written out rather than left to the singer.   **Music: NAWM 51**

10. *Euridice*

Euridice treated the legend of Orpheus and Euridice. Peri's version was performed for a court wedding, with some of Caccini's music interpolated. Caccini's setting was more lyrical, and Peri's was more dramatic, varying the style with the dramatic situation.

11. Peri and recitative style

In *stile recitativo* or *recitative style,* Peri sought to imitate speech by harmonizing the syllables that were naturally stressed or intoned in speech and setting the syllables in between to notes that might be either consonant or dissonant with the bass, thus suggesting the continuous motions of speech. He used this and other types of monody in *Euridice* to represent the actions and emotions of the drama.   **Music: NAWM 52**

12. Monteverdi's *Orfeo*

Monteverdi's opera *Orfeo* (Mantua, 1607) is on the same subject as Peri's *Euridice* and uses more contrast of styles. The recitative is more continuous and tonally organized; there are more airs and madrigals; repeating ritornellos and choruses create large-scale form; and the orchestra is large and varied. **Music: NAWM 54**

13. Francesca Caccini

Only a few more operas were staged through the 1620s. The Florentine court preferred ballets and intermedi, such as *La liberazione di Ruggiero* (1625), an opera-like blend of ballet and intermedio by *Francesca Caccini* (1587–ca. 1640). The daughter of Giulio Caccini, she was known as both a singer and a composer and was the highest-paid musician at court.

14. Rome

Opera was established in Rome in the 1620s. Subjects included mythology, epics, and the lives of saints, and comic opera became a separate type.

15. Luigi Rossi's *Orfeo*

By mid-century, operas (such as Luigi Rossi's *Orfeo*) often included scenic spectacle, comic episodes, extraneous characters, and other elements that were entertaining as theater but no longer conformed to the Florentine ideal of a unified drama akin to that of ancient Greece. Solo singing separated into two distinct types, *recitative* and *aria,* the former more speech-like than Peri's, the latter melodious and usually strophic.

16. Venetian opera

Opera was introduced to Venice in 1637 in a public theater. This marked the first time opera was staged for a paying public.

Etude: Opera in Seventeenth-Century Venice

Venice was ideal for opera, with many visitors in Carnival season (from the day after Christmas to the day before Lent), wealthy backers, and a steady audience. Plots were drawn from mythology, epics, and Roman history.

17. Monteverdi's *Poppea*

Monteverdi's last two operas, *Il ritorno d'Ulisse* (The Return of Ulysses, 1641) and *L'incoronazione di Poppea* (The Coronation of Poppea, 1642), were written for Venice. They alternate passages of recitative, aria, and *arioso* (a style between recitative and aria) as appropriate to convey the drama.   **Music: NAWM 55**

18. Cavalli and Cesti

Pier Francesco Cavalli (1602–1676) and *Marc' Antonio Cesti* (1623–1669) were important opera composers in Venice. Their arias are fully developed and use a new idiom later known as *bel canto* (beautiful singing), with smooth diatonic lines and easy rhythms.   **Music: NAWM 56**

19. Characteristics of opera

By the mid-seventeenth century, Italian opera was characterized by a focus on solo singing, with little ensemble or instrumental music; a separation of recitative and aria; the use of distinctive types of aria; and the primacy of music over the words, opposite to the original Florentine conception.

III. Vocal Chamber Music (CHWM 190–96, NAWM 59–60)

Most secular vocal music was chamber music. Like opera, chamber works used monody and basso continuo.

1. Strophic aria

Strophic arias used the same music for each strophe or stanza. *Strophic variations* used the same harmonic and melodic plan for each stanza, but varied the melodic details.

Etude: Baroque Ostinato Patterns

Composers often based works on the romanesca and other standard patterns for singing poetry or on a repeating bass figure called a *ground bass* or *basso ostinato*. The *chaconne* and *passacaglia* both feature a repeating bass figure in a slow triple meter.

2. The concertato medium

The seventeenth-century *concerto* brought together contrasting sounds in a harmonious whole, in what is called the *concertato medium*. A *concertato madrigal* uses instruments as well as voices; a *sacred concerto* is a sacred vocal work with instruments; and an *instrumental concerto* pits groups of instruments against each other, usually soloists against a larger group.

3. Monteverdi's concertato madrigals

Monteverdi's later books of madrigals include concertato madrigals.

Etude: Monteverdi's Eighth Book of Madrigals

Monteverdi's Book 8, *Madrigali guerrieri et amorosi* (Madrigals of War and Love, 1638), includes a variety of concerted pieces, along with two staged ballets and *Il Combattimento di Tancredi e Clorinda* (The Combat of Tancred and Clorinda), a theatrical piece of 1624. The latter uses pictorial music to suggest the action and introduces a new style, *stile concitato* (excited style), to suggest warlike feelings and actions.

4. Genres of vocal solo music
Monodies were very popular in early-seventeenth-century Italy and were published in large numbers.

5. Cantata
The *cantata* was a work for solo voice and continuo. Later ones, such as those by *Barbara Strozzi* (1619–after 1664) alternated recitatives and arias, like an operatic scene.   **Music: NAWM 57**

6. Church music
Monody, the basso continuo, and the concertato medium were used in church music as well as in secular music. But Renaissance polyphony was not abandoned; the counterpoint of Palestrina became the model for the elevated church style, known as *stile antico* (old style).

Window: Barbara Strozzi, Renaissance Woman (CHWM 196–97)

Barbara Strozzi won fame as a singer and composer of cantatas and other vocal works focused on the theme of love.

IV. The Venetian School (CHWM 196–98, NAWM 58)

Venice was an independent city-state and a major trading center with the East. *Saint Mark's Church* was a center of music and pageantry, and many great composers served as choirmaster, including Willaert, Rore, Zarlino, and Monteverdi. Venetian music was often homophonic, richly textured, and varied in sonority.

1. Venetian polychoral motets
Many works of the late 1500s and early 1600s used two or more choirs, each accompanied by instruments and placed apart from the others. In the motets for *cori spezzati* (divided choirs), called *polychoral motets,* by Giovanni Gabrieli, the choirs sing alone, answer each other in antiphony, and join together for large climaxes.   **Music: NAWM 58**

2. Venetian influence
The Venetian style influenced composers throughout Europe.

V. Genres of Sacred Music: Catholic and Lutheran (CHWM 199–203, NAWM 59–62)

1. Grand concerto
A *grand concerto* was a large work for singers and instruments, often arranged in two or more separate choirs.

2. Concerto for few voices
More common were concertos for one to three voices with organ continuo. *Lodovico Viadana* (1560–1627) was among the first to use this medium,

in his 1602 collection *Cento concerti ecclesiastici* (One Hundred Sacred Concertos). *Alessandro Grandi* (ca. 1575/80–1630) was noted for his sacred works in the new style.   **Music: NAWM 59–60**

3. Oratorio
An *oratorio* was an unstaged sacred drama performed in a church hall.

4. Carissimi's *Jephte*
Giacomo Carissimi (1605–1674) was the leading Italian composer of oratorios in the mid-seventeenth century. In *Jephte,* he mixes dialogue and lament in recitative with choral effects.   **Music: NAWM 61**

5. Oratorio vs. opera
Both oratorios and operas featured recitatives, arias, ensembles, and instrumental preludes and ritornellos, but oratorios were sacred, often included a narrator, used chorus more prominently, and had no staging or costumes.

6. Lutheran church music
Lutheran composers in Germany in the seventeenth century also wrote grand concertos and concertos for few voices, along with chorale motets.

7. Sacred concerto in Germany
An important collection of small sacred concertos was *Opella nova* (1618 and 1626) by *Johann Hermann Schein* (1586–1630).

8. Heinrich Schütz
Heinrich Schütz (1585–1672) was the leading German composer of his time. He studied in Venice and was chapelmaster for the elector of Saxony at Dresden for over half a century. He is renowned for his church music. He apparently wrote no independent instrumental music, and most of his secular vocal music is lost. His sacred music includes polychoral works, small sacred concertos, and concertato motets.

9. Schütz's *Symphoniae sacrae*
Schütz's most important concertato motets are his three books of *Symphoniae sacrae* (1629, 1647, and 1650). Several in the last book are like dramatic scenes.   **Music: NAWM 62**

Window: The Ecstasy of Saint Teresa (CHWM 200–201)

Bernini's sculpture *The Ecstasy of Saint Teresa* is typical of Baroque art in being theatrical, representing action and seeking to move our emotions.

VI. Instrumental Music (CHWM 203–13, NAWM 66–68)

Over the first half of the seventeenth century, instrumental music gradually became the equal of vocal music in quantity and content.

A. *Dance Music*

Dances and other types of pieces often used dance rhythms.

1. Suites
German composers cultivated the *dance suite,* a series of dances of varied character that often were melodically related.

2. Schein

Johann Hermann Schein's *Banchetto musicale* (Musical Banquet, 1617) blends Italian and German traits. Each suite is unified by key and by a common motive or melodic similarity.

3. French lute and keyboard music

French composers arranged dances for lute and later for harpsichord. **Music: NAWM 63**

4. Influence of lute technique

Lutenists typically played chords one note at a time, a manner called *style brisé* (broken style), and used ornaments called *agréments* to highlight or prolong a note. These features were adapted to the harpsichord and became characteristic of French keyboard music and French style in general.

5. Denis Gaultier

Denis Gaultier (1603–1672) was the most important French lute composer of the seventeenth century.

6. Froberger

Johann Jakob Froberger (1616–1667) took the French style to Germany and standardized the dances in the suite as *allemande, courante, sarabande,* and *gigue*.   **Music: NAWM 64**

B. *Improvisatory Compositions*

1. Frescobaldi's toccatas

Among the best-known early Baroque toccatas are those by *Girolamo Frescobaldi* (1583–1643), organist at St. Peter's in Rome., which feature a series of overlapping sections.   **Music: NAWM 65**

2. Froberger's toccatas

Froberger's toccatas alternate free improvisatory passages with sections in imitative counterpoint.

C. *Contrapuntal or Fugal Genres (in Continuous or Nonsectional Imitative Counterpoint)*

1. Ricercare

Most seventeenth-century *ricercares* are short, serious pieces for keyboard that treat a single subject in imitation throughout. Frescobaldi composed organ ricercares for use in church services.

2. Fantasia

A longer imitative work on a single subject was usually called a *fantasia*.

3. English consort music

English composers wrote imitative fantasias or fancies for viol consort.

D. *Canzona or Sonata (Sectional Genres)*

1. Canzona

Canzonas featured a series of sections, most in imitative counterpoint. A *variation canzona* uses variants of the same subject in each section.

2. Sonata

In the seventeenth century, *sonata* came to refer to works for one or two instruments with basso continuo. The solo writing was often idiomatic and expressive, as in solo vocal works.

3. Biagio Marini

Biagio Marini (ca. 1587–1663) wrote some of the earliest sonatas for solo violin and continuo. They tend to be sectional, with contrasting mood and figuration in each section. Some sections imitate vocal melodies, and others are in an idiomatic violin style that includes runs, trills, double stops, and improvised embellishments. A common scoring for a sonata was two treble instruments and continuo, called a *trio sonata*.

E. *Variations*

Variations were common in the seventeenth century, sometimes under titles such as *partite* (divisions). There were several types:

1. In *cantus firmus variations,* the melody was largely unchanged and was surrounded by other contrapuntal lines.
2. In another type, the melody was in the top voice and was embellished differently in each variation.
3. Other types of variations are based on a bass or harmonic plan rather than on a melody.

1. Frescobaldi's partite

Frescobaldi wrote variations on the bass and harmony of airs for singing poetry.

2. Chorale variations

German composers wrote variations on chorale melodies.

3. Scheidt

An important collection of organ works is Samuel Scheidt's *Tabulatura nova* (1624), which includes several variation sets on chorale tunes.

STUDY QUESTIONS

Prelude (CHWM 172–74)

1. Which famous artists, writers, philosophers, and scientists were active in the seventeenth century? How does music show a similar intellectual ferment?

General Characteristics of Baroque Music (CHWM 174–79, NAWM 53)

Music to Study
>   **NAWM 53:** Claudio Monteverdi, *Cruda Amarilli,* madrigal (ca. 1600)
>   3.59–63 (Concise 2.13–17)

2. How does Monteverdi use dissonances, and particularly unprepared dissonances, to convey the meaning of the text in *Cruda Amarilli* (NAWM 53)?

3. What was the *seconda pratica* ("second practice")? With what other practice does it contrast, and how do the two practices differ? How is the second practice reflected in *Cruda Amarilli*?

4. How did the Renaissance ideal of writing music that could be performed by any combination of voices and instruments change in the seventeenth century? What was the effect on composition?

5. What are the *affections*? How does the representation of affections in music differ from the later idea of expressing an individual artist's feelings?

6. What is new about rhythm in seventeenth-century music, in contrast to earlier music?

7. Define the following terms, and explain the significance of each concept.

   basso continuo or thorough bass

   figured bass

   continuo instruments

8. How did the emphasis on the bass and the use of basso continuo change how counterpoint was conceived and written and how dissonance was defined?

9. Why was figured bass important in the development of *major-minor tonality* as a replacement for the older system of modes?

Early Opera (CHWM 179–90, NAWM 53–58)

10. What is a *pastoral*? What is the importance of pastoral subjects and poetry in the development of opera? In what sense is *L'Euridice* (excerpted in NAWM 52) a pastoral?

11. In what sense was ancient Greek tragedy a model for opera? Who were Girolamo Mei and Vincenzo Galilei, and what did each do to promote the revival of Greek ideals that ultimately led to opera?

12. What were the roles of Ottavio Rinuccini, Jacopo Peri, and Giulio Caccini in the creation of the first operas?

13. What does the term *monody* mean? What different types of monody did Peri and Caccini use in their vocal music?

Music to Study

NAWM 51: Giulio Caccini, *Vedrò 'l mio sol,* continuo madrigal (ca. 1590)
CD 3.51–53
NAWM 52: Jacopo Peri, *Le musiche sopra l'Euridice* (The Music for *The Euridice*), opera (1600), excerpts
52a: Prologue, *Io, che d'alti sospir,* strophic air with ritornello
CD 3.54
52b: *Nel pur ardor,* canzonet (dance-song) with ritornello
CD 3.55
52c: *Per quel vago boschetto,* recitative   CD 3.56–58
NAWM 54: Claudio Monteverdi, *L'Orfeo,* opera (1607), excerpts
54a: Prologue, *Dal mio Permesso,* strophic variations
CD 4.1–6
54b: *Vi ricorda o boschi ombrosi,* strophic canzonet (excerpt)
CD 4.7–8 (Concise 2.18–19)
54c: *In un fiorito prato,* recitative; *Tu se' morta,* expressive recitative; and *Ahi caso acerbo,* chorus (madrigal)
CD 4.9–15 (Concise 2.20–26)

14. How does Caccini's madrigal *Vedrò 'l mio sol* (NAWM 51) differ from other madrigals we have seen?

    What traits does it share with other sixteenth-century Italian madrigals? Why is it a madrigal, and not an air?

15. What kinds of ornaments does Caccini use in the vocal line of *Vedrò 'l mio sol,* and where do they appear?

16. What is the *stile recitativo* or *recitative style*? How does Peri describe it in the preface to *Euridice* (excerpted in CHWM, p. 184)? How does the dialogue from his setting of *Euridice* (NAWM 52c) reflect his conception?

17. How does Peri use harmony, dissonance, and rhythm in Orfeo's response to the death of Euridice (mm. 63–87) to convey the meaning of the words and the feelings they reflect?

18. What style of monody does Peri use in the other excerpts from *Euridice* (NAWM 52a and 52b)? How does this style differ from recitative style?

19. Compare and contrast Monteverdi's *Orfeo* with Peri's *Euridice,* including the excerpts in NAWM 54 and 52 respectively and the description of each in CHWM. In what ways is the Monteverdi similar and different?

20. Monteverdi's prologue (NAWM 54a) is a *strophic variation,* in which the harmony and general melodic contour are the same for each strophe of the text, but details in the music are changed to fit the new text. How are the first two strophes different? Note the changes Monteverdi has made.

How does the last strophe differ from the others in the way it ends, and how does that illustrate the text? (Hint: Look at the melody, the harmony, and the last few words of the text.)

21. How does Monteverdi convey the meaning of the text and the feelings it reflects in Orfeo's recitative *Tu se' morta* (NAWM 54c, mm. 43–64)?

22. In *Orfeo,* Monteverdi uses particular musical forms and styles to convey the changing dramatic situation and the feelings of the characters. What characteristics make each of the following forms and styles appropriate for the scene in which it is used?

54a: La Musica, strophic variation with ritornello

54b: Orfeo, strophic canzonet with ritornello

54c: Messenger, recitative

Orfeo, expressive recitative

Chorus, choral madrigal

23. Who was Francesca Caccini, when and where did she live and work, and for what was she renowned?

24. When and where was opera first made available to the paying public?

What made this city ideal for opera?

Music to Study
    NAWM 55: Claudio Monteverdi, *L'incoronazione di Poppea* (The Coronation of Poppea) opera (1642), Act I, Scene 3
      CD 4.16–20
    NAWM 56: Marc' Antonio Cesti, *Orontea,* opera (1649), Act II, Scene 17, *Intorno all'idol mio*
      CD 4.21–22

25. Compare and contrast the scene from Monteverdi's *L'incoronazione di Poppea* in NAWM 55 with the scene from *Orfeo* in NAWM 54c. For each, what devices does Monteverdi use to depict the text and portray the dramatic situation?

26. In this scene from *L'incoronazione di Poppea,* the music shifts back and forth often between recitative and aria styles. Why does Monteverdi set Poppea's "Deh non dir di partir" (mm. 280–87) as recitative, and her words "Vanne, vanne ben mio" (mm. 303–9) as a brief aria? (Hint: Do not be fooled by the notation of the latter; it is in a fast triple time.)

27. Contrast the aria from Cesti's *Orontea* (ca. 1649) in NAWM 56 with the airs from Peri's *Euridice* (1600) in NAWM 52a and 52b. How has the style of operatic song changed from the beginning to the middle of the seventeenth century?

28. How does the aria from *Orontea* exemplify the *bel canto* style?

29. What important operatic conventions took shape in Italy by the middle of the seventeenth century? How did opera in Rome and Venice at mid-century differ from Florentine operas of about 1600?

Vocal Chamber Music (CHWM 190–96, NAWM 57)

30. Define the following terms:

    strophic aria

    strophic variation

    ground bass or basso ostinato

    concertato medium

    concertato madrigal

    sacred concerto

    instrumental concerto (in the seventeenth century)

31. What is the *stile concitato*? Who first used it? When, and in what piece?

32. What is a *cantata* in the seventeenth century? How does it resemble opera, and how is it different?

Music to Study
   NAWM 57: Barbara Strozzi, *Lagrime mie,* cantata (published 1659)
      CD 4.23–27

33. In her cantata *Lagrime mie* (NAWM 57), Strozzi uses sections of recitative, aria, and arioso (a style between recitative and aria, usually more metric than recitative). Where is each kind of monody used? (Indicate by measure numbers.)

   recitative _____

   aria   _____

   arioso   _____

   In what ways are the sections of text set as aria particularly appropriate for that style of music?

34. What musical devices does Strozzi use to represent the following words and the feelings or actions behind them?

   "lagrime" (tears)

   "respiro" (breath)

   "tormenti" (torments)

35. What new and old styles were used in seventeenth-century church music?

The Venetian School (CHWM 196–98, NAWM 58)

Music to Study
> **NAWM 58:** Giovanni Gabrieli, *In ecclesiis,* motet or grand concerto (pub-
> lished 1615)
> CD 4.28–33

36. What are *cori spezzati*? What is a *polychoral motet*? How does Gabrieli's
    motet *In ecclesiis* (NAWM 58) exemplify the characteristics of the genre?

Genres of Sacred Music: Catholic and Lutheran (CHWM 199–203, NAWM 59–62)

37. What varieties of sacred concerto were written in the seventeenth century? For
    what circumstances and occasions was each type suited?

38. What is an *oratorio*? From what does its name derive? How is it like opera,
    and how does it differ?

Music to Study

> **NAWM 59:** Lodovico Viadana, *O Domine, Jesu Christe,* sacred concerto (ca. 1602)
>> CD 4.34
>
> **NAWM 60:** Alessandro Grandi, *O quam tu pulchra es,* motet (1625)
>> CD 4.35–37
>
> **NAWM 61:** Giacomo Carissimi, *Historia di Jephte,* oratorio (ca. 1650), excerpt
>> 61a: *Plorate colles,* expressive recitative   CD 4.38
>> 61b: *Plorate filii Israel,* chorus   CD 4.39
>
> **NAWM 62:** Heinrich Schütz, *Saul, was verfolgst du mich* (SWV 415), grand concerto (ca. 1650)
>> CD 4.40–41 (Concise 2.27–28)

39. How is Viadana's *O Domine, Jesu Christe* (NAWM 59) like a sixteenth-century motet, such as Victoria's *O magnum mysterium* (NAWM 48a), and how is it different?

40. How is Viadana's sacred concerto like secular monody of around the same time, such as Caccini's *Vedrò 'l mio sol* (NAWM 51), and how is it different?

41. How is Grandi's *O quam tu pulchra es* (NAWM 60) like a sixteenth-century motet, and how is it different?

42. How does Grandi's motet compare to the alternation of recitative and aria styles in the scene from Monteverdi's *L'incoronazione di Poppea* in NAWM 55? How does each work respond to its text?

43. Compare the excerpt from Carissimi's *Historia di Jephte* in NAWM 61 with the scene from Monteverdi's *Orfeo* in NAWM 54c. What elements does each use?

How do Monteverdi and Carissimi use harmony to convey emotions?

How does each use the chorus?

44. How does Schütz use changes of texture and other musical effects to depict the events and text of *Saul, was verfolgst du mich* (NAWM 62)? What types of style and texture does he use?

Instrumental Music (CHWM 203–13, NAWM 63–65)

45. What is a dance *suite*? What dances typically appear in a suite by Froberger?

46. What is *style brisé* (broken style)?

What are *agréments*?

On what instrument did *style brisé* and *agréments* originate? _____

Why were they necessary or useful on that instrument?

To what instrument were they later adapted? _____

Music to Study
> **NAWM 63a:** Ennemond Gaultier, *La Poste,* gigue for lute (early to mid-
>   seventeenth century)
>   CD 4.42
> **NAWM 63b:** Jean-Henri D'Anglebert, arrangement for harpsichord of
>   Ennemond Gaultier's *La Poste* (seventeenth century)
>   CD 4.43
> **NAWM 64:** Johann Jakob Froberger, *Lamentation on the Death of Emperor
>   Ferdinand III* (1657)
>   CD 4.44
> **NAWM 65:** Girolamo Frescobaldi, Toccata No. 3 (1615, rev. 1637)
>   CD 4.45 (Concise 2.29)

47. Compare Gaultier's gigue for lute (NAWM 63a) with its arrangement for
    harpsichord (NAWM 63b). How does the keyboard version imitate the style
    of the lute?

48. What features of Froberger's *Lamentation on the Death of Emperor Ferdinand III* (NAWM 64) mark it as a piece in French style?

    What features are particularly appropriate to its subject?

49. How is Frescobaldi's Toccata No. 3 (NAWM 65) divided into sections? Where does the style or figuration change?

50. In the first half of the seventeenth century, what is the difference between a ricercare and a fantasia?

    What is the difference between a canzona and a sonata?

51. What kinds of variations were written in the seventeenth century? In each type, what stayed the same in each variation, and what changed?

TERMS TO KNOW

Terms Related to the Baroque Period

Baroque period
prima pratica, seconda pratica
the affections
measures
thorough bass

basso continuo
continuo instruments
figured bass
realization of a basso continuo
tonality (major-minor tonality)

Terms Related to Early Opera

opera
intermedio (pl., intermedi) or
    intermezzo (pl., intermezzi)
pastoral
monody
air

solo madrigal
recitative style (stile recitativo)
recitative
aria
arioso
bel canto

Terms Related to Vocal Music

strophic aria
strophic variation
ground bass or basso ostinato
chaconne
passacaglia
concerto (seventeenth-century)
concertato medium
concertato madrigal
sacred concerto

instrumental concerto
  (seventeenth century)
stile concitato
cantata (seventeenth century)
stile antico
cori spezzati
polychoral motet
grand concerto
oratorio

Terms Related to Instrumental Music

dance suite
style brisé
agréments
allemande, courante, sarabande,
    gigue
ricercare (seventeenth-century)
fantasia (seventeenth-century)

canzona (seventeenth-century)
variation canzona
sonata (seventeenth-century)
trio sonata
partita or partite
cantus firmus variations

NAMES TO KNOW

Names Related to Early Opera

Girolamo Mei
Florentine Camerata
Giovanni Bardi
Vincenzo Galilei
L'Euridice
Ottaviano Rinuccini
Jacopo Peri
Giulio Caccini

Le nuove musiche
L'Orfeo
Francesca Caccini
La liberazione di Ruggiero
Il ritorno d'Ulisse
L'incoronazione di Poppea
Pier Francesco Cavalli
Marc' Antonio Cesti

Names Related to Vocal Music

Madrigali guerrieri et amorosi
Il Combattimento di Tancredi e
  Clorinda
Barbara Strozzi
Saint Mark's Church
Lodovico Viadana
Cento concerti ecclesiastici

Alessandro Grandi
Giacomo Carissimi
Jephte
Opella nova
Johann Hermann Schein
Heinrich Schütz
Symphoniae sacrae

Names Related to Instrumental Music

Banchetto musicale
Denis Gaultier
Johann Jakob Froberger
Girolamo Frescobaldi

Biagio Marini
Samuel Scheidt, *Tabulatura*
  nova

REVIEW QUESTIONS

1. Make a time-line for the pieces, composers, treatises, and theorists discussed in this chapter.

2. What are the principal characteristics that distinguish music of the Baroque period from music of the Renaissance?

3. What new concepts or procedures were developed in the period 1600–1650 as composers sought to find ways to capture human emotions in music?

4. Trace the development of opera in Italy from its origins to 1650. Include in your answer changes of aesthetic aims and ideas as well as changes of style and procedure.

5. What connections do you see between Monteverdi's madrigals and his operas? What effects do you think his experience as a madrigal composer had on his operas?

6. What new forms and styles of secular vocal music were introduced in the first half of the seventeenth century?

7. How was sacred music affected by the new developments in secular music in the first half of the seventeenth century? What new forms or styles of sacred music emerged during this time?

8. What was the concertato medium, and where was it used?

9. What types of instrumental music were practiced during the early seventeenth century? Which of these genres and styles were new, and which continued trends from the sixteenth century? Of the latter, how were the older genres or styles changed in the seventeenth century?

10. What are some elements that distinguish French from Italian instrumental style in the early Baroque?

OPERA AND VOCAL MUSIC IN THE LATE SEVENTEENTH CENTURY

10

CHAPTER OBJECTIVES

After you complete the reading, study of the music, and study questions for this chapter, you should be able to

1. describe developments in Italian opera in the second half of the seventeenth century and the beginning of the eighteenth century;
2. trace the origins and development of musical theater in France, England, and Germany during the seventeenth and early eighteenth centuries and explain what makes each national tradition distinctive;
3. describe the cantata and other secular vocal genres in the late seventeenth century;
4. describe the varieties of sacred music being composed in the late seventeenth and early eighteenth centuries; and
5. define and use the most important terms and identify some of the composers and works associated with opera and vocal music in the late seventeenth and early eighteenth centuries.

CHAPTER OUTLINE

Prelude (CHWM 214–15)

In the second half of the seventeenth century, opera spread across Italy and Europe, with important centers at Venice and Naples and distinctive traditions in Germany and France. Operatic styles influenced vocal chamber music and sacred music.

I. Opera (CHWM 215–24, NAWM 66–70)

A. *Venice*

1. Singers

Singers were the stars of opera, often commanding much higher fees than composers, and arias were the main musical attraction.

137

2. Aria types

There were many types of aria, including strophic, two-part, and three-part forms, and arias over ostinato basses or in dance rhythms. Arias often featured a dance rhythm or distinctive motive reflecting the text. Many Italian composers made careers writing Italian operas in Germany.

Etude: An Aria by Agostino Steffani

A typical Italian aria of the time included *coloratura* passages and mood or text painting. Many arias featured a *motto,* in which the singer states the opening motive (the motto), the instruments interrupt, and then the singer begins again. Also common was a *walking-bass* accompaniment.

B. *Naples*

A new operatic style that emphasized elegant melodies over dramatic effect developed in Naples and became dominant in the early eighteenth century.

1. Alessandro Scarlatti

The later operas of *Alessandro Scarlatti* (1660–1725) are in the new style.

2. Kinds of recitative

There were two types of recitative, later called *recitativo secco* or *semplice* (dry or simple recitative, with basso continuo), for dialogue or monologue, and *recitativo accompagnato* or *obbligato* (accompanied recitative, with orchestra), for especially dramatic situations.

3. Da capo aria

The principal aria type was the *da capo aria,* in which the first section (with or without the opening ritornello) is repeated after a contrasting middle section. An aria expressed a single mood, sometimes with an opposing or related mood in the middle section.   **Music: NAWM 66**

C. *France*

The French resisted Italian opera, but a distinctive style of opera developed in France in the 1670s under the patronage of Louis XIV.

1. *Tragédie lyrique*

Jean-Baptiste Lully (1632–1687) drew on two strong French traditions, court ballet and classical French tragedy, to create the *tragédie lyrique.*

2. Lully

Lully was born in Italy, came to Paris at a young age, was a violinist with Louis XIV's string orchestra, and composed music for court ballets. In 1672 he was put in charge of sung drama in France.   **Music: NAWM 67**

3. Quinault

His librettos by *Jean-Phillippe Quinault* featured mythological plots with frequent *divertissements,* long interludes of choral singing and dancing.

4. Lully's recitative

Lully adapted recitative to the rhythms and inflections of French.

5. *Recitative simple* and *mesuré*

There were two types: *récitatif simple,* in freely shifting meter, and *récitatif mesuré,* in a more songlike, measured style.   **Music: NAWM 68b**

6. Ouverture

Lully codified the *ouverture,* or *French overture,* as an introduction to a ballet, opera, suite, or other large work. A French overture usually has two parts, the first slow, stately, homophonic, and marked by dotted rhythms, and the second fast and imitative, often closing with a return to the slower first tempo.   **Music: NAWM 68a**

7. Orchestra

Lully's orchestra of strings and winds influenced others across Europe.

D. *England*

1. Masque

Musical theater in seventeenth-century England included the *masque,* akin to the French court ballet; plays with extensive incidental music, called *semi-operas*; and only two full operas.

2. Purcell

Henry Purcell (1659–1695) wrote a large amount of music for chorus, voice, chamber ensembles, and keyboard, and incidental music for forty-nine plays.   **Music: NAWM 70**

3. *Dido and Aeneas*

Purcell's opera *Dido and Aeneas* (1689) blended French overture, dance, and choral styles with Italian and English vocal styles, including Italian ground bass arias and a distinctively English style of recitative.   **Music: NAWM 69**

E. *Germany*

While German courts supported Italian opera, some German cities, notably Hamburg, supported opera in German, called *Singspiel* (play with music). These usually used spoken dialogue instead of recitative.

1. Reinhard Keiser

Reinhard Keiser (1674–1739) was the foremost composer of German opera in the early eighteenth century, unifying German and Italian traits.

II. Vocal Music for Chamber and Church (CHWM 224–31)

1. Italian cantata

In the second half of the seventeenth century, the Italian *cantata* was a dramatic narrative or soliloquy for voice and continuo laid out as a series of two or three recitative-aria pairs. It was like a scene from an opera, but performed in a chamber setting and without staging. Many opera composers wrote cantatas.

2. Alessandro Scarlatti

Scarlatti wrote over six hundred cantatas. His music uses diminished seventh chords, distant modulations, and unusual harmonies for expressive effect.

3. France and Germany

French and German composers also wrote cantatas after Italian models.

4. England

English composers wrote songs in a native style; *catches,* unaccompanied humorous canons; and *odes,* large works for soloists, chorus, and orchestra celebrating state occasions and holidays.

5. Church music

Catholic church music in Italy and Germany mixed old and new styles.

6. Oratorio

Oratorios were written in the same style as operas and substituted for opera during Lent and other seasons when theaters were closed.

7. French church music

Marc-Antoine Charpentier (1634–1704) brought the Latin oratorio to France, combining Italian and French traits.

8. Motet

At Louis XIV's chapel, the leading genres were the motet for solo voice and continuo and the *grand motet* for soloists, choruses, and orchestra.

9. François Couperin

François Couperin and others wrote sacred concertos for few voices, called *petits motets* (little motets).

10. Lutheran church music

Lutheran music reached its height in the period 1650–1750.

11. Chorales

Much Lutheran music was based on chorales. *Dieterich Buxtehude* (ca. 1637–1707) and *Johann Pachelbel* (1653–1706) wrote sacred concertos for Lutheran services, some of which used chorale texts or melodies.

12. Buxtehude

Buxtehude was an organist and presented much of his church music in public concerts following afternoon church services. Orthodox Lutheran beliefs and practices were challenged by *Pietism,* which emphasized individual freedom and simple, direct expression of feelings in music.

13. Lutheran church cantata

The *Lutheran church cantata* was devised around 1700 by *Erdmann Neumeister* (1671–1756) as a series of recitatives and arias meditating on a biblical text and closing with a chorale. Neumeister blended orthodoxy with Pietism, and composers setting his cantata texts to music blended elements of chorale settings, solo song, the sacred concerto, and opera.

Etude: The Passion

The *historia* was a German genre setting a Bible story to music. The most important type was the *Passion,* telling the story of the suffering and death of Jesus. In the late seventeenth century a new type appeared that resembled an oratorio and is known as the *oratorio Passion.* Beyond relating the Bible story, Passions came to include chorales sung by the choir or congregation and poetic texts set as solo arias.

STUDY QUESTIONS

Opera (CHWM 215–24, NAWM 66–70)

1. What were the most important elements of Italian opera in the late seventeenth and early eighteenth centuries? How did drama and music relate in Italian opera of this period, and how did this compare with the ideals of the Florentine Camerata?

2. Describe each of the following. In what circumstances was each used?

   recitativo semplice or secco

   recitativo obbligato or accompagnato

Music to Study
   NAWM 66: Alessandro Scarlatti, *Griselda,* opera (1721), Act II, Scene 1,
      Mi rivedi
   CD 4.46–48

3. What type of aria is Scarlatti's *Mi rivedi, o selva ombrosa* (NAWM 66)? Chart the form of this aria as it would be performed.

4. Look at the words of this aria in translation. What emotions is Griselda experiencing? How does Scarlatti's music convey Griselda's feelings? How does the musical form help to capture the conflicting emotions Griselda feels?

5. On what two French traditions did French opera draw?

    _____   _____

    Name the composer and librettist who founded the French opera tradition.

    _____   _____

Music to Study

NAWM 67: Jean-Baptiste Lully, *Le bourgeois gentilhomme: Ballet des nations* (1670), excerpt: L'Entrée et Chaconne des Scaramouches, Trivelins et Arlequins
CD 4.49–50

NAWM 68: Jean-Baptiste Lully, *Armide,* opera (1686), excerpts
68a: Ouverture   CD 5.1–3
68b: Act II, Scene 5: *Enfin il est en ma puissance*
                                        CD 5.4–6

6. In the excerpts from Lully's *Ballet des nations* in NAWM 67, what dances are used, and what musical elements indicate these particular dances? How does the music suggest the comic character of the figures it accompanies?

7. What characteristics of the overture to *Armide* (NAWM 68a) are typical of the French overture?

8. How does the musical setting of Armide's recitative *Enfin il est en ma puissance* (NAWM 68b) reflect the form and accentuation of the text?

9. How does the musical setting reflect the dramatic situation and the emotional conflict Armide is feeling?

10. How does this scene from *Armide* differ from the recitative and aria of Italian opera?

11. What are the characteristics of these genres of musical theater? What nation is each from, and how does it differ from Italian opera?

   masque

   semi-opera

   Singspiel

Music to Study
   NAWM 69: Henry Purcell, *Dido and Aeneas,* opera (1689), Act III, Scene 2
      Recitative: *Thy hand, Belinda*   CD 5.7 (Concise 2.30)
      Aria: *When I am laid in earth*   CD 5.8–9 (Concise 2.31–32)
      Chorus: *With drooping winds*   CD 5.10
   NAWM 70: Henry Purcell, *The Fairy Queen,* semi-opera (1692), *Hark! the
      ech'ing air a triumph sings*
      CD 5.11

12. Compare Purcell's recitative *Thy hand, Belinda* (in NAWM 69) to Lully's
    recitative from *Armide* (in NAWM 68b) and Peri's recitative in *L'Euridice* (in
    NAWM 52c). How does Purcell's music follow the accentuation of the
    English text? How does the music convey Dido's emotions?

13. Laments in Italian operas were often written over a descending ground bass,
    and Purcell's aria *When I am laid in earth* (in NAWM 69) follows this tradi-
    tion. Part of the expressivity comes from dissonances or conflicts in phrasing
    between the ostinato bass and the vocal line. Where do these dissonances or
    conflicts in phrasing occur?

    Besides these conventions, what other devices does Purcell use to give this
    music the feeling of a lament?

14. In the closing chorus of *Dido and Aeneas* (in NAWM 69), how does the
    music reinforce the mood of lamentation?

15. How does the air from Purcell's *The Fairy Queen* (NAWM 70) compare to
the aria from Scarlatti's *Griselda* (NAWM 66) and the air from Lully's
Armide (in NAWM 68b)? Would you say this Purcell air is more Italian or
more French in style?

Vocal Music for Chamber and Church (CHWM 224–31)

16. Describe the form and style of the secular Italian cantata in the late seventeenth and early eighteenth centuries. How does it compare to opera?

17. Describe the Lutheran church cantata. Who devised it, and when? What was
the text like? What was the music like, and from which traditions did it draw?

TERMS TO KNOW

Terms Related to Opera

coloratura
motto (motto beginning)
walking bass
recitativo secco (or semplice)
recitativo accompagnato (or
    obbligato)
da capo aria
tragédie lyrique

divertissement
récitatif simple
récitatif mesuré
French overture (ouverture)
masque
semi-opera
Singspiel

Terms Related to Other Vocal Music

cantata (in late-seventeenth-
    century Italy)
catch
ode
grand motet, petit motet

Pietism
Lutheran church cantata
historia
Passion
oratorio Passion

NAMES TO KNOW

Alessandro Scarlatti
Jean-Baptiste Lully
Jean-Phillippe Quinault
Henry Purcell
Dido and Aeneas

Reinhard Keiser
Marc-Antoine Charpentier
Dieterich Buxtehude
Johann Pachelbel
Erdmann Neumeister

REVIEW QUESTIONS

1. Make a time-line for the pieces, composers, librettists, and theorists discussed in this chapter.

2. How did Italian opera develop and change during the seventeenth and early eighteenth centuries, from Monteverdi through Scarlatti?

3. Trace the development of musical theater in France during the seventeenth century and explain what distinguishes it from Italian opera.

4. What factors influenced the development of English musical theater in the seventeenth century? What genres did the English use? What did the English borrow from the French and Italian traditions?

5. Describe the secular Italian cantata of the late seventeenth century, using Scarlatti's *Lascia, deh lascia* as an example (see CHWM, pp. 224–25).

6. Describe the varieties of Lutheran sacred music being composed in the late seventeenth and early eighteenth centuries.

INSTRUMENTAL MUSIC IN THE LATE BAROQUE PERIOD

11

CHAPTER OBJECTIVES

After you complete the reading, study of the music, and study questions for this chapter, you should be able to

1. name and describe the genres of instrumental music composed in the second half of the seventeenth century and the early eighteenth century;
2. trace the development of keyboard music in this period and describe the styles of various regions and individual composers; and
3. trace the development of ensemble music and orchestral music in this period and describe the style of Corelli.

CHAPTER OUTLINE

Prelude (CHWM 233–34)

In the latter seventeenth and early eighteenth centuries, the medium for which instrumental music was intended helped to determine how it was composed. There were two main categories, keyboard and ensemble music. The principal genres of keyboard music were these:
   1. Toccata, prelude, or fantasia and fugue;
   2. Settings of chorales or chants, such as a chorale prelude;
   3. Variations;
   4. Passacaglia and chaconne;
   5. Suite; and
   6. Sonata (after 1700).
The principal genres of ensemble music were these:
   1. Sonata (sonata da chiesa), sinfonia, and related genres;
   2. Suite (sonata da camera) and related genres; and
   3. Concerto.
This was a golden age of instrument making and composition for the church organ, especially in Germany; for the harpsichord, especially in France; and for strings, especially in Italy.

I. Music for Organ (CHWM 234–38, NAWM 71–72)

Much organ music was written for Protestant services, where it served as a prelude to part of the service.

1. Toccata

The seventeenth-century German toccata includes both sections in improvisatory style and sections in imitative counterpoint.

2. Fugal sections

Buxtehude's toccatas alternate short sections in improvisatory style with longer fugal ones. From this contrast evolved the eighteenth-century form of toccata (or prelude) and fugue.   **Music: NAWM 71**

3. Fugue

The ricercare was gradually replaced by the *fugue,* which was composed as an independent piece or as part of a prelude or toccata. A fugue opens with an *exposition,* in which the *subject* in the tonic is imitated by the *answer* in the dominant and the other voices alternate subject and answer. Later appearances of the subject are also called expositions and alternate with *episodes* where the subject is absent and modulation may occur.

4. Chorale compositions

Lutheran chorales were used in several types of organ composition.

5. Organ chorales

In simple organ settings, chorales were accompanied with harmonizations or counterpoint.

6. Chorale variation

In *chorale variations* (also called *chorale partita*), the chorale tune was varied through a series of different settings.   **Music: NAWM 72**

Etude: Key Cycles and Equal Temperament

Lute players could play in all twenty-four major and minor keys because their frets were equally spaced, giving *equal temperament,* and keyboard players gradually adopted this system.

7. Chorale fantasia

In a *chorale fantasia,* the chorale is fragmented and its motives developed.

8. Chorale prelude

A *chorale prelude* presents a chorale once, varied melodically or given a contrapuntal setting.

II. Music for Harpsichord and Clavichord (CHWM 239–43, NAWM 73)

The main genres for stringed keyboard instruments were the *theme and variations* and the *suite.*

1. Theme and variations

Composers often wrote variations on an original melody rather than on an existing tune.

2. Suite

The German suite (or *partita*) always contained an allemande, courante, sarabande, and gigue, and might also contain an introductory prelude or one or more dances added after one of the last three standard dances.

Etude: Characteristic Dances of the Keyboard Suite

The allemande, probably a German dance, moves in continuous eighth or sixteenth notes in a moderately fast duple meter, with a short upbeat. The French courante is in moderate 6/4 or 3/2 meter. The Mexican-Spanish sarabande is in a slow triple meter with an emphasis on the second beat, and is the most homophonic. The Anglo-Irish gigue is usually in a fast compound triple meter and often features imitative counterpoint.

3. Jacquet de la Guerre

French *clavecinists* (harpsichordists) such as *Elisabeth-Claude Jacquet de la Guerre* (1665–1729) and *François Couperin* (1668–1733) wrote suites that include a wider variety of dance types. Jacquet de la Guerre was renowned for her harpsichord, ensemble, and vocal music.

4. Couperin's *ordres*

Couperin's *ordres* contain any number of short movements, most of them in dance rhythms and most with evocative titles.   **Music: NAWM 73**

5. Passacaglia and chaconne

The passacaglia and chaconne often appeared in suites or as independent works. Couperin's treatise *L'Art de toucher le clavecin* (The Art of Playing the Harpsichord, 1716) detailed how to play the harpsichord, including fingering and performing the agréments (French ornaments).

III. Ensemble Music (CHWM 243–54, NAWM 74–75)

1. Ensemble sonatas

The sonata was a work in several contrasting sections or movements for a small number of instruments with basso continuo. After about 1660, there were two main types: *sonata da chiesa* (church sonata), a series of mostly abstract movements, often ending with a dance, and *sonata da camera* (chamber sonata), a suite of stylized dances, often opening with a prelude.

2. Trio sonatas

A *trio sonata* is a sonata (of either type) for two treble instruments (usually violins) and basso continuo. This is the most common instrumentation for a sonata after about 1670.   **Music: NAWM 74**

3. Solo sonatas

The *solo sonata* for one treble instrument and continuo gained popularity after about 1700.

Etude: Emergence of the Baroque Sonata

The Baroque sonata gradually evolved from the canzona, as the contrasting sections lengthened and separated into independent movements.

A. *Arcangelo Corelli*

Arcangelo Corelli (1653–1713) was the greatest master of seventeenth-century instrumental music. After studies at Bologna, he lived in Rome. He published two sets each of trio sonatas da chiesa and da camera, a set of solo violin sonatas, and a set of concerti grossi, with twelve works per set.

1. Trio sonatas
Corelli's trio sonatas feature lyrical violin lines without virtuosic display. They served as models for composers for the next fifty years.

2. Harmonic sequences
Sequences drive Corelli's music forward and help create the directed harmonic motion characteristic of common-practice tonality (which was new in Corelli's generation).

3. Church sonatas
Corelli's church sonatas most often include four movements in the pattern slow-fast-slow-fast, with a majestic prelude, a fugue, a slow aria or duet, and a fast binary dance.

4. Chamber sonatas
Corelli's chamber sonatas typically begin with a prelude and include two or three dance movements in binary form.

5. Unity of key
Most of the movements in a sonata are in the same key, but often a slow movement is in the relative minor key.

6. Unity of theme
Each movement presents and develops a single melodic idea, as is typical of the late Baroque.   **Music: NAWM 75**

7. Solo sonatas
Corelli's violin sonatas use the same format as his trio sonatas but demand more virtuosity from the violin.

8. Improvisation in musical performance.
Performers in the Baroque period were expected to elaborate on written music by adding ornaments and embellishments.

Etude: Baroque Ornamentation
Ornamentation was not only decorative but added interest and helped to convey the affections. There were two ways to ornament a melody: with small figures such as trills, turns, appoggiaturas, and mordents or with freer embellishment such as scales, runs, and arpeggios. Performers could also omit movements or sections and add instruments as desired. (In sum, pieces were seen as opportunities for performance, not as hallowed works that were only to be performed as the composer intended.)

9. Influence outside Italy
Purcell, Handel, and others wrote trio sonatas influenced by Corelli.

10. François Couperin
François Couperin sought a union of French and Italian styles, represented by Lully and Corelli, in his trio sonatas and other ensemble music.

B. *Larger Ensembles*

Sonatas, dance suites, and other types of composition were also written for larger ensembles.

1. Ensemble music in Germany

The ensemble sonata and suite were popular in Germany. Many German cities had a *collegium musicum,* a group that played and sang music for their own pleasure, and a town band, the *Stadtpfeifer.*

2. Orchestral music

In the late seventeenth century, musicians began to distinguish between *chamber music* for one player on a part and *orchestral music.* Until then, the same music was often played by either size ensemble. Only overtures and dances from operas and ballets were specifically for orchestra.

3. The orchestral suite

The German *orchestral suite* (or *ouverture,* after the opening movement) was modeled on suites from Lully's operas and ballets.

4. The concerto

The instrumental concerto was a new genre that emerged in the late seventeenth century and became the most important Baroque orchestral genre. The *concerto grosso* contrasted a small ensemble (*concertino*) with a large ensemble (*concerto grosso*), and the *solo concerto* set a solo instrument with continuo against the orchestra. In both, the full orchestra was called *tutti* (all) or *ripieno* (full).

5. Corelli's concertos

Corelli's concerti grossi were like sonatas punctuated by changes of texture between larger and smaller groups.

6. Concerto in Germany

Many German composers followed Corelli's example.

7. Giuseppe Torelli

Giuseppe Torelli (1658–1709) helped to codify the concerto as a work in three movements in the pattern fast-slow-fast.

8. Ritornello

In the concertos of Torelli, the fast movements are in *ritornello form,* in which the full orchestra states a *ritornello* in the tonic at the beginning; the soloist or soloists contribute an episode, which usually modulates; the large group states the ritornello (or a part of it) in the new key; this alternation of episode and ritornello continues for some time; and the movement ends with the reappearance of the ritornello in the tonic.

9. Other composers of concerti

Later composers adopted and extended Torelli's approach.

Window: Queen Christina of Sweden and Her Circle (CHWM 250–51)

Queen Christina of Sweden (1626–1689) abdicated her throne and settled in Rome in 1655 as a patron of intellectual life and the arts. Corelli dedicated his first publication to her and later served her as a musician.

STUDY QUESTIONS

Prelude (CHWM 233–34)

1. What are the main types of keyboard music in the later Baroque period? How do these compare to the types of keyboard music practiced in the sixteenth century and in the early seventeenth century?

2. What are the main types of ensemble music in the later Baroque period? How do these compare to the main types of instrumental ensemble music practiced in the sixteenth century and in the early seventeenth century?

Music for Organ (CHWM 234–38, NAWM 71–72)

> *Music to Study*
> **NAWM 71:** Dieterich Buxtehude, Praeludium in E Major, BuxWV 141, prelude for organ (late seventeenth century)
>   CD 5.12–16
>
> 3. How does Buxtehude's Praeludium in E Major (NAWM 71) fit the definition of a late-seventeenth-century toccata or prelude given in CHWM, pp. 234–36? What types of texture and figuration does it use? How does it fall into sections?

4. What types of organ composition in the late seventeenth and early eighteenth centuries were based on chorales? In each type, how was the chorale treated?

Music to Study
> **NAWM 72:** Dieterich Buxtehude, *Danket dem Herrn,* BuxWV 181, chorale variations (late seventeenth century)
> CD 5.17–19

5. How does Buxtehude treat the chorale melody in his variations on *Danket dem Herrn* (NAWM 74)?

Music for Harpsichord and Clavichord (CHWM 239–43, NAWM 73)

6. What four dances are typically part of the German keyboard suite, and in what order? What is the meter, relative speed, nation of origin, and character of each?

dance	meter	speed	nation of origin	other characteristics
————	——	————	————	————————
————	——	————	————	————————
————	——	————	————	————————
————	——	————	————	————————

What other movements might be part of a German suite?

Music to Study
    NAWM 73: François Couperin, *Vingt-cinquième ordre* (Twenty-fifth Order), keyboard suite (1730)
        73a: *La Visionaire* (The Dreamer)   CD 5.20–21
        73b: *La Misterieuse* (The Mysterious One)
                                         CD 5.22
        73c: *La Monflambert*   CD 5.23 (Concise 2.33)
        73d: *La Muse victorieuse* (The Victorious Muse)
                                         CD 5.24 (Concise 2.34)
        73e: *Les Ombres errantes* (The Roving Shadows)
                                         CD 5.25

7. In what sense is *La Visionaire* (NAWM 73a) a "French overture," as it is described in CHWM, p. 242?

8. What elements of *La Misterieuse* (NAWM 73b) suggest that it is an allemande? What in *La Monflambert* (NAWM 73c) suggests that it is a gigue?

9. What are the names of the following *agréments* in the upper melody of *La Misterieuse* (NAWM 73b), and how is each one played? (Hint: See CHWM, p. 242.)

first measure, second note (E)

first measure, notes 6–7 (A–B)

measure 25, fifth note (A)

Ensemble Music (CHWM 243–54, NAWM 74–75)

10. What two main types of sonata began to be distinguished after about 1660? Describe each type as practiced by Corelli.

11. What was the most common instrumentation for sonatas in the late seventeenth century? What was a sonata in this instrumentation called?

Music to Study
> **NAWM 74:** Giovanni Legrenzi, *La Raspona,* trio sonata (published 1655)
>   CD 5.26–27
> **NAWM 75:** Arcangelo Corelli, Trio Sonata in D Major, Op. 3, No. 2 (published 1689)

1. Grave	CD 5.28
2. Allegro	CD 5.29
3. Adagio	CD 5.30 (Concise 2.35)
4. Allegro	CD 5.31–32 (Concise 2.36–37)

12. In what ways are the violin melodies in Legrenzi's *La Raspona* (NAWM 74) idiomatic for instruments and unlike vocal style?

13. Is Corelli's Op. 3, No. 2 (NAWM 75) a church sonata or a chamber sonata? What traits mark it as this type of sonata?

14. Corelli's trio sonatas are marked by sequences and by suspensions, especially chains of suspensions in sequence. For each of these techniques, find two passages in which it is prominent.

   sequences   _____   _____

   chain of suspensions   _____   _____

   How do these techniques help to give these passages a sense of forward momentum toward the next cadence?

15. In what ways are Corelli's solo violin sonatas like his trio sonatas, and in what ways are they different?

16. How did Baroque musicians regard ornamentation of written melodies?

17. Describe the two main ways of ornamenting a melody in the Baroque period.

18. Why did Couperin seek to unite the French and Italian styles of instrumental music? Which composers did he invoke as representative of each style?

19. What is the difference between *chamber music* and *orchestral music*? In the seventeenth century, what kinds of pieces might have been played by either type of ensemble?

20. Name and describe the two main types of *concertos* composed around 1700. How were Baroque principles of contrast embodied in each of them?

21. How many movements does a typical concerto by Giuseppe Torelli have, and what is the relative tempo of each movement?

22. Describe *ritornello form* as used by Torelli. How does this form embody the Baroque interest in contrast, and how does it draw contrasting parts into a unified whole?

TERMS TO KNOW

Terms Related to Keyboard Music

fugue
fugue subject, answer,
   exposition, episode
equal temperament
chorale variations (or partita)
chorale fantasia

chorale prelude
theme and variations
suite (or partita)
clavecinist
ordre

Terms Related to Ensemble Music

sonata da chiesa
sonata da camera
trio sonata
solo sonata
sequences (in Baroque music)
collegium musicum
Stadtpfeifer
chamber music

orchestral music
orchestral suite (or ouverture)
concerto grosso
solo concerto
concertino, concerto grosso
tutti or ripieno
ritornello
ritornello form

NAMES TO KNOW

Elisabeth-Claude Jacquet de la
   Guerre
François Couperin
L'Art de toucher le clavecin

Arcangelo Corelli
Giuseppe Torelli
Queen Christina of Sweden

REVIEW QUESTIONS

1. Make a time-line for the pieces, composers, and treatises discussed in this chapter.

2. Name the varieties of keyboard music being composed in the late seventeenth and early eighteenth centuries. Name and briefly describe an example for as many of these genres as you can.

3. What functions did keyboard music serve in the late seventeenth and early eighteenth centuries? Name the functions for as many genres as you can.

4. As a review of this and previous chapters, trace the evolution of keyboard music from about 1500 to about 1720.

5. Name the varieties of ensemble music composed in the period 1650–1720. Name and briefly describe an example for as many varieties as you can.

6. As a review of this and previous chapters, trace the development of music for instrumental chamber ensemble from about 1500 to around 1720.

7. What did Corelli and Torelli contribute to the development of instrumental ensemble music?

MUSIC IN THE EARLY EIGHTEENTH CENTURY

CHAPTER OBJECTIVES

After you complete the reading, study of the music, and study questions for this chapter, you should be able to

1. summarize the careers, describe the musical styles, and name and describe some of the most significant works by each of four major composers of the early eighteenth century: Antonio Vivaldi, Jean-Philippe Rameau, Johann Sebastian Bach, and George Frideric Handel;
2. compare the music of each to that of his predecessors and contemporaries; and
3. explain the historical significance of each of these composers.

CHAPTER OUTLINE

Prelude (CHWM 256–57)

Between 1720 and 1750, music of the high Baroque competed with a simpler, more songful style. Antonio Vivaldi, Jean-Philippe Rameau, Johann Sebastian Bach, and George Frideric Handel were the most eminent composers of the early eighteenth century, and each created a unique idiom within the established Baroque genres.

I. Antonio Vivaldi (CHWM 257–62, NAWM 76–77)

1. Venice

In the early eighteenth century, Venice was in decline but still famous for its music, including public festivals, church music, and opera.

2. The Pietà

Antonio Vivaldi (1678–1741) was music director, teacher, conductor, and composer at the *Pio Ospedale della Pietà* in Venice, a home and school for orphaned or abandoned girls. Music was an important part of the curriculum, and the concerts at the Pietà were well attended.

3. Vivaldi's life

Vivaldi was trained as a musican and priest. It addition to his duties at the Pietà, he composed and led operas and concerts throughout Italy and Europe. At this time, there were no musical "classics," and audiences expected new music each season.

4. Vivaldi's works

Vivaldi composed quickly and always for a specific occasion, writing concertos and church music for the Pietà and 49 operas for theaters in Venice and other cities. About five hundred of his concertos survive, along with about ninety sonatas and many operas and religious works.

5. Vocal works

Vivaldi is best known today as an instrumental composer, but was also successful and prolific as a composer of church music and of opera.

6. Concertos

Vivaldi's concertos are marked by clear forms, memorable melodies, rhythmic energy, and skillful contrasts of sonority and texture.

7. Solo concertos

Two-thirds of Vivaldi's concertos are for solo with orchestra, usually violin, but also cello, flute, or bassoon. Others feature two soloists or a concertino group of which one or two members are the main soloists.

8. Instrumentation of the concertos

Vivaldi's orchestra was about twenty-five strings with harpsichord or organ continuo, sometimes with winds.

9. Form of the concertos

Most of Vivaldi's concertos are in three movements, with fast outer movements in ritornello form and a slow aria-like middle movement in a closely related key. The soloist is a real virtuoso, standing apart from the orchestra as a singer does in an opera.

10. Form of the Allegro

In Vivaldi's hands ritornello form is infinitely variable, not at all a rigid scheme. **Music: NAWM 76**

11. Slow movements

Vivaldi's slow movements resemble slow opera arias and are equal in importance to the Allegros. **Music: NAWM 77**

12. Changing style

Vivaldi's music shows both conservative and progressive traits. His sinfonias mark him as a founder of the Classic-era symphony.

II. Jean-Philippe Rameau (CHWM 262–66, NAWM 78)

1. La Pouplinière

The leading patron of the arts in France, outside the royal court, was Alexandre-Jean-Joseph Le Riche de la Pouplinière, a rich nobleman and avid patron of music. He sponsored the career of *Jean-Philippe Rameau* (1683–1764), the foremost eighteenth-century French composer.

2. Rameau's life

Rameau had a unique career, becoming known first as a theorist and only later as a composer, and writing his major works late in life. In 1722 he published his *Traité de l'harmonie* (Treatise on Harmony). In 1731 be became organist, conductor, and composer for La Pouplinière.

3. Rameau's operas

From the 1730s, Rameau wrote operas and opera-ballets which were produced in Paris with the backing of La Pouplinière. His operas secured his reputation but inspired a debate between his devotées and those who attacked him for subverting the tradition of Lully.

Etude: Rameau's Theoretical Works

Rameau sought to put music theory on a solid acoustical basis. He founded the theory of tonal music (or functional harmony), as opposed to modal music, and all later tonal theory is derived from his work. He posited the chord as the basic unit in music, derived from divisions of a string (or the overtone series); said chords were built in thirds; suggested that chords maintain their identity and original roots when inverted, and that root progressions determine successions of chords; and established the tonic, dominant, and subdominant chords as the pillars of harmony and related all other chords to them.

4. Characteristics of French opera

French interest in spectacle is illustrated in Rameau's *Les Indes galantes* (The Gallant Indies, 1735), an opera-ballet in four acts set in exotic locales in Asia and North and South America.

5. Rameau's musical style

Rameau's operas are like Lully's in alternating realistically declaimed recitatives with airs, choruses, overtures, instrumental interludes, and long divertissements. But his style is quite different.

6. Melodic style

Rameau believed that melody was rooted in harmony. His melodies are often triadic and make clear their underlying harmony

7. Harmonic style

Rameau used harmonic dissonance and modulation for expression.

8. Airs

Rameau's airs, like those of other French composers, are restrained in comparison to Italian arias, but gain drama through harmonic dissonance and other means. **Music: NAWM 78**

9. Choruses

Rameau often used the chorus in dramatically effective ways.

10. Instrumental music

Rameau's instrumental interludes are remarkable in their ability to depict scenes.

11. Clavecin pieces

Rameau's harpsichord pieces recall those of Couperin.

III. Johann Sebastian Bach (CHWM 266–82, NAWM 79–82)

Johann Sebastian Bach (1685–1750) was not the most famous composer of his time but has become so in the last two centuries.

1. Bach's life and works

Bach was born into a family of professional musicians and was trained by his father and elder brother. He blended German, French, and Italian styles, which he learned by copying and arranging music by leading composers of each region. He served as church organist at Arnstadt (1703–7) and Mühlhausen (1707–8), organist and concertmaster for the duke of *Weimar* (1708–17), music director for a prince in *Cöthen* (1717–23), and cantor of *St. Thomas Church* and school in *Leipzig* (1723–50), writing music for his immediate use in each post.

A. *Bach at Arnstadt, Mühlhausen, and Weimar: The Organ Works*

Bach's first positions were as an organist, and his first major works were for the organ. His early works were influenced by Buxtehude. At Weimar, he arranged Vivaldi concertos for keyboard, learned the Italian style, and adopted many Vivaldi traits in his own works. From Italian, French, and German elements he forged his own style.

1. Preludes and fugues

Some of Bach's organ toccatas intersperse fugue and toccata sections, but more common are works with separate fugues. Most of Bach's important organ preludes and fugues date from his Weimar years, and many use elements from the Italian concerto, such as the alternation of the subject (like a ritornello) with episodes that resemble solo sections. **Music: NAWM 79**

2. *Orgelbüchlein*

Bach wrote about 170 chorale settings for organ, using all current types of setting. His *Orgelbüchlein* (Little Organ Book) contains short chorale preludes.

3. Pedagogic aims

Like several of his collections, the *Orgelbüchlein* had pedagogical aims.

4. Chorale preludes

The chorale preludes in the *Orgelbüchlein* state the chorale once, usually in the soprano, accompanied with counterpoint or embellished. Some preludes suggest visual images in the chorale texts through appropriate figures in the accompaniment.   **Music: NAWM 80**

B. *Bach at Cöthen and Leipzig: The Harpsichord and Clavichord Music*

Bach wrote in all keyboard genres of his time, and they show the intermingling of Italian, French, and German elements in Bach's style.

1. *The Well-Tempered Keyboard*

Bach's best-known keyboard work is *The Well-Tempered Keyboard,* two cycles of 24 preludes and fugues in all twelve major and minor keys.

Book I (ca. 1722) is a teaching manual in several ways, whereas Book II (ca. 1740) includes pieces from many periods in Bach's life.

2. Preludes

The preludes offer the player varied technical challenges and exemplify different types of keyboard composition.

3. Fugues

The fugues illustrate the range of possibilities for a fugue with a single subject.

4. Suites

Bach wrote three sets of six suites each, the English Suites (ca. 1715), the French Suites (1722–25), and the six Partitas (1726–31). All contain the standard four dances with additions, and the English Suites begin with preludes.

5. *Goldberg Variations*

The *Goldberg Variations* (published 1741 or 1742) is a set of thirty variations on a sarabande. Every third variation is a canon; the interval of imitation grows from a unison in variation 3 to a ninth in variation 27. The last variation is a *quodlibet* incorporating two popular songs of the time, followed by a reprise of the theme. The noncanonic variations are of many types.

C. *Bach at the Princely Court of Cöthen: Solo and Ensemble Music*

Bach's sonatas, partitas, and suites for unaccompanied violin, cello, and flute suggest a polyphonic texture by playing two or more strings at once jumping back and forth between implied independent lines. Most of his sonatas for violin, viola da gamba, or flute and harpsichord have four movements, slow-fast-slow-fast, like a sonata da chiesa, and are like trio sonatas, with the right hand of the harpsichord acting as the other solo instrument while the left hand supplies the continuo.

1. Brandenburg Concertos

Bach's six *Brandenburg Concertos,* written for the Margrave of Brandenburg (1721) follow Italian models, but expand the form.

2. Harpsichord concertos

Bach was among the first to write or arrange concertos for one or more harpsichords and orchestra.

3. Orchestral suites

Bach's orchestral suites (or ouvertures) are sprightly and attractive.

4. Other instrumental works

Two works are surveys of musical possibilities. *A Musical Offering* (1747) presents a trio sonata, two ricercares, and ten canons based on a theme by King Frederick the Great of Prussia, on which Bach improvised while visiting the king. *The Art of Fugue* (1749–50) sums up the fugue in a series of eighteen canons and fugues of increasing complexity, all based on the same subject.

D. *Bach at Leipzig: The Vocal Music*

As cantor in Leipzig, Bach oversaw the music at St. Thomas and St. Nicholas churches and taught Latin and music in St. Thomas's School. Each Sunday, Bach directed a cantata, alternating between the two churches. The service also included a motet, a Lutheran Mass (Kyrie and Gloria), and chorales, using a choir of at least twelve singers (three for each part). The cantata followed the Gospel reading in the liturgy and often was related in subject. Bach composed four complete cycles of cantatas for the church year (1723–29), plus cantatas for various occasions such as weddings.

1. Church cantatas

About two hundred cantatas survive, representing many forms and approaches. Many of Bach's cantata movements are reworkings of music he had written for other purposes.

2. Neumeister cantatas

Bach set five cantata texts by Erdmann Neumeister and was influenced by his combination of chorale verses, Bible passages, and new poetry. In his cantatas, Bach frequently combined secular genres such as French overture, recitative, and da capo aria with chorale settings.

3. Chorale cantatas

Bach's cantatas use chorales in various ways. He often based the opening chorus on a chorale in an elaborate setting and ended with the same chorale in simple four-part harmony, with independent solos and duets and an occasional chorale setting in between.   **Music: NAWM 81**

4. Secular cantatas

Bach also wrote secular cantatas for various occasions. In some he experimented with the newer operatic style.

5. Passions

Bach's *St. John Passion* (1724) and *St. Matthew Passion* (1727) were performed during Good Friday services. In both, the Bible story is narrated by the tenor soloist, with characters played by other soloists and the crowd by the chorus, and chorales, recitatives, and arias are interpolated as commentary on the story.

6. Large-scale design

Bach arranged several of his major works according to a single large design, aiming at comprehensive treatment of the matter at hand.

7. Mass in B Minor

One such work is Bach's *Mass in B Minor,* compiled in 1747–49 from existing and some new movements. It includes styles from stile antico and cantus firmus to the modern galant style. Bach may have intended it as a universal statement of religious feeling.   **Music: NAWM 82**

E. *Reception History*

Even before his death, Bach's music was viewed as old-fashioned in comparison to the newer, more tuneful style of contemporary Italian opera. His music was known to some in the latter eighteenth century, then revived and popularized in the nineteenth century, culminating in a complete edition of his works.

IV. George Frideric Handel (CHWM 282–92, NAWM 83–84)

George Frideric Handel (1685–1759) was a truly international composer, working in Germany, Italy, and England.

1. London

Handel spent the majority of his career in London, where he composed Italian operas for the *Royal Academy of Music,* then turned to oratorios in English, which attracted a broad middle-class audience. King George I was his patron, continuing a sponsorship that began when the future king was elector of Hanover and Handel's employer.

2. Handel's life

Handel was born in Halle and studied organ and composition. In 1703 he moved to Hamburg, where he wrote his first opera. In 1706 he went to Italy, where he met the leading patrons and composers, including Corelli and Alessandro Scarlatti. In 1710 he was named music director for the elector of Hanover, later crowned king of England. Handel preceded his patron to London and soon established himself as a composer of Italian opera. During the 1720s, Handel composed operas for the Royal Academy of Music; after that company failed, he formed his own opera company. When rising costs and falling interest made opera no longer viable, Handel wrote oratorios in English, which were less costly to perform and won an enthusiastic following. The oratorios gave him a great and enduring popularity in England.

3. Instrumental music

Handel's most significant instrumental works are the orchestral suites *Water Music* (1717) and *Music for the Royal Fireworks* (1749) and twelve concerti grossi, Op. 6.

4. Concertos

Handel's concertos are modeled on those of Corelli, with a sequence of movements and general style like a sonata da chiesa for orchestra.

5. Operas

Handel's operas were among the most successful of his time. The plots are freely adapted from history and literature, and the music consists mainly of recitatives (both dry and accompanied) to forward the action and arias that reflect on the characters' feelings.

6. Arias

Handel used a variety of aria types, from coloratura to folklike melodies and from contrapuntal to concertato accompaniments. His later operas adopt the light melodic style then current in Italy.   **Music: NAWM 83**

7. Oratorios

Handel's oratorios blend operatic recitative and aria with elements from the English masque and choral anthem, the German historia, and French and ancient Greek drama. The oratorios were in English and often used Old Testament stories.

8. Choruses

The prominence of the chorus in Handel's oratorios is indebted to choral music in both Germany and England. The chorus often comments on the action, as in a Greek drama, or participates in the action. Handel often uses musical figures to depict images in the text or convey a feeling.   **Music: NAWM 84**

9. Handel's borrowings

Handel often borrowed and reworked material from his own music and from other composers. Borrowing, transcribing, and reworking were universally accepted practices. When Handel borrowed, he "repaid with interest," using the borrowed material in new and more ingenious ways.

Window: Farinelli, the Adored Castrato (CHWM 288–89)

Castratos were males castrated before puberty to preserve their soprano or contralto voices. Castratos sang in church and took leading roles (playing male characters) in operas. Their voices were prized for their strength, agility, and thrilling sound. Leading castratos, such as *Farinelli* (1705–1782), were adored by listeners and commanded enormous fees.

STUDY QUESTIONS

Antonio Vivaldi (CHWM 257–62, NAWM 76–77)

1. For what institution did Vivaldi work for most of his career? Describe the institution's purpose, the role of music in it, and Vivaldi's role.

2. What was the eighteenth-century attitude toward new music? How did this attitude affect Vivaldi?

3. In Vivaldi's concertos, which instruments does he favor as soloists?

4. What is the typical pattern of movements in Vivaldi's concertos, including the number of movements and their tempo, forms, and key relationships?

Music to Study
    NAWM 76: Antonio Vivaldi, Concerto Grosso in G minor, Op. 3, No. 2
        (published 1712), excerpts
        76a: Adagio e spiccato (first movement)   CD 5.33
        76b: Allegro (second movement)   CD 5.34–40 (Concise 2.38–44)
    NAWM 77: Antonio Vivaldi, Concerto for Violin and Orchestra, Op. 9,
        No. 2 (published 1728), Largo (second movement)
        CD 5.41

5. How does Vivaldi treat texture and contrasts of texture in his concertos? How is this exemplified in the concerto movements in NAWM 76 and 77?

---

6. Chart the form of the second movement of Vivaldi's Op. 3, No. 2 (NAWM 76b) by completing the table below. Use the abbreviations "Rit" for ritornello, "Solo" for the solo episodes, and letters for the melodic material of the ritornello as it returns. (See the discussion of ritornello form in Chapter 11, if needed, and the discussion of this work in NAWM.)

Before you begin, what is the relationship between b and c in the table below?

Beginning measure	Section	Tutti or soloists	Melodic material	Key
14	Rit	Tutti	a	g minor
17	↓	↓	b	↓
20	↓	↓	c	↓
23	Solo	Soloists		↓

Jean-Philippe Rameau (CHWM 262–66, NAWM 78)

7. Briefly trace Rameau's career. What were his various occupations? How did he earn a living? What (and who) made it possible for him to write operas and opera-ballets?

8. What were Rameau's contributions to the theory of music?

Music to Study
    NAWM 78: Jean-Philippe Rameau, *Hippolyte et Aricie,* opera (1733), Act
           IV, Scene 1, *Ah! faut-il*
       CD 5.42 (Concise 2.45)

9. At the opening of Act IV of Rameau's *Hippolyte et Aricie,* the noble young
man Hippolyte is alone in the woods, banished from home, and despairing.
How does Rameau use harmony, melody, rhythm, and choice of instrument
in the instrumental prelude (NAWM 78, mm. 1–13) to convey his situation
and mood? In particular, what suggests that he is in despair? In a rural setting? Alone?

10. Diagram the form of this excerpt. Use letters to designate the melodic material of the orchestral introduction (A starting in m. 1, B in m. 4, C in m. 9, D
in m. 11) and "Recit" to indicate passages in recitative.

How would you describe this form? How does it reflect Hippolyte's emotions?

11. How does this excerpt compare with the scene from Lully's *Armide* in NAWM 68b? How are Rameau's approach and style similar to Lully's, and how are they different? What is the role of dissonance in each excerpt?

Johann Sebastian Bach (CHWM 266–82, NAWM 79–82)

12. How did Bach learn music? How did he absorb the Italian style?

13. Where did Bach work, and when? What were his duties in each position? How did his employment affect the music he composed?

Music to Study

NAWM 79: Johann Sebastian Bach, Praeludium et Fuga in A minor for organ, BWV 543 (1710s?)

79a: Praeludium (Prelude) CD 5.43 (Concise 2.46)
79b: Fuga (Fugue) CD 5.44 (Concise 2.47)

14. How do the melodies in Bach's Praeludium et Fuga in A minor for organ (NAWM 79) show the influence of Italian violin style? Use the solo violin portions of Vivaldi's Concerto Grosso in G minor, Op. 3, No. 2, second movement (NAWM 76b) for comparison.

15. Bach's fugue alternates between statements of the subject (first presented in mm. 1–5) with episodes of other figuration, often moving in sequence. How does this format resemble the ritornello form of Vivaldi's concertos?

16. How does this Bach fugue compare to the first fugal section of Buxtehude's Praeludium in E (NAWM 71) in form and in other respects?

17. Based on the comparisons you have made above, write a brief summary of how Bach's prelude and fugue blends North German and Italian influences.

Music to Study
    NAWM 80: Johann Sebastian Bach, *Durch Adams Fall,* BWV 637, cho-
        rale prelude from the *Orgelbüchlein* (ca. 1716–23)
    80a: Chorale melody   not on recordings
    80b: Bach setting   CD 5.45

18. How does Bach employ musical imagery in his chorale prelude on *Durch
    Adams Fall* (NAWM 80b) to convey the images in the chorale text?

19. What does *The Well-Tempered Keyboard* contain? When was it written?

20. What types of chamber music and orchestral music did Bach write?

21. What were Bach's duties as Cantor of St. Thomas and Music Director of
    Leipzig?

> *Music to Study*
>   **NAWM 81:** Johann Sebastian Bach, *Wachet auf, ruft uns die Stimme* [Cantata No. 140], BWV 140 (1731)
>   1: Chorus, *Wachet auf*   CD 6.1–5 (Concise 2.48–52)
>   2: Tenor recitative, *Er kommt*   CD 6.6
>   3: Duet for soprano and bass, *Wann kommst du, mein Heil?*
>   CD 6.7
>   4: Chorale, *Zion hört die Wächter singen*   CD 6.8
>   5: Bass recitative, *So geh herein zu mir*   CD 6.9
>   6: Duet for soprano and bass, *Mein Freund ist mein!*
>   CD 6.10–11
>   7: Chorale, *Gloria sei dir gesungen*   CD 6.12
>   **NAWM 82:** Johann Sebastian Bach, Mass in B Minor, BWV 232 (1747–49), excerpts from the Credo (*Symbolum Nicenum*)
>   82a: Bass Aria, *Et in Spiritum sanctum Dominum*
>   CD 6.13–14
>   82b: Chorus, *Confiteor*   CD 6.15–17
>   82c: Chorus, *Et expecto resurrectionem*   CD 6.18–19

22. For which day of the church calendar did Bach write the cantata *Wachet auf, ruft uns die Stimme* (NAWM 81)? Where in the liturgy was the cantata performed? How do the words of the chorale Bach uses and of the added texts relate to the Gospel reading for the day?

23. How are the words and images of the text reflected in the music for the opening chorus (1) and the two duets (3 and 6)?

24. How is the chorale tune *Wachet auf, ruft uns die Stimme* used in the first movement?

In the fourth movement?

In the final movement?

25. What Italian forms and textures, adapted from opera, concerto, and sonata, are used in this cantata, and in which movements? What other Italian traits do you notice?

26. In what ways does the music of *Et in Spiritum sanctum Dominum* from Bach's Mass in B Minor (NAWM 82a) show traces of an up-to-date style?

27. Where and in which voices does the cantus firmus appear in the chorus Confiteor (NAWM 82b)? How is it treated?

28. In addition to cantus firmus technique, what other Renaissance traits can you find in the *Confiteor*? What Baroque traits make clear that this is a Baroque composition in *stile antico,* not a work from the Renaissance?

29. How does Bach use changes of musical style and texture to convey the sense of the words "and I await the resurrection of the dead"? (Note that these words are set twice, in two different styles, to bring out two different aspects of their meaning.)

George Frideric Handel (CHWM 282–92, NAWM 83–84)

30. By the age of twenty-five, where had Handel lived, studied, and worked? What genres had he tried? What influences had he absorbed? What made his music "international" in style?

31. In which genre was Handel first successful in England? Why and when did his success fade? Which new genre supplanted the first and allowed Handel to continue his career?

Music to Study

> **NAWM 83:** George Frideric Handel, *Giulio Cesare* (Julius Caesar), opera
>   (1724), Act II, Scene 2, Recitative and Aria, *V'adoro pupille*
>   CD 6.20–24 (Concise 2.53–57)

32. Baroque opera plots typically centered on love, drew on history or mythology, created opportunities for spectacle, and often involved secrecy and disguise. How are these elements reflected in the libretto for Handel's *Giulio Cesare,* particularly in this excerpt (NAWM 83)?

33. A typical operatic scene involved recitative followed by a da capo aria with an opening ritornello, first section, contrasting middle section, and reprise of the first section. In this excerpt, how does Handel modify this series of events? How do these changes aid the drama? How do they make the final statement of the aria's first section more than a conventional repetition?

34. What elements does Handel draw from instrumental forms, including the concerto and the dance? How does he use these elements expressively?

35. What national styles and genres did Handel combine in his oratorios?

36. What language is used in Handel's oratorios? How did the language and the subject matter influence the success of his oratorios? Where were they performed, and for whom?

37. How did Handel use the chorus in his oratorios? How does this differ from the practice of Italian composers? What traditions influenced Handel in this regard?

Music to Study
  NAWM 84: George Frideric Handel, *Saul,* oratorio (1739), Act II, Scene 10
    84a: Accompagnato, *The Time at length is come*
                    CD 6.25
    84b: Recitative, *Where is the Son of Jesse?*
                    CD 6.26
    84c: Chorus, *O fatal Consequence of Rage*
                    CD 6.27–29

38. In the recitatives from *Saul* (NAWM 84a and 84b), how does the music portray Saul's rage?

39. In the following chorus (NAWM 84c), how does Handel use musical symbolism to convey the meaning of the text?

40. In this chorus, where does Handel use fugue? What other textures does he employ? Why do you think he used these elements in this way? How do the changes of texture delineate the form and convey the meaning of the text?

41. How does Handel's choral writing in this work differ from that of Bach in the choral movements from his cantata *Wachet auf* (NAWM 81) and Mass in B Minor (NAWM 82), and how is it similar?

42. What is the role of borrowing in Handel's music? What is borrowed in these excerpts from *Saul,* and how is this material treated? How does this example illustrate the comment in CHWM, p. 292, that when Handel borrowed he "repaid with interest"?

TERMS TO KNOW

quodlibet   castrato

NAMES TO KNOW

Antonio Vivaldi   *Goldberg Variations*
Pio Ospedale della Pietà   *Brandenburg Concertos*
Jean-Philippe Rameau   *A Musical Offering*
Traité de l'harmonie   *The Art of Fugue*
Les Indes galantes   *St. John* and *St. Matthew Passions*
Johann Sebastian Bach   Mass in B Minor
Weimar   George Frideric Handel
Cöthen   Royal Academy of Music
St. Thomas Church and School   *Water Music*
Leipzig   *Music for the Royal Fireworks*
Orgelbüchlein   Farinelli
The Well-Tempered Keyboard

REVIEW QUESTIONS

1. Add to the time-line you made for the previous chapter the *Traité de l'harmonie* and the composers and pieces discussed in this chapter.

2. Describe the career and music of Vivaldi. How did the circumstances of his employment relate to the music he wrote? How are his concertos similar to those of Corelli and Torelli, and how are they different?

3. How do the operas and opera-ballets of Rameau continue the tradition of Lully, and how do they differ?

4. Trace Bach's career and explain how his training and employment influenced the types of music he wrote and the styles he drew upon.

5. What did Bach's instrumental music draw from German sources? What did he draw from Italian models and from French models? Describe a piece by Bach that blends at least two of these national traditions, and explain how Bach combined elements from different nations into a coherent idiom.

6. Adopting the aesthetic position of Johann Adolph Scheibe (as quoted on p. 281 of CHWM), describe what is wrong with Bach's Praeludium et Fuga in A minor (NAWM 79) and the opening chorus of his cantata *Wachet auf, ruft uns die Stimme* (NAWM 81).

7. Trace Handel's career and explain how his experiences as a composer influenced the types of music he wrote and the styles he drew upon.

8. Compare and contrast the musical ideals and styles of Bach and Handel, focusing particularly on their vocal music.

9. What was the historical significance of Vivaldi, Rameau, Bach, and Handel? What trends did each absorb, what influence did each have on later music, and in what respects did each achieve a unique musical idiom?

THE EARLY CLASSIC PERIOD: OPERA AND INSTRUMENTAL MUSIC IN THE EIGHTEENTH CENTURY

CHAPTER OBJECTIVES

After you complete the reading, study of the music, and study questions for this chapter, you should be able to

1. briefly describe the intellectual, cultural, and aesthetic background to music in the Classic period;
2. name and describe the principal musical styles, genres, and forms current in the second half of the eighteenth century; and
3. name some of the composers of the period, describe their individual styles, and identify some of their works.

CHAPTER OUTLINE

Prelude (CHWM 294–97)

> The music of Haydn and Mozart was later called *classic,* and the term is now applied to the entire period 1730–1815. The term *galant* (elegant) was used in the eighteenth century for the new style that featured melody in clearly demarked phrases over light accompaniment. *Empfindsamkeit* (sentimentality) was a related style that added surprising harmonies, chromaticism, nervous rhythms, and speech-like melody. All were influenced by *Enlightenment* ideals of reason, knowledge, naturalness, and humanitarianism. Politics, culture, and the arts were cosmopolitan. The flutist and composer *Johann Joachim Quantz* held that the best music combined features of many nations and thus was universally pleasing. A growing middle-class public pursued learning and the arts and supported the new institution of the public concert. The latter eighteenth century preferred music that was universal in appeal, both noble and entertaining, expressive yet tasteful, natural, simple, and immediately pleasing.

Etude: Cosmopolitan Vienna

Musicians from across western Europe were active in Vienna, enabling a mixing of styles and the synthesis of the "Viennese" classical style.

I. General Characteristics of the New Style (CHWM 298–302)

1. Melody

The new styles of the mid-to-late eighteenth century focused on melody, but in a way very different from the constant spinning-out of Bach or Vivaldi.

2. Melodic periodicity

The new styles of melody were *periodic,* divided into short *phrases* that combine into *periods* and larger sections, like the phrases, sentences, and paragraphs of a speech.

3. Harmonic periodicity

In contrast to the continuous drive of Baroque harmony, the pace of harmonic change slowed down in the new styles.

4. Alberti bass

To compensate, composers animated the texture through devices such as the *Alberti bass.*

5. Emotional contrasts

Composers no longer sought to express one single *affection* in a movement, as in the Baroque period, and instead presented contrasting styles and feelings within a single movement. This corresponded to current views that a person's feelings were continuously in flux.

Window: Musical Style and Social Custom in British Society (CHWM 300–301)

Amateur music-making was important in British society in the eighteenth and nineteenth centuries, especially for women, but relatively few in Britain pursued music as a career.

II. Opera buffa (CHWM 302–6, NAWM 85 and 87)

Many style elements of the Classic era derive from Italian opera, especially comic opera. An *opera buffa* was a full-length comic opera with both comic and serious characters. It was sung throughout, the dialogue in rapid *recitative* with keyboard accompaniment and the *arias* in short tuneful phrases over simple harmonies.

1. Intermezzo

An *intermezzo* was a series of short comic scenes performed between acts of a serious opera or play. It used recitatives and arias as in opera buffa.

2. Pergolesi, *La serva padrona*

The best-known intermezzo is *La serva padrona* (The Maid as Mistress, 1733), by *Giovanni Battista Pergolesi* (1710–1736). Comic opera grew in importance after 1760. Each nation or region had its own type, using the national language and musical styles. Comic opera exercised an important influence on later music, in its style, its preference for naturalness, and its use of national characteristics. **Music: NAWM 85**

3. French *opéra comique*
French *opéra comique* began as a show with popular airs (called "vaude-villes") or other simple tunes. The 1752 visit of an Italian comic opera troupe to Paris inspired French composers to write comic operas in a mixed style with original airs (called "ariettes"). Although the Italians set dialogue as recitative, the French and other national comic opera traditions used spoken dialogue. Later in the century, opéra comique was also used for serious subjects.

4. English ballad opera
Ballad opera became popular in England after *John Gay*'s success with *The Beggar's Opera* (1728), a mostly spoken play which set new words to popular tunes and parodied operatic conventions. **Music: NAWM 87**

5. German Singspiel
The success of ballad opera inspired a revival of *Singspiel* in Germany. Some Singspiel tunes became so popular that they have virtually become folksongs. In the north, Singspiel merged with native opera in the early nineteenth century; in the south, it was influenced by Italian comic opera.

III. Opera Seria (CHWM 306–10, NAWM 86)

An *opera seria* was a serious opera on a heroic classical subject without comic interludes.

1. Metastasio
The form was codified by the librettist *Pietro Metastasio* (1698–1782), whose librettos were set hundreds of times. His plots show a conflict of passions that is resolved through heroism or renunciation, and his aim was to promote morality and to show examples of enlightened rulers.

2. Musical structure
The action in an opera seria proceeds in recitative, and characters comment on the situation in arias.

3. The aria
The standard aria form was the *da capo aria,* featuring a large A section with two vocal statements surrounded by orchestral ritornellos, a shorter contrasting B section with a new text and in a related key, and a reprise of the A section.

4. Abbreviated da capo
The da capo aria format was sometimes shortened by omitting the first ritornello on the reprise of A.

5. Reign of the singers
The main interest in opera lay in the arias. Singers often sought changes in arias or substituted arias from other operas. Often the embellishments that singers added did more to display their voices than to further the drama.

6. New features of da capo arias

The da capo aria form evolved over time, as composers introduced a greater variety of moods and figuration and borrowed formal ideas from the sonata and concerto.

7. Hasse

Johann Adolf Hasse (1699–1783), music director at the Saxon court in Dresden, was the leading composer of opera seria, writing in an Italianate style. **Music: NAWM 86**

8. Faustina Bordoni

Hasse's wife *Faustina Bordoni* (1700-1781) was one of the century's leading sopranos and sang in most of Hasse's operas.

9. Vocal embellishment

Singers always embellished the written line, especially at the reprise.

IV. Opera Reform (CHWM 310–13, NAWM 88)

Nicolò Jommelli (1714–1774) and *Tommaso Traetta* (1727–1779) sought to make opera more natural and varied, blending French and Italian traits.

1. Gluck

Christoph Willibald Gluck (1714–1787) had a cosmopolitan career and was deeply influenced by the reform movement in opera.

2. Aims of reform

Working with librettist *Raniero de Calzabigi* (1714–1795), Gluck reformed opera by making music once again subservient to the poetry and plot. His *Orfeo ed Euridice* (1762) and *Alceste* (1767) blend Italian, German, and French traits; emphasize the chorus, dance, and orchestra and link them to the dramatic action; restrict the vocal display of singers; lessen the gulf between aria and recitative; and unify a variety of elements in extended scenes. Gluck brought his new style to Paris with *Iphigénie en Aulide* in 1774 and scored a great triumph. **Music: NAWM 88**

3. Influence

Gluck's operas became models for later composers and began a new tradition of serious opera in French

Etude: The *Querelle des bouffons*

Serious French opera had been in decline since the *Querelle des bouffons* (quarrel of the comic actors), a debate in 1752 about the relative merits of traditional French opera and the new comic Italian opera. Gluck appealed to the public by showing that good opera could be written in French.

V. Instrumental Music: Sonata, Symphony, and Concerto (CHWM 313–23, NAWM 89–93)

A. *Sonata*

In the late eighteenth century, "sonata" has several meanings, including a work for keyboard or a formal plan for a movement.

1. Domenico Scarlatti

Domenico Scarlatti (1685–1757), son of Alessandro Scarlatti, worked in Portugal and Spain.

2. Harpsichord sonatas

Scarlatti's 555 harpsichord *sonatas* are typically in one movement (or two paired movements) in rounded binary form: two sections, both repeated, the first moving from tonic to dominant or relative major, the second modulating back to the tonic and ending with a tonic-key restatement of the material that closed the first section. Rather than themes, Scarlatti presents a series of strongly marked ideas that plainly project the key through pedal points, arpeggiation, and other figuration.   **Music: NAWM 89**

2. Early symphonies

The Italian opera overture or *sinfonia* of the early eighteenth century had three movements in the order fast-slow-fast, ending with a dance. These were also performed independently, and composers such as *Giovanni Battista Sammartini* (1701–1775) began to write *symphonies* for concert performance.   **Music: NAWM 90**

3. Sonata form

Sonatas, symphonies, and chamber works typically have three or four movements in contrasting moods and tempos. The first movement is usually in *sonata form,* which comprises (1) an *exposition* with a first theme in the tonic (P), a modulatory transition (T), and a second theme (S) and closing theme (K) in the dominant or relative major; (2) a *development* section which modulates to new keys and may fragment and vary the themes; and (3) a *recapitulation,* restating all three themes in the tonic, sometimes followed by a *coda.* (The exposition was usually repeated and the development and recapitulation normally repeated as a unit, showing the derivation of this form from rounded binary form as used by Scarlatti and Sammartini.)

B. *The* **Empfindsam** *Style*

The *empfindsam* style was adopted by several German composers around the middle of the century.

1. Wilhelm Friedemann Bach

Wilhelm Friedemann Bach, the eldest son of Johann Sebastian Bach, used the *empfindsam* style.

2. Carl Philipp Emanuel Bach

Carl Philipp Emanuel Bach (1714–1788), the most famous of Johann Sebastian Bach's sons, was an influential composer in his own right, best known for his keyboard music. He preferred the *clavichord* for his earlier sonatas and the *pianoforte* (now called *fortepiano*) for his later ones, as they permit a variety of dynamic levels from soft to loud.

3. Main characteristics of *empfindsam* style

C. P. E. Bach was a leading exponent of the *empfindsam* style, as shown in several sets of keyboard sonatas marked by constantly changing rhythms, sudden surprising changes of harmony, texture, or dynamic level, and instrumental evocations of recitative and aria. **Music: NAWM 91**

4. *Sturm und Drang*

The expressive style reached a climax in the 1760s and 1770s with the trend known as *Sturm und Drang* (storm and stress).

C. *German Symphonic Composers*

1. Mannheim and Stamitz

Composers at *Mannheim,* Vienna, and Berlin were the leading German symphonists at mid-century. The Mannheim orchestra, led by *Johann Stamitz* (1717–1757), was renowned for its virtuosity, dynamic range, and controlled crescendo. **Music: NAWM 92**

2. Vienna

Viennese taste tended to pleasant lyricism and contrasting themes.

3. Berlin

Berlin symphonists preferred less contrast and adopted a more serious tone marked by thematic development and counterpoint.

Etude: The Eighteenth-Century Orchestra

The Classic-era orchestra had about twenty to thirty-five players, including strings, winds in pairs, horns, and harpsichord. The use of basso continuo was gradually abandoned, and conducting duties passed to the leader of the violins. The winds, often used to double the strings and fill in harmonies, gained more independent roles late in the century.

D. *J. C. Bach's Concertos*

Johann Christian Bach (1735–1782), J. S. Bach's youngest son, studied and worked in Italy before going to London. There he had a successful career and met the young Mozart, on whom he had a profound influence. His *concertos* for piano or harpsichord and orchestra follow in their first movements a form that alternates orchestral ritornellos with solo episodes, as in the Baroque concerto, but also features the key structure and contrasting themes of sonata form. **Music: NAWM 93**

Postlude (CHWM 323)

The early Classic period saw many innovations, especially in comic opera. The desire to reach a wide and varied audience led to music, both vocal and instrumental, that was simple, natural, and easy to grasp. Its intelligibility made possible the increasing independence—and thus ever greater significance—of instrumental music in the Classic period.

STUDY QUESTIONS

Prelude (CHWM 294–97)

1. What was the Enlightenment? How did the wider cultural climate of the eighteenth century affect music? How did musical life change in response to a growing public that was interested in music?

2. According to Johann Joachim Quantz (quoted in CHWM, p. 297) and others in the late eighteenth century, what were the characteristics of the best music?

General Characteristics of the New Style (CHWM 298–302)

3. What general characteristics distinguish music of the later eighteenth century from music of the Baroque period?

4. According to Johann Nikolaus Forkel (as quoted in CHWM, p. 302), how is a piece of music like a speech?

Opera Buffa (CHWM 302–6, NAWM 85 and 87)

5. What are the characteristics of an *opera buffa*? How does an *intermezzo* differ, and how are the two genres similar?

Music to Study

> **NAWM 85:** Giovanni Battista Pergolesi, *La serva padrona* (The Maid as Mistress), intermezzo (1733), excerpt
>
> Recitative: *Ah, quanto mi sta male*   CD 7.1–2 (Concise 3.1–2)
> Aria: *Son imbrogliato io*   CD 7.3–6 (Concise 3.3–6)

6. What is funny in Uberto's recitative soliloquy in this scene from Pergolesi's *La serva padrona* (NAWM 85)? How do his vocal line, the changes of harmony, and the interjections of the string orchestra convey yet parody his emotions?

7. How are repeated notes and phrases and sudden changes of texture and mood used in Uberto's aria *Son imbrogliato io* to create a comic flavor? What other humorous touches do you notice?

8. What are the distinctive features of comic opera in France, England, and Germany in the eighteenth century?

Music to Study
  NAWM 87: John Gay (librettist and arranger), *The Beggar's Opera*, ballad
      opera (1728), Scenes 11–13
    CD 7.12–16

9. In what ways does *The Beggar's Opera* differ from Italian opera and French comic opera? What is this type of musical theater called? What did John Gay do to "compose" this work?

Opera Seria (CHWM 306–10, NAWM 86)

10. What are the characteristics of the *opera seria* libretto as established by Pietro Metastasio? What moral lessons did his operas aim to teach?

11. What does "da capo" mean, and what does it ask the performer to do?

    What does "dal segno" mean, and what does it signify?

Music to Study
>   **NAWM 86:** Johann Adolf Hasse, *Cleofide,* opera seria (1731), Act II, Scene
>   9, *Digli ch'io son fedele*
>   CD 7.7–11

12. Compare Cleofide's aria *Digli ch'io son fedele* (NAWM 86) to the standard
    da capo form in CHWM, p. 307. Where does each section begin and end? In
    what respects does it follow this form? Where does it deviate?

13. In what ways does the B section contrast with the A section?

14. What characteristics of the new Classic-era styles (as described in the first sec-
    tion of this chapter) are apparent in the music of both sections of this aria?

15. How does the embellished melody in the upper staff of Example 13.3 in
    CHWM (p. 309) relate to the written melody in the staff below? It was tran-
    scribed (by King Frederick the Great of Prussia, no less) from a live perfor-
    mance. What can you deduce from this example about how singers embel-
    lished arias in opera seria? (You may also consider the embellishments added
    by Emma Kirkby in the performance that accompanies NAWM.)

Opera Reform (CHWM 310–13, NAWM 88)

16. How did Jommelli and Traetta seek to reform Italian opera in the 1750s?

Music to Study
> **NAWM 88:** Christoph Willibald Gluck, *Orfeo ed Euridice,* opera (1762),
>   excerpt from Act II, Scene 1
>   CD 7.17–21

17. What operatic reforms did Gluck introduce in *Orfeo ed Euridice* and *Alceste*? How are those reforms apparent in the scene from *Orfeo ed Euridice* in NAWM 88? How does this differ from the other operas we have seen so far in this chapter, and particularly from Hasse's *Cleofide* as composed and performed?

18. What dramatic musical devices does Gluck use to set the scene and portray the characters (the Furies in the underworld, and Orfeo, who has come down to bring back his beloved Euridice)?

Instrumental Music: Sonata, Symphony, and Concerto (CHWM 313–23, NAWM 89–93)

Music to Study
    NAWM 89: Domenico Scarlatti, Sonata in D Major, K. 119 (ca. 1749)
        CD 7.22–23 (Concise 3.7–8)

19. In the first half of his Sonata in D Major, K. 119 (NAWM 89), Scarlatti introduces a string of ideas with contrasting figuration and function. For each of the following passages (indicated by measure numbers), indicate the implied key when it is tonally stable or "mod" (for modulation) if it changes key, and briefly describe the figuration (e.g., arpeggios, scales, octaves, repeated notes or chords, trills, stepwise melody, or a combination of these).

    Of these ideas, some return in the second half, and some do not. For those that do, indicate where in the second half they begin and in what key they are presented.

	Mm.	Implied key	Figuration	Where in 2nd half?
a.	1–5			
b.	6–13			
c.	14–17			
d.	18–35			
e.	36–55			
f.	56–64			
g.	65–72			
d'.	73–95			

20. Based on your answers above, write a brief description of the form and the kinds of figuration Scarlatti uses in his sonata.

21. In this sonata, how does Scarlatti imitate the sound or style of Spanish guitar music?

22. What role did opera play in the birth of the independent symphony?

Music to Study
 NAWM 90: Giovanni Battista Sammartini, Symphony in F Major, No. 32 (ca. 1744), Presto (first movement)
   CD 7.24–26
 NAWM 91: Carl Philipp Emanuel Bach, Sonata in A Major, H. 186, Wq. 55/4 (1765), Poco adagio (second movement)
   CD 7.27–28 (Concise 3.9–10)
 NAWM 92: Johann Wenzel Anton Stamitz, Sinfonia a 8 in E-flat Major (published 1758), Allegro assai (first movement)
   CD 7.29–33

23. How does the first movement of Sammartini's Symphony in F Major, No. 32 (NAWM 90) compare in style to the aria from Pergolesi's *La serva padrona* in NAWM 85 or the Scarlatti sonata in NAWM 89? What elements does it have in common with each?

24. In the second movement of C. P. E. Bach's Sonata in A Major (NAWM 91), where does the opening material repeat, and in what key? What else is repeated, and in what key does it appear each time? Diagram the form of the piece. How does it relate to sonata form, and how is it different?

25. What elements of this movement are typical of Bach's expressive style?

26. Compare the melodic writing in this sonata movement to the vocal embellishments added to Hasse's aria from *Cleofide* (NAWM 86), as shown in the upper staff of Example 13.3 in CHWM (p. 309; see also question 15, above). Although the melodic range is too wide for a singer, how does Bach create the sense in this instrumental work of a vocal melody, like a slow aria?

27. Compare the Stamitz symphony movement in NAWM 92 to the Sammartini symphony movement in NAWM 90. How are they similar, and how are they different, in instrumentation, style, and form?

28. How large was the orchestra in the Classic period? In addition to the strings, what other instruments were members, about how many of each were there, and what was their function?

Who conducted? _____

Music to Study
   NAWM 93: Johann Christian Bach, Concerto for Harpsichord or Piano and Strings in E-flat Major, Op. 7, No. 5 (ca. 1770), Allegro di molto (first movement)
      CD 7.34–46

29. What traits mark Johann Christian Bach's keyboard concerto movement (NAWM 93) as *galant* in style? How does it differ from the *Empfindsamkeit* of C. P. E. Bach's sonata movement (NAWM 91)?

30. How does the form of this first movement resemble a Baroque concerto movement in ritornello form (in which the orchestra interjects transposed and often abbreviated statements of the ritornello between solo episodes), and how does it differ? How does it resemble a Classic-era movement in sonata form, and how does it differ?

TERMS TO KNOW

Terms Reviewed from Earlier Chapters

affection
recitative
aria

Singspiel
da capo aria

Terms Related to the Classic Style

Classic period, Classic style
galant style
Empfindsamkeit (*empfindsam*
   style)

the Enlightenment
periodic, periodicity
phrase, period
Alberti bass

Terms Related to Opera

opera buffa
intermezzo (eighteenth-century)
opéra comique

ballad opera
opera seria
querelle des bouffons

Terms Related to Instrumental Music

keyboard sonata (late-
   eighteenth-century)
sinfonia (eighteenth-century)
symphony
sonata form
exposition, development,
   recapitulation, coda

clavichord
pianoforte (fortepiano)
Sturm und Drang
concerto (late-eighteenth-century)

NAMES TO KNOW

Names Related to the Classic Style and to Opera

Joseph Joachim Quantz
La serva padrona
Giovanni Battista Pergolesi
John Gay
The Beggar's Opera
Pietro Metastasio
Johann Adolf Hasse
Faustina Bordoni

Nicolò Jommelli
Tommaso Traetta
Christoph Willibald Gluck
Raniero de Calzabigi
Orfeo ed Euridice
Alceste
Iphigénie en Aulide

Names Related to Instrumental Music

Domenico Scarlatti
Giovanni Battista Sammartini
Carl Philipp Emanuel Bach

Mannheim
Johann Stamitz
Johann Christian Bach

REVIEW QUESTIONS

1. Make a time-line for the pieces, composers, librettists, and theorists discussed in this chapter.

2. How did the Enlightenment ideals of reason and naturalness help to create a climate in which the older Baroque styles were replaced by simpler, immediately pleasing styles with wide appeal?

3. Describe the varieties of comic opera in the eighteenth century in Italy, France, England, and Germany.

4. Describe opera seria of the 1730s to 1750s. How is the reform opera of Gluck and Calzabigi different?

5. What elements of form do all or most of the instrumental works in NAWM 89–93 have in common? (For instance, do they all have similar harmonic plans? Do they repeat musical material in similar ways? What elements does each share with the standard model of sonata form?) Can you distill from these five movements a short list of formal strategies that are shared by all or most of these pieces?

THE LATE EIGHTEENTH CENTURY: HAYDN AND MOZART

CHAPTER OBJECTIVES

After you complete the reading, study of the music, and study questions for this chapter, you should be able to

1. trace the careers of Haydn and Mozart and the development of their musical idioms;
2. describe the principal genres and forms practiced by Haydn, Mozart, and their contemporaries; and
3. name several important works by each of these composers and describe some works by each in their mature styles.

CHAPTER OUTLINE

Prelude (CHWM 324–25)

The greatest composers of the Classic era were *Franz Joseph Haydn* (1732–1809) and *Wolfgang Amadeus Mozart* (1756–1791). They were friends and influenced each other, yet had strikingly different careers.

I. Franz Joseph Haydn (1732–1809) (CHWM 325 and 328–29)

1. Early life
Haydn learned music through lessons, as a choirboy, and by studying counterpoint and composition.

2. Esterházy service
Haydn served the Esterházy family for most of his career, from 1761 through the end of his life.

Etude: Music at Eszterháza and Haydn's Career
Haydn's patron from 1762 to 1790 was *Prince Nicholas Esterházy,* who lived most of the year at his country estate, *Eszterháza.* Haydn's duties were to compose music as requested, conduct frequent performances, train and supervise the musicians, and maintain the instruments. Writing so

much music for immediate performance allowed Haydn to experiment and develop a fresh, effective style that made him the most popular composer in Europe. He also wrote music for publication and on commission. When Prince Nicholas died in 1790, his son Anton disbanded the orchestra and gave Haydn a pension. In 1791–92 and 1794–95 Haydn went to London, where he gave concerts for the impresario *Johann Peter Salomon* and wrote symphonies Nos. 93–104 (the *London* Symphonies). He returned to Vienna as music director for Anton's son Prince Nicholas II with much lighter duties. His major late works are Masses and two oratorios, *The Creation* (1798) and *The Seasons* (1801).

II. Haydn's Instrumental Music (CHWM 325–39, NAWM 94–98)

A. *Symphonic form*

Many early Haydn symphonies use the three-movement plan of the opera sinfonia or four movements in the order Andante, Allegro, Minuet, Presto. Soon he adopted a standard pattern of four movements: Allegro, Andante, *Minuet and Trio,* and Allegro or Presto.

1. First-movement form
   The first movement is in sonata form, alternating harmonically stable and symmetrically phrased themes with unstable transitions and developments. There may be a slow introduction.

2. Exposition
   Haydn often repeats and alters the opening theme to lead into the transition, a tutti (passage for full orchestra) which modulates to the dominant or relative major. The second thematic section may introduce a new theme or rework the opening idea, and the exposition closes with a cadential tutti.

3. Development
   The development varies and recombines elements from the exposition, often with sudden digressions or silences.

4. Recapitulation
   The recapitulation recalls the themes in the tonic, sometimes altered, and often amplifies the transition and closing section.

5. Minuet and Trio
   The Minuet and Trio pairs two minuets, graceful triple-meter dances in rounded binary form. The second (the Trio) is more lightly scored and is followed by a return of the first, for an overall A B A form. In a symphony, the slow movement offers a lyrical respite after the strong contrasts of the first, and the Minuet and Trio is relatively brief and in a popular style.

6. Finale
   The fourth movement is faster and shorter than the first and is usually full of high spirits and surprises.

B. *The Symphonies of 1768–74*

The symphonies of 1768–74 are longer and more serious than earlier and require the listener's full attention.

1. *Sturm und Drang*

The agitated emotions of some Haydn symphonies in minor keys from this period has been linked to the slightly later literary movement *Sturm und Drang* (storm and stress). They feature startling dynamic contrasts, rich harmonies, distant modulations, and more counterpoint.

2. Slow movements

The slow movements are expressive and lyrical.

3. *Farewell* Symphony

A famous symphony from this time is the *Farewell Symphony,* which ends with each group of players in turn finishing its part and leaving the stage.

C. *The Symphonies of 1774–88*

The symphonies after 1774 are cheerful and infused with the style of comic opera.

1. Symphony No. 56

Symphony No. 56 is one of twenty in C major. Like other symphonies of the 1770s, it is impressive yet clear and appealing.   **Music: NAWM 94**

2. *Paris* symphonies

The six *Paris Symphonies* (Nos. 82–87) were commissioned for a concert series in Paris in 1785–86.

3. Symphonies Nos. 88 to 92

In Symphonies Nos. 88–92 (1787–88), Haydn often begins with a slow introduction; uses contrasting second themes less often; features the winds; and infuses the finale with counterpoint, increasing its weight without sacrificing popular appeal.   **Music: NAWM 95**

D. *London Symphonies*

Haydn wrote music to suit particular occasions, performers, and halls and to please both the expert and the untutored music lover. His *London Symphonies* (Nos. 93–104) were aimed at the public, with greater tunefulness, variety of orchestration, harmonic daring, and rhythmic drive.

1. Special effects

Haydn used effects he knew would appeal to the London public, including dynamic surprises and folklike melodies.   **Music: NAWM 96**

2. Orchestration

Haydn included trumpets, timpani, and clarinets in his *London* symphonies and gave the parts more independence.

3. Harmony

The slow introductions are harmonically imaginative, often emphasizing the minor mode.

4. Movement forms

First movements tend to focus on the first theme rather than introducing a contrasting second theme. The slow movements use theme and variation or a variant of sonata form. The Minuet-and-Trio movements are fast and often humorous.

5. Finales

The finales use sonata form, *rondo form* (A B A C A or A B A C A B A are typical), or a blend of the two such as *sonata-rondo,* in which A functions as a sonata-form first theme, B the second theme, and C the development.

E. *The String Quartets*

1. Quartets through 1781

Haydn's Opp. 17 (1771) and 20 (1772) collections confirmed him as the first great master of the *string quartet.* The same movement types are used as in the symphony, although the minuet may precede the slow movement.

2. Fugues

Three finales in Op. 20 are fugal.

3. Sonata-form movements

In sonata-form movements, the first violin usually dominates in the first theme, followed by dialogue punctuated by unison.

4. Opus 33

The Op. 33 quartets (1781) are lighter, with the minuet transformed into a *scherzo* (joke) through fast tempos and unusual rhythms.

5. Humor in Opus 33

Quartets were intended primarily for amateurs to play for their own pleasure, and Haydn's playfulness adds to the fun.   **Music: NAWM 97**

6. The quartets of 1785–90

The quartets of 1785–90 tend toward monothematic first movements.

7. The last quartets

Haydn's late quartets, written 1793–1803, are marked by widely ranging harmonies and stark juxtapositions of contrasting moods and styles.

8. Opus 76, No. 3

The slow movement of Op. 76, No. 3 is a set of variations on Haydn's hymn for Kaiser Franz Joseph I, which later became the national anthem of Austro-Hungary and of Germany.   **Music: NAWM 98**

9. Opus 76, Minuets

The Minuets of Op. 76 are full of offbeat accents and other witty touches.

F. *Keyboard Sonatas*

Haydn's early keyboard sonatas are suitable for harpsichord, clavichord, or piano, but his later ones require the piano's dynamic range. His sonatas generally develop in parallel with his symphonies and quartets.

III. Haydn's Vocal Works (CHWM 340–42)

Haydn apparently valued his vocal works above his instrumental music, but posterity has reversed this judgment.

1. Operas

Haydn wrote many operas, most of them Italian comic operas. They met with success in his day but are now rarely heard.

2. Church music

Haydn's church music is often remarkably cheerful.

3. Masses

Haydn's most important works for church were six festive Masses he wrote between 1796 and 1802 for Prince Esterházy. These were in symphonic style, with full orchestra, soloists, and chorus.

4. Oratorios

While in England, Haydn heard and admired some of Handel's oratorios.

5. *Creation* and *Seasons*

Haydn's own late oratorios *Die Schöpfung* (The Creation, 1798) and *Die Jahreszeiten* (The Seasons, 1801), both on librettos by *Baron Gottfried van Swieten,* show Handel's influence.

IV. Wolfgang Amadeus Mozart (1756–1791) (CHWM 342–45)

1. Early life

Mozart was born in Salzburg, where his father *Leopold Mozart* served the archbishop. Wolfgang and his sister Marianne ("Nannerl") were child prodigies, and their father took them on tour around Europe. Mozart began composing at age five. His more than six hundred works are identified by their number in the catalogue of his works by Ludwig von Köchel.

Etude: Mozart's Teachers

Mozart's first teacher was his father Leopold. Through touring, Mozart learned every style of music then current in western Europe and imitated each one in his own compositions. His mature works synthesize these various styles and types in music of unprecedented variety.

V. Mozart's Years in Salzburg (CHWM 345–47)

Mozart was in Salzburg for most of 1774–81 but actively sought a position elsewhere. He was commissioned to write an opera seria, *Idomeneo,* for Munich.

1. Piano sonatas

Mozart wrote piano variations for his pupils and piano sonatas for his own concert performances. The sonatas are varied in form, style, and content.

2. Themes

Mozart's themes are often graceful, singing melodies that grow without apparent effort from the initial ideas.

3. Other instrumental music

Mozart also wrote sonatas for violin and piano, *serenades* and *divertimentos,* and violin concertos.

VI. Mozart's Vienna Years (CHWM 347–60, NAWM 99–100)

Mozart moved to Vienna in 1781, hoping to earn a living as a freelance performer and composer. He met with great initial success, but he failed to find a permanent position and his popularity and earnings later declined.

His music struck a perfect balance between immediate universal appeal and the depth of feeling and technique that earned the respect of the learned. He was strongly influenced by Haydn.

1. Van Swieten
Mozart was introduced to the music of Johann Sebastian Bach by Baron Gottfried van Swieten, and he was deeply influenced by Bach.

2. Solo piano works
Mozart's most important piano works from this time are the Fantasia and Sonata in C Minor, K. 475 and 457

3. The Haydn quartets
In 1785 Mozart published six quartets dedicated to Haydn (known as the *Haydn quartets*). The fruit of long effort and much revision (unusual for Mozart, who normally wrote quickly and easily), they show his ability to absorb Haydn's techniques yet remain original.

4. Quintets
Mozart's string quintets and Clarinet Quintet fully reveal his genius.

A. *Symphonies*
Mozart wrote only six symphonies after 1781, but they were longer and more substantial than their predecessors. Each is highly individual, but together they are characterized by striking openings, more difficult wind parts, more harmonic and contrapuntal complexity, weightier finales, and frequent witty and unexpected touches.

1. Introductions
The slow introductions to three of the symphonies adopt aspects of the French overture and create suspense through modulation.

2. Finales
The finales combine seriousness and counterpoint with wit. The finale of Symphony No. 41 in C Major (*Jupiter*) combines its fugal first theme in counterpoint with five other motives.

B. *Piano Concertos*
Mozart wrote seventeen piano concertos in Vienna for his own performances as a soloist, primarily during his first five years there. In them, as in all his music, he sought to please both the connoisseur and the less learned listener, although they challenge the best players.

1. Form
Mozart's concertos are in three movements in the order fast-slow-fast.

2. Baroque elements
The first movements of Mozart's concertos are like those of Johann Christian Bach in blending aspects of Baroque ritornello form and sonata form.   **Music: NAWM 99**

3. Typical second movement
Mozart's second movements are like slow arias in a closely related key.

4. Typical finale

The concerto finales are rondos or sonata-rondos.

5. Cadenzas

Before the final tutti in the fast movements, the orchestra pauses on a tonic six-four chord and the soloist plays a *cadenza*.

C. *Operas*

In Vienna, Mozart composed a Singspiel, *Die Entführung aus dem Serail* (The Abduction from the Harem, 1786); three Italian comic operas on librettos by *Lorenzo da Ponte* (1749–1838), *Le nozze di Figaro* (The Marriage of Figaro, 1786), *Don Giovanni* (premiered at Prague in 1787), and *Così fan tutte* (Women Are Like That, 1790); an opera seria, *La clemenza di Tito* (The Clemency of Titus, 1791); and a German opera, *Die Zauberflöte* (The Magic Flute, 1791).

1. *Figaro*

Figaro followed operatic convention, but Mozart's music captured each character, and the ensembles showed them interacting in dramatic ways.

2. *Don Giovanni*

Don Giovanni was the first opera on the Don Juan story to take the central character seriously, resulting in characters and a drama of unprecedented depth. **Music: NAWM 100**

3. *Così fan tutte*

Così fan tutte includes some of Mozart's most melodious music.

4. *Die Entführung*

Die Entführung aus dem Serail is a Singspiel on a "Turkish" plot.

5. *Die Zauberflöte*

Die Zauberflöte mixes comedy with the humanistic imagery and symbolism of the Freemasons, and Mozart's music blends elements of Singspiel, opera seria, opera buffa, accompanied recitative, sacred choral style, and Baroque counterpoint.

D. *Church Music*

Mozart wrote church music from an early age.

1. Masses

Mozart's Masses are written in symphonic-operatic style, alternating chorus and soloists.

2. Requiem

Mozart's Requiem was left unfinished at his death and completed by his student and collaborator Franz Xaver Süssmayr.

Window: Mozart and His Father (CHWM 358–59)

Mozart had a complex relationship with his father Leopold, who was an unselfish mentor when Mozart was young but turned unforgiving when Mozart moved to Vienna and married against Leopold's wishes.

STUDY QUESTIONS

Prelude (CHWM 324–25)

1. What are some significant differences between the careers of Haydn and Mozart? (See also the accounts of their careers throughout the chapter.)

Franz Joseph Haydn (1732–1809) (CHWM 325 and 328–29)

2. Who was Haydn's main patron? What was Haydn required to do as part of his employment?

3. Trace Haydn's career after 1790, including his sources of income and his major compositions.

Haydn's Instrumental Music (CHWM 325–39, NAWM 94–98)

4. What are the standard four movements of a Haydn symphony, and what are the main characteristics of each?

Music to Study

NAWM 94: Franz Joseph Haydn, Symphony No. 56 in C Major, Hob. I:56
   (1774), Allegro di molto (first movement)
   CD 7.47–53 (Concise 3.11–17)
NAWM 95: Franz Joseph Haydn, Symphony No. 92 in G Major (*Oxford*),
   Hob. I:92 (1789), Adagio cantabile (second movement)
   CD 7.54–57
NAWM 96: Franz Joseph Haydn, Symphony No. 104 in D Major, Hob.
   I:104 (1795), Finale (fourth movement)
   CD 7.58–68

(Note: Instruments like horn and clarinet are notated as they are fingered to
allow players to move easily between members of the same family. Horns in
F and D, for instance, use the same fingering when they see a C, but the instrument will produce an F and a D respectively. In most scores, these "transposing instruments" are shown as notated for the player, so the conductor or
score-reader must transpose as the instrument does to determine the pitch
that will sound. In the latter two movements, Haydn uses horns in D, which
sound a minor seventh lower than written—D when C is notated; in Symphony No. 104, he also uses trumpets in D, sounding a whole step higher, and
clarinets in A, sounding a minor third lower—A when C is notated.)

5. In the exposition of Haydn's Symphony No. 56, first movement (NAWM
   94), how are the following sections distinguished from each other? Mention
   these and other features you find significant: harmonic stability or instability;
   key (when stable); use of chromaticism; phrasing (clearly articulated or continuous and overlapping); dynamics; orchestration; and melodic content.

   first theme area (mm. 1–28)

   transition (mm. 29–52)

   second theme area (mm. 53–67, with a contrasting extension in mm. 68–78)

   closing group (mm. 79–99)

6. Based on your findings in the previous question, how do these elements work together to make this music intelligible to a wide range of listeners?

7. In what measure does the recapitulation begin? _____

The recapitulation repeats material from the exposition, with some changes. What is different in the recapitulation, in comparison to the exposition?

8. What happens in the development, in terms of harmony and key?

How are orchestration and dynamics used in the development?

What ideas from the exposition are used in the development, where do they appear, and how are they changed from the exposition?

9. Chart the form of the slow movement of Haydn's Symphony No. 92 (NAWM 95), and give the key of each main section.

How do the opening motives of the first two sections relate?

What elements of both sections appear in the coda (mm. 94–111)?

10. Compare the melodic writing in this movement to the vocal embellishments added to Hasse's aria from *Cleofide* (NAWM 86 and Example 13.3 in CHWM, p. 309) and to the melodic style in the slow movement from C. P. E. Bach's piano sonata (NAWM 91; see also Chapter 13, questions 15 and 26). How does Haydn embellish his melodies?

11. How are the wind instruments used in this movement? How does this compare to the earlier Haydn symphony movement in NAWM 94?

12. What elements give the finale of Symphony No. 104 (NAWM 96) its popular character?

13. In what ways does the exposition of this sonata-form movement differ in form from the first movement of Haydn's Symphony No. 56 (NAWM 94)? How are these differences typical of Haydn's later symphonies?

14. String quartets were written primarily for amateurs to play for their own enjoyment. What aspects of Haydn's quartets were particularly well suited to give pleasure to the players themselves?

Music to Study
   NAWM 97: Franz Joseph Haydn, String Quartet in E-flat Major, Op. 33, No. 2 (*The Joke*), Hob. III:38 (1781), Presto (fourth movement)
      CD 8.1–6 (Concise 3.18–23)
   NAWM 98: Franz Joseph Haydn, String Quartet in C Major, Op. 76, No. 3, Hob. III:77 (1797), Poco adagio, cantabile (second movement)
      CD 8.7–11

15. The theme of a rondo is normally a little binary form with two repeated sections, often a rounded binary form (in which both halves end with the same music) in the pattern ‖: a :‖: b a :‖. This is true of the finale of Haydn's String Quartet in E-flat Major, Op. 33, No. 2 (NAWM 97), where the theme appears in mm. 1–36. In this theme, b (mm. 9–28) is much longer than a. What does Haydn do to extend b and prepare for the return of a?

16. In what measures does the theme reappear in its entirety, including both sections but without the repeat signs?

Where does it appear in varied or abridged form? What is changed?

How do the passages just before the return of the theme prepare for it?

17. This quartet acquired the nickname "The Joke" because of this movement. Describe what is witty or funny in this finale.

18. In the second movement of his String Quartet in C Major, Op. 76, No. 3 (NAWM 98), Haydn presents a series of variations on a tune that later became the Austrian and German national anthems. In each variation, how is the tune varied? How is the accompaniment changed?

variation I:

variation II:

variation III:

variation IV:

Haydn's Vocal Works (CHWM 340–42)

19. Whose music was a major influence on Haydn's late Masses and oratorios?

Wolfgang Amadeus Mozart and Mozart's Years in Salzburg (CHWM 342–47)

20. Describe Mozart's career and the influences on his music to 1781.

Mozart's Vienna Years (CHWM 347–60, NAWM 99–100)

21. How did Mozart become acquainted with the music of Johann Sebastian Bach? How was he influenced by Bach's music?

Music to Study
> **NAWM 99:** Wolfgang Amadeus Mozart, Piano Concerto in A Major, K. 488 (1786), Allegro (first movement)
>   CD 8.12–27

22. In the first movement of Mozart's Piano Concerto in A Major (NAWM 99), what segments of the opening orchestral ritornello return later in the work, and where does each return? How is it varied on its return?

23. How does the form of this first movement resemble a Baroque concerto movement in ritornello form, how does it resemble a sonata-form first movement, and how does it differ from each? How does it compare with the first movement of J. C. Bach's concerto in NAWM 93 (see Chapter 13, question 30)?

---

24. In Mozart's view, what was the proper relationship between the words and the music in opera?

Music to Study
  NAWM 100: Wolfgang Amadeus Mozart, *Don Giovanni*, K. 527, opera
        (1787), Act I, Scene 5
    100a: No. 3, Aria, *Ah, chi mi dice mai*, and Recitative, *Chi è là?*
      CD 8.28–30 (Concise 3.24–26)
    100b: No. 4, Aria: *Madamina! Il catalogo è questo*
      CD 8.31–32 (Concise 3.27–28)

25. How does Mozart's music help to delineate the three characters and portray their feelings in *Ah, chi mi dice mai* from *Don Giovanni* (NAWM 100a)?

26. In what ways does the form of this aria resemble sonata form? What element of sonata form does it omit?

27. In Leporello's "catalogue" aria (100b), how are the different characteristics of Don Giovanni's victims depicted in the music? That is, what musical means does Mozart use to depict the images in the text?

TERMS TO KNOW

Minuet and Trio
rondo form
sonata-rondo
string quartet

scherzo
serenade
divertimento
cadenza

NAMES TO KNOW

Franz Joseph Haydn
Wolfgang Amadeus Mozart
Prince Nicholas Esterházy
Eszterháza
Johann Peter Salomon
the *Farewell* Symphony
the *Paris* Symphonies
the *London* Symphonies
Die Schöpfung (The Creation)
Die Jahreszeiten (The Seasons)
Baron Gottfried van Swieten
Leopold Mozart

Idomeneo
Mozart's *Haydn* quartets
Jupiter symphony
Die Entführung aus dem Serail (The
   Abduction from the Harem)
Lorenzo da Ponte
Le nozze di Figaro (The Marriage of
   Figaro)
Don Giovanni
Così fan tutte (Women Are Like
   That)
Die Zauberflöte (The Magic Flute)

REVIEW QUESTIONS

1. Add Haydn, Mozart, and the major events and works discussed in this chapter to the time-line you made for Chapter 13.

2. Compare the careers of Haydn and Mozart, including the circumstances of their lives and the genres and styles they cultivated. What are the main similarities between their careers, and what are the major differences?

3. Briefly describe each of the following genres as practiced by Mozart and Haydn in terms of form, style, content, and social function: symphony, string quartet, piano sonata, concerto, and comic opera.

4. Describe the principal characteristics of Haydn's mature style in his instrumental works. Use NAWM 94–98 as examples for your discussion, referring to and describing passages as appropriate.

5. Building on the previous question, what aspects of Haydn's style did Mozart absorb into his own? And in what ways does Mozart's mature music differ from that of Haydn? Use NAWM 99–100 and other works described in CHWM as examples for your discussion, referring to and describing passages as appropriate.

LUDWIG VAN BEETHOVEN (1770–1827)

CHAPTER OBJECTIVES

After you complete the reading, study of the music, and study questions for this chapter, you should be able to

1. briefly recount Beethoven's career and the circumstances of his life;
2. list the main characteristics of the music of each of his three periods; and
3. name several important works and describe at least one complete movement for each period.

CHAPTER OUTLINE

Prelude (CHWM 361–63)

Ludwig van Beethoven (1770–1827) was born in Bonn in northwest Germany and was taught music by his father and a local organist. In 1792, he went to Vienna and studied with Haydn and other composers. He was neither as prolific nor as speedy a composer as Haydn or Mozart, but took each piece through many drafts and revisions, as we can see in his surviving *sketchbooks*. His career is divided into three periods. In the first, to about 1802, he assimilated the musical language, genres, and styles of his time. In the second, from about 1803 to around 1816, his works were more individual, longer, and grander than before. In the third period, his music became more introspective (and often more difficult to play and understand).

I. First Period (CHWM 363–66, NAWM 101–2)

1. Patrons

Beethoven was supported by aristocratic patrons, three of whom gave him an annuity to keep him in Vienna. He also sold his works to publishers, performed as a pianist, and taught piano. Thus he was able to make a living without being employed by a single patron, as Haydn had been.

2. Piano Sonatas

Beethoven's piano sonatas follow Haydn's example but include individual features. Several traits of his piano style may be indebted to the sonatas of *Muzio Clementi* (1752–1832).   **Music: NAWM 101–2**

3. Chamber music

Beethoven's first six string quartets, Op. 18 (1798–1800), follow Haydn in motivic development and use of counterpoint but show Beethoven's individuality in their themes, surprising modulations and turns of phrase, and formal structure. Other chamber works of the first period include piano trios, violin sonatas, cello sonatas, and a septet for strings and winds.

4. First Symphony

Beethoven's Symphony No. 1 in C Major (1800) has a scherzo as the third movement and features long codas in the other movements.

5. Second Symphony

Beethoven's Second Symphony in D Major (1802) is longer than previous symphonies, with more thematic material and long codas that develop the main ideas.

II. Second Period (CHWM 366–75, NAWM 103)

By his early thirties, Beethoven was renowned as a pianist and composer, had many aristocratic patrons, and was sought after by publishers.

1. *Eroica* Symphony

The *Third Symphony* (*Eroica,* 1803) was unprecedented in length and complexity, with many unusual features. It celebrates the ideal of heroism. **Music: NAWM 103**

2. Dramatization of themes in the *Eroica*

The symphony's opening theme is treated like a character in a drama, struggling and finally triumphing.

3. Beethoven, Napoleon, and the *Eroica*

 Beethoven first titled the work *Bonaparte,* after Napoleon, but changed the title to *Sinfonia Eroica* (Heroic Symphony).

4. Funeral march in the *Eroica*

The symphony's second movement is a funeral march that evokes the style of French Revolutionary marches.

5. *Fidelio*

Beethoven's opera *Fidelio* (1804–5, rev. 1806 and 1814) glorifies heroism and the humanitarian ideals of the Revolution. Leonore assumes the disguise of a man in order to free her husband from wrongful imprisonment. Beethoven revised the work repeatedly before it was a success.

6. *Rasumovsky* Quartets

Beethoven's second set of string quartets was Op. 59 (1806), dedicated to Count Rasumovsky, Russian ambassador to Vienna. Two movements use Russian themes.

7. Op. 59, No. 1

The quartets were so novel that musicians were slow to accept them.

8. Middle symphonies

Beethoven worked on the Fourth, Fifth, and Sixth Symphonies between 1806 and 1808. The Fourth is jovial.

9. Fifth Symphony

The *Fifth Symphony* portrays struggle and final triumph, moving from C minor to C major.

10. *Pastoral* Symphony

The *Sixth (Pastoral) Symphony* in F Major is in five movements and evokes country scenes.

Etude: Beethoven's Deafness

Starting in his twenties, Beethoven gradually went deaf, writing movingly of his suffering in an 1802 letter called the *Heiligenstadt Testament*. His deafness tended to isolate him from society.

11. Seventh Symphony

The Seventh Symphony in A Major (1811–12) is expansive.

12. Eighth Symphony

By contrast, the Eighth in F Major (1812) is quite condensed.

13. Overtures

Beethoven also wrote several overtures, which resemble in form the first movement of a symphony (without the reprise of the exposition).

14. Piano sonatas

Many of Beethoven's sonatas show individual features. The *Moonlight* Sonata, Op. 27, No. 2 (1801) begins with a fantasia, and the Sonata in D Minor, Op. 31, No. 2 (1802) uses a melody that resembles a recitative.

15. *Waldstein* and *Appassionata* sonatas

The *Waldstein* Sonata in C Major, Op. 53 (1804) and the *Appassionata* Sonata in F Minor, Op. 57 (1805) both stretch the traditional forms with intense themes and strongly contrasting textures.

16. Piano concertos

Beethoven's first three piano concertos belong to his first period, and the Fourth in G Major (1805–6) and Fifth (*Emperor*) in E-flat Major (1809) to his middle period, along with his one Violin Concerto (1806).

III. Third Period (CHWM 375–82, NAWM 104)

Although Beethoven was famous across Europe and well supported by patrons and publishers, his deafness led to greater social isolation. His music became more abstract and introspective.

1. Characteristics of Beethoven's late style

Beethoven's late works are marked by extremes from the meditative to the grotesque. Classical conventions are invoked but disrupted. His late compositions work out the full potential of themes and motives.

2. Variations

Many of Beethoven's late slow movements are variations. The *Diabelli Variations,* Op. 120 (1819–23) for piano do not simply embellish the theme as do earlier variation sets but rework material from it to create a new design, mood, and character in each variation.

3. Continuity

In his late works, Beethoven creates a new sense of continuity by blurring phrase and section divisions and deemphasizing cadences.

4. Improvisatory passages

Many late works include passages that have an improvisatory character or resemble recitative.

5. Fugal texture

Beethoven's late works often feature fugal textures in developments, and several movements or large sections are fugues.

6. New sonorities

The late works use new sonorities, including wide spacings and unusually dense textures. Several also feature an unusual number of movements and unusual kinds of movements.

7. Quartet Op. 131

The *String Quartet in C-sharp Minor,* Op. 131 (1826) has an unusual seven-movement structure.   **Music: NAWM 104**

8. *Missa solemnis*

The *Missa solemnis* (1819–23), or Mass in D, is a grand, complex work.

9. Debt to Handel

The *Missa solemnis* recalls the choral style of Handel while resembling the symphonic conception and mix of chorus and soloists typical of Haydn's late Masses.

10. Ninth Symphony

Beethoven's *Ninth Symphony* is longer than his others. At its premiere it was a popular success but not a financial one.

11. Form of Ninth Symphony finale

The Ninth Symphony's finale is novel in recalling themes from the earlier movements and introducing soloists and chorus to sing stanzas from Friedrich von Schiller's *Ode to Joy.*

Window: The Immortal Beloved (CHWM 376–77)

Beethoven never married, but an impassioned love letter found in his effects after his death has left the mystery of the identity of the woman he called his "Immortal Beloved." The most likely candidate is Antonie Brentano, a Viennese woman married to a businessman in Frankfurt.

Postlude (CHWM 383)

Building on the genres, styles, and procedures of the Classic era, Beethoven created highly individual works that brought him unprecedented success and became models for later composers. His middle-period works were the most influential, particularly for the concept of music as a vehicle to express the composer's own feelings and experiences. (This was the most novel aspect of Beethoven's music; this idea became so influential that modern listeners often assume that this is what all composers have had in mind, when earlier composers sought only to convey the feelings in a text or represent the generalized affections.) Through this and his innovations in form and procedure, he became a revolutionary force in music history.

STUDY QUESTIONS

Prelude (CHWM 361–63)

1. What are two reasons that Beethoven wrote fewer symphonies than Haydn or Mozart? (For a reason that he could afford to do so, see question 3 below.)

2. Beethoven's career is often divided into three periods. Provide the dates for each period and a brief characterization of each.

   First period:

   Second period:

   Third period:

First Period (CHWM 363–66, NAWM 101–2)

3. How did Beethoven make a living in Vienna? How was his situation different from that of Haydn?

Music to Study
    NAWM 101: Ludwig van Beethoven, *Sonate pathétique* for piano, Op. 13,
        (1797–98), Rondo, Allegro (third movement)
       CD 8.33–42 (Concise 3.29–38)
    NAWM 102: Muzio Clementi, Piano Sonata in G Minor, Op. 34, No. 2
        (1795), Largo e sostenuto / Allegro con fuoco (first movement)
       CD 8.43–51

4. In what ways is the finale of Beethoven's *Pathétique* Sonata (NAWM 101)
   like traditional rondos?

   In what ways is it different?

5. What are some of the effects Beethoven uses to make this rondo dramatic?

6. Compare the later repetitions of the rondo refrain to its initial presentation.
   What changes are made, if any? How do these changes contribute to the dramatic quality of the music?

7. Compare the rondo's first episode (mm. 25–61) to the reprise of this episode near the movement's end (mm. 134–69). In the reprise, how is it changed from its initial presentation? How does this reflect the influence of sonata form?

8. Both the first movement of Clementi's Sonata in G Minor, Op. 34, No. 1 (NAWM 102) and the finale of Beethoven's *Pathétique* Sonata use sudden changes in harmony, texture, or dynamic level for dramatic effect or to demarcate the form. Find and describe two such moments of sudden change in each movement.

9. Name the string quartets and symphonies Beethoven wrote during his first period, and give a date and a brief description for each.

Second Period (CHWM 366–75, NAWM 103)

Music to Study
   NAWM 103: Ludwig van Beethoven, Symphony No. 3 in E-flat Major
         (*Eroica,* 1803), Allegro con brio (first movement)
      CD 8.52–66

10. According to CHWM and NAWM, the principal theme of the first movement
    of Beethoven's *Eroica* Symphony (NAWM 103) is treated as a person in a
    drama, struggling against other players and triumphing in the end. How does
    Beethoven use changes in the principal motive (mm. 3–8) to convey struggle
    and triumph? (Hint: Look at the versions of this idea in the development, at
    mm. 408 and 424 in the recapitulation, and at mm. 639ff. in the coda.)

11. What other devices does Beethoven use in this movement to suggest a heroic
    struggle ending in triumph? How do the very long development and coda
    contribute to this effect?

12. What unusual features of this movement can be explained or understood
    better through an examination of the sketches (as shown in NAWM, pp.
    268–74)?

13. What do Beethoven's *Eroica* Symphony and his opera *Fidelio* owe to the arts and politics of France in the Revolutionary period?

14. Name the string quartets and symphonies Beethoven wrote during his second period, and give a date and a brief description for each.

15. How does the music of Beethoven's Sixth Symphony (the *Pastoral*) suggest scenes from life in the country?

16. What is the *Heiligenstadt Testament*? What does it discuss, and what attitudes does Beethoven express? What does Beethoven say in it about his relations with other people and about the role of his art in his life?

Third Period (CHWM 375–82, NAWM 104)

17. For each of the following aspects of music, how does Beethoven's late style differ from Haydn, Mozart, and his own earlier style?

   a. juxtaposition of disparate elements

   b. variation technique

   c. delineation of phrases and sections

   d. evocation of improvisation and recitative

   e. use of fugue

   f. sonority

   g. number of movements

Music to Study
> **NAWM 104:** Ludwig van Beethoven, String Quartet in C-sharp Minor, Op.
> 131 (1826), excerpts
> 104a: Adagio ma non troppo e molto espressivo (first movement)
>   CD 8.67–69 (Concise 3.39–41)
> 104b: Allegro molto vivace (second movement)
>   CD 8.70 (Concise 3.42)

18. Beethoven's String Quartet in C-sharp Minor, Op. 131 is in seven move-
    ments. Give the tempo marking, meter, key, and form for each movement.

	Tempo	Meter	Key	Form
1.	_____	_____	_____	_____
2.	_____	_____	_____	_____
3.	_____	_____	_____	_____
4.	_____	_____	_____	_____
5.	_____	_____	_____	_____
6.	_____	_____	_____	_____
7.	_____	_____	_____	_____

How can this sequence of movements be reconciled with the traditional four-
movement plan of a string quartet?

19. The quartet's key scheme is unusual, and there is a correspondence between
    the keys used for each movement and the important pitches of the subject of
    the opening fugue (NAWM 104a). Write out the following notes for the
    fugue subject in violin I (mm. 1–4) and answer in violin II (mm. 4–8):

	first note (same as last note)	highest note	lowest note	longest and loudest note
subject in violin I	_____	_____	_____	_____
answer in violin II	_____	_____	_____	_____

Of these notes, circle the ones that are used as the key of one of the movements in the quartet, as you listed them in question 18.

20. What aspects of the music give the second movement (NAWM 104b) its particularly light and folklike character?

21. Where in the second movement is there a recollection of the key of the first movement, to match the hint in the first movement of the key of the second?

22. In what ways does this quartet exemplify the characteristics of Beethoven's late style as you described them in question 17 above? (Hint: Answers for part d. of question 17 will be found in CHWM and for parts e. and g. in the questions above. For parts a., b., c., and f., look both in CHWM and at the two movements in NAWM 104.)

a. juxtaposition of disparate elements

b. variation technique

c. delineation of phrases and sections

d. evocation of improvisation and recitative

e. use of fugue

f. sonority

g. number of movements

23. What does Beethoven's *Missa solemnis* owe to Handel, and what does it owe to Haydn?

24. What is unusual about Beethoven's Ninth Symphony? Describe the sequence of events in the finale.

Postlude (CHWM 383)

25. What was Beethoven's impact on later composers? In what ways was he "one of the great disruptive forces in the history of music"?

TERMS TO KNOW

Beethoven's sketchbooks   Beethoven's three periods

NAMES TO KNOW

Ludwig van Beethoven   *Waldstein* Sonata
Muzio Clementi   *Diabelli* Variations, Op. 120
Eroica Symphony   String Quartet in C-sharp Minor,
Fidelio   Op. 131
Heiligenstadt Testament   *Missa solemnis*
Beethoven's Fifth Symphony   Beethoven's Ninth Symphony
Pastoral Symphony   *Ode to Joy*

REVIEW QUESTIONS

1. Write an essay in which you recount Beethoven's career, including the changing circumstances of his life, his three major style periods, and major compositions of each period.

2. What other composers particularly influenced Beethoven's music, and what did he absorb from each?

3. You have examples in NAWM 101, 103, and 104 of movements from each of Beethoven's three periods. For each of these works, describe the form and other significant features of the movements in NAWM and explain what makes this work characteristic of its period.

ROMANTICISM AND NINETEENTH-CENTURY ORCHESTRAL MUSIC

CHAPTER OBJECTIVES

After you complete the reading, study of the music, and study questions for this chapter, you should be able to

1. describe some of the differences between music of the Classic and Romantic periods, particularly in their aesthetic orientation;
2. explain how nineteenth-century symphonic composers responded to the example and influence of Beethoven;
3. identify some of the most important symphonic composers in the nineteenth century and suggest what makes each composer individual; and
4. briefly describe one or more characteristic works for each one.

CHAPTER OUTLINE

Prelude (CHWM 384–85)

There is more historical continuity than contrast between the Classic and Romantic periods. *Romanticism* held that instrumental music could convey emotion without words, and orchestral music was a central focus.

I. Romanticism (CHWM 385–86)

Romanticism is less a set of style traits than a state of mind, characterized by individuality, intense expressivity, and transcending conventions.

1. Music as a Romantic art
Some writers saw instrumental music as the ideal Romantic art, since it could convey emotion without words and feelings inexpressible in words.

2. Music and literature
Music was also closely identified with literature and poetry, especially in the *art song*. Many composers wrote about music.

3. Program music
Program music refers to instrumental music associated with poetic, descriptive, or narrative subject matter, combining the Romantic interest in music as the ideal expressive medium with composers' literary orientation.

II. Orchestral Music (CHWM 386–401, NAWM 105)

Orchestral music increasingly centered on public concerts for middle-class audiences. Such concerts were rare in comparison to other kinds of music-making, but orchestral music was considered of great importance by audiences, critics, and composers.

A. *Schubert (1797–1828)*

Franz Schubert composed almost one thousand works in his short life, including more than six hundred lieder and nine symphonies.

1. *Unfinished* Symphony
Schubert's *Unfinished Symphony* has only two movements, an opening fast movement and a slow movement. It has been called the first Romantic symphony for its lyrical themes and striking harmony and orchestration.

2. Great C-major symphony
Schubert's *"Great" C-major Symphony* expanded to a "heavenly length" and is marked by beautiful melodies and orchestral effects.

B. *Berlioz (1803–1869)*

1. *Symphonie fantastique*
The *Symphonie fantastique* (1830) by *Hector Berlioz* is a symphony conceived as a musical drama whose words are not spoken or sung but are written in a program handed out to the audience.   **Music: NAWM 105**

2. *Idée fixe*
The central theme, or *idée fixe* (fixed idea or fixation), stands for the artist's beloved and appears in all five movements, sometimes transformed.

3. *Harold en Italie*
Harold en Italie (Harold in Italy, 1834) is also a program symphony, with a recurring theme played by solo viola, representing the protagonist.

4. *Roméo et Juliette*
Roméo et Juliette (1839) is a "dramatic symphony" in seven movements for orchestra, soloists, and chorus.

5. Berlioz's influence
These innovative works influenced all later program music and began a new era of colorful orchestration.

C. *Mendelssohn (1809–1847)*

In two of his symphonies, *Felix Mendelssohn* combined Classical forms with themes reminiscent of foreign lands.

1. *Italian* Symphony

Mendelssohn's Symphony No. 4 (*Italian,* 1833) features melodies in Italian operatic and folk styles.

2. *Scottish* Symphony

His Symphony No. 3 (*Scottish,* 1842) achieves a Scottish flavor through Scotch snaps, pentatonic melodies, and grace notes.

3. Overtures

Among Mendelssohn's other important orchestral works are his *concert overtures* (one-movement works, usually descriptive or dramatic) and his incidental music for Shakespeare's *A Midsummer Night's Dream.*

D. *Liszt (1811–1886)*

1. Symphonic poem

Franz Liszt wrote twelve *symphonic poems* between 1848 and 1858 and another in 1881–82. He was the first to use the term, which designates a programmatic work in one movement that evokes ideas and feelings associated with its subject.

2. Thematic transformation

Liszt used *thematic transformation,* transforming a theme or motive into new themes and thus providing both motivic unity and variety of mood

3. *Les Préludes*

In the symphonic poem *Les Préludes,* Liszt used thematic transformation to create a wide range of moods.

4. *Faust* Symphony

Liszt's *Faust Symphony* is also programmatic, on characters and episodes drawn from Goethe's *Faust.*

5. Liszt's influence

Many later composers wrote symphonic poems, and Liszt's harmonies influenced Wagner and others.

E. *Brahms (1833–1897)*

Johannes Brahms composed four symphonies, two overtures, and four concertos.

1. First Symphony

Brahms's First Symphony combines Classic structure with Romantic melodic gesture and intensity. Typical of his symphonies, the third movement is more lyrical than a scherzo, and the middle movements are in keys a third away from the main key of the symphony, instead of in the dominant or subdominant.

2. Third Symphony

Also typical of Brahms are conflict between the minor and major modes and superimposition of duple and triple divisions of the beat, as in the Third Symphony.

3. Fourth Symphony

Brahms's Fourth Symphony utilizes chains of thirds in the first movement. The finale is a chaconne movement, showing his interest in Baroque music.

F. Dvořák *(1841–1904)*

Antonín Dvořák is best known for his Symphony No. 9 (*From the New World,* 1893), written during his sojourn in the United States.

Window: The Symphony Orchestra (CHWM 392–93)

The Romantic orchestra was more than twice the size of that of Haydn and Mozart, with many more strings and a greater number and variety of winds, brass, and percussion. Individual instruments were also more powerful. The orchestra now required a permanent conductor rather than being directed from the harpsichord or by the leader of the violins.

Postlude: The Beethoven Legacy (CHWM 401–3)

Beethoven cast a long shadow. Later composers sought to differentiate their music from his, typically by extending some elements of his music while rejecting others. Schubert introduced song-like themes into the symphony; Berlioz found precedents in Beethoven's symphonies for the programmaticism and thematic drama of his *Symphonie fantastique*; Mendelssohn and Brahms continued the symphony in individual ways; and Wagner saw the choral finale of Beethoven's Ninth Symphony as pointing to the union of music with words and drama.

STUDY QUESTIONS

Romanticism (CHWM 385–86)

1. According to Liszt and Schopenhauer, what is special about music as an art?

2. What are some of the links between music and literature in the nineteenth century?

Orchestral Music (CHWM 386–401, NAWM 105)

3. What was the role of orchestral music in the nineteenth century? Who was its audience, and what was its status?

4. How do Schubert's symphonies differ in approach from those of Beethoven?

5. What does Schumann praise in Schubert's "Great" Symphony in C Major (see the passage in CHWM, p. 387)?

Music to Study
> **NAWM 105:** Hector Berlioz, *Symphonie fantastique* (1830), excerpts
> III. *Scène aux champs* (Scene in the Country)
> not on recordings
> IV. *Marche au supplice* (March to the Scaffold)
> CD 9.1–6 (Concise 3.43–48)

6. What devices of orchestration, melody, and rhythm does Berlioz use to suggest that the third movement of his *Symphonie fantastique* (NAWM 105) is set in the country? (One device not mentioned in the commentary is the dotted siciliano rhythm, long associated with pastoral settings, first introduced in mm. 28–30.)

7. Where does the *idée fixe* (printed in NAWM p. 327 and CHWM, Example 16.2, p. 390) appear in this movement? How is it transformed, and how is it introduced and developed, to suit the program (in NAWM, pp. 327–28)?

8. Where does the *idée fixe* appear in the fourth movement, *Marche au supplice*? How is it treated, and how do its treatment and the surrounding music fit the program of the movement?

9. What special instrumental effects does Berlioz use in this movement, and how do they suit the program? What other aspects of the music help to support the program?

10. What was Berlioz's significance for later generations?

11. What is "Italian" in Mendelssohn's *Italian* Symphony (No. 4)? What is "Scottish" in his *Scottish* Symphony (No. 3)?

12. What is a *symphonic poem*? Who invented it, and when?

13. How did Liszt use thematic transformation in his *Les Préludes*? What did this procedure allow him to accomplish?

14. In what ways do the Brahms symphonies continue the Classic tradition, and in what ways are they Romantic? What are some distinctive traits of Brahms's music?

Window: The Symphony Orchestra (CHWM 392–93)

15. How did the nineteenth-century orchestra differ from that of Haydn's time, in size, composition, sound, and method of direction? How is this reflected in the differences between Romantic orchestral works such as the *Symphonie fantastique* (NAWM 105) and a symphony of Haydn (NAWM 94–96)?

Postlude: The Beethoven Legacy (CHWM 401–3)

16. According to CHWM, how did each of the following composers confront the influence of Beethoven's symphonies and find an individual path?

Schubert

Berlioz

Brahms

Wagner

TERMS TO KNOW

Romanticism
art song
program music
idée fixe

concert overture (nineteenth-
century)
symphonic poem
thematic transformation

NAMES TO KNOW

Franz Schubert
Unfinished Symphony
"Great" Symphony in C major
Hector Berlioz
Symphonie fantastique
Harold en Italie
Roméo et Juliette
Felix Mendelssohn

Italian Symphony
Scottish Symphony
Franz Liszt
Les Préludes
Faust Symphony
Johannes Brahms
Antonín Dvořák

REVIEW QUESTIONS

1. Make a time-line for the nineteenth century, and place on it the composers and most significant pieces discussed in this chapter. Add to it the three periods of Beethoven's career and his most important works, as discussed in Chapter 15. Make your time-line large enough to allow further additions, as you will be adding to it in Chapters 17–19.

2. How are Classic and Romantic orchestral music similar, and how are they different? Use examples from the orchestral works you know by Haydn (NAWM 94–96) and Berlioz (NAWM 105) to illustrate these similarities and differences. Include consideration of the size and composition of the orchestra, forms and genres used, the artistic aims of the composers, and matters of style and procedure.

3. Describe the symphonic works of Schubert, Berlioz, Mendelssohn, Liszt, and Brahms. What characteristics distinguish each composer's works from those of Beethoven, and from the other composers discussed here?

SOLO, CHAMBER, AND VOCAL MUSIC IN THE NINETEENTH CENTURY

CHAPTER OBJECTIVES

After you complete the reading, study of the music, and study questions for this chapter, you should be able to

1. name some of the principal nineteenth-century composers of piano music and chamber music, characterize their styles, trace influences upon them, and describe representative works by Schumann, Chopin, and Brahms; and
2. describe the nineteenth-century German lied as practiced by Schubert, Robert Schumann, and Clara Schumann.

CHAPTER OUTLINE

Prelude (CHWM 404–5)

> While orchestras were expanding and orchestral music becoming more monumental, composers also cultivated more intimate genres for solo piano, voice and piano, and chamber ensembles. The nineteenth-century piano had a larger range, more varied dynamics, and faster response than the eighteenth-century piano, allowing greater expressivity and virtuosity and making it an attractive medium. The best chamber music of the period came from composers who felt closest to the Classic tradition. The *lied* or German art song, combining literary and lyrical tendencies, reached its peak in this era.

I. Solo Music for Piano (CHWM 405–14, NAWM 106–10)

> The piano (now mass-produced and thus widely available and affordable) became the most common household instrument. This created a demand for music that amateurs could play at home, and many composers wrote for this market.

A. *Schubert*

Schubert wrote marches, dances, and lyrical piano works that create a distinctive mood. His longer works include eleven sonatas and the *Wanderer Fantasy* (1822), which uses a theme from his song *The Wanderer*.

1. Sonatas

Schubert's piano sonatas often present three keys in the exposition, rather than two, and while following Classic form use lyrical themes that resist development.

B. *Mendelssohn*

Mendelssohn wrote a variety of works for piano, including preludes and fugues that show his interest in Bach.

1. *Lieder ohne Worte*

Mendelssohn's most popular piano pieces are his *Lieder ohne Worte* (Songs without Words), short works which are like songs for piano alone. **Music: NAWM 106**

C. *Robert Schumann (1810–1856)*

Robert Schumann aimed to be a concert pianist, but after injuring his right hand he turned to composition and to writing about music in the journal he founded, the *Neue Zeitschrift für Musik*. All his published music before 1840 was for piano.

1. Character pieces

Schumann specialized in short *character pieces* grouped into collections. His pieces carry titles that suggest extramusical associations. In his criticism and his music, he used the imaginary characters Florestan, Eusebius, and Raro to reflect different sides of his own character.

2. *Phantasiestücke*

In his collection *Phantasiestücke* (Fantasy Pieces, 1837), Schumann sought to depict a variety of moods and images.   **Music: NAWM 107**

D. *Chopin (1810–1849)*

Fryderyk Chopin wrote almost exclusively for piano. He was born in Poland and lived in Paris from 1831.

1. Mazurkas

Chopin's *mazurkas* are stylized Polish dances and are among the first nationalist works of the nineteenth century.

2. Polonaises

The *polonaise* was a Polish dance already familiar in Western Europe, but Chopin's show a national character.

3. Performing style

Chopin's playing style was more personal than theatrical, and his music is accordingly introspective. He used *tempo rubato,* in which the right hand pushes forward or holds back the tempo while the left hand accompanies in strict time.

4. Nocturnes

Chopin followed *John Field* (1782–1837) in composing *nocturnes,* which suggest the quiet or dreaminess of night.   **Music: NAWM 108–9**

5. Preludes

Chopin's preludes show the influence of Bach.

6. Ballades and Scherzos

Chopin also wrote larger works. He coined the term *ballade* for works that suggest the changing moods of a narrative ballad. His scherzos are quirky and passionate rather than humorous.

7. Études

Chopin's *études* are studies in piano technique, but are unusual for études in that they are also poetically meaningful works for concert performance.

E. *Liszt*

Born in Hungary and trained in Vienna, Liszt was a touring virtuoso from a young age. He ceased touring in 1848 and became court music director at Weimar, later moving to Rome.

1. Style

Liszt's eclectic style combined Hungarian national traits, French Romanticism, pianistic virtuosity, and Chopin's lyricism.

2. Paganini's influence

As performer and composer, Liszt sought to match on the piano the dazzling virtuosity of the violinist *Nicolò Paganini* (1782–1840).

3. *Un sospiro*

Liszt often combined rapid figuration in both hands with a slow melody shared between them.   **Music: NAWM 110**

4. Transcriptions

Liszt made many transcriptions for piano of other music. His Hungarian rhapsodies use Hungarian tunes and ornamentation.

5. Concertos

Liszt wrote two piano concertos and other works for piano and orchestra.

6. Sonata in B minor

His one-movement Piano Sonata in B minor uses thematic transformation.

7. Late works

Liszt experimented with chromatic harmony, especially in his late works.

Window: A Ballad of Love (CHWM 412–13)

George Sand (1804–1876) left her husband, adopted a male name and men's clothing, and wrote more than eighty novels. Her romantic relationship with Chopin coincided with his most productive years.

II. Chamber Music (CHWM 415–19)

A. *Schubert*

Schubert wrote several significant chamber works. The most popular from his earlier period is the *Trout* Quintet for piano and strings.

1. Last three quartets

Three string quartets from 1824–26 are intensely expressive. Two movements are based on songs by Schubert.

2. String Quintet in C major

Schubert's String Quintet in C major (1828) is widely regarded as his best chamber work.

B. *Brahms*

Brahms is Beethoven's true successor in the realm of chamber music, with a large body of works of high quality.

1. Piano Quintet

Like most of Brahms's music, the Piano Quintet in F Minor, Op. 34 (1864) uses *developing variation,* in which a musical idea is varied to create a string of interrelated but different ideas.

2. Later works

Brahms also wrote string quartets, piano trios, a string quintet, and a quintet for clarinet and strings, one of the peaks of the clarinet literature.

3. Sonatas

There are also sonatas for solo instrument with piano, three for violin, two for cello, and two for clarinet.

III. Vocal Music: The Lied (CHWM 419–23, NAWM 111–14)

1. Ballads

Ballads were long narrative poems that required more variety and drama in the music than did a lyrical strophic poem. The piano became equal with the voice in conveying the meaning of the poetry.

A. *Schubert*

Schubert's song melodies are both lovely in themselves and well suited to the text.

1. Harmonic style

Schubert often used chromaticism, complex modulations, and harmonic contrast to create drama or highlight the meaning of the words.

2. Form

Many Schubert songs are strophic. Those that are through-composed are based on recurring themes and a clear tonal structure.

3. Accompaniments

Schubert's piano accompaniments often include figures that convey an image or feeling in the text.

4. *Gretchen am Spinnrade*

In *Gretchen am Spinnrade* (Gretchen at the Spinning Wheel, 1814), a constant figuration in the piano suggests the spinning wheel and Gretchen's agitation. **Music: NAWM 111**

5. *Der Erlkönig*

In *Der Erlkönig* (The Erlking), triplets in the accompaniment suggest a galloping horse and the anxiety of a father, while the three characters in the drama are each given distinctive music.

6. *Der Doppelgänger*

In *Der Doppelgänger* (The Double) the piano conveys ghostly horror.

7. Texts

Schubert set dozens of poems by Goethe and composed two *song cycles* (groups of songs intended to be performed in sequence and often implying a story) to poems by Wilhelm Müller, *Die schöne Müllerin* (The Pretty Miller-Maid, 1823) and *Winterreise* (Winter's Journey, 1827).

8. *Winterreise*

In *Winterreise,* a lover returns in winter to places associated with a failed summer romance, with eerie effects. **Music: NAWM 112**

B. *Robert Schumann*

Schumann's lieder are often restless and intense.

1. *Dichterliebe*

In 1840, the year of his marriage, Schumann wrote more than one hundred songs. These include the song cycle *Dichterliebe* (A Poet's Love) on poems by Heinrich Heine about unrequited love. The piano equals the voice in interest and expressivity, often providing preludes and postludes. **Music: NAWM 113**

C. *Clara Schumann (1819–1896)*

Clara Wieck Schumann was a child prodigy on the piano and became an important soloist and composer. Her marriage to Robert Schumann and raising a family limited her touring, but she continued to perform, compose, and teach. Her works include a piano concerto, a piano trio, pieces for piano solo, and lieder. Her songs capture poetic imagery in music in subtle and original ways. **Music: NAWM 114**

STUDY QUESTIONS

Prelude (CHWM 404–5)

1. How did the nineteenth-century piano differ from earlier keyboard instruments, including eighteenth-century pianos?

Solo Music for Piano (CHWM 405–14, NAWM 106–10)

2. How do Schubert's sonatas differ from Beethoven's?

Music to Study
NAWM 106: Felix Mendelssohn, *Lieder ohne Worte* (Songs without Words), excerpts
106a: Op. 85, No. 4 in D major (1845)   CD 9.7–8
106b: Op. 67, No. 4 in C major (1845)   CD 9.9–11

3. In what ways do the examples from Mendelssohn's *Songs without Words* in NAWM 106 resemble songs?

4. Describe the figuration and textures in these pieces. How do they exploit the capabilities of the nineteenth-century piano? How does the figuration here differ from or resemble the keyboard figuration used by eighteenth-century composers such as Domenico Scarlatti (NAWM 89), C. P. E. Bach (NAWM 91), J. C. Bach (NAWM 93), or Mozart (NAWM 99)?

Music to Study
  NAWM 107: Robert Schumann, *Phantasiestücke* (Fantasy Pieces), Op. 12
      (1837), excerpts
  107a: No. 4, *Grillen* (Whims)   CD 9.12–14 (Concise 3.49–51)
  107b: No. 5, *In der Nacht* (In the Night)   CD 9.15–17

5. Diagram the form of Schumann's *Grillen* (NAWM 107a).

   How does it compare to a traditional ABA form?

   How does this piece, titled "Whims," convey a sense of whims or whimsy?

6. Diagram the form of Schumann's *In der Nacht* (NAWM 107b).

   How does this piece convey passionate emotions? How does its form resemble a narrative—that is, how does it suggest that it is relating a story?

7. What textures does Schumann use in these piano pieces that are different from textures used by Classic-era composers such as C. P. E. Bach (NAWM 91), Mozart (NAWM 99), or Beethoven (NAWM 101)?

8. What was Chopin's national heritage, and how is this reflected in his music?

Music to Study

    NAWM 108: John Field, Nocturne in A Major, No. 8 (1815)
        CD 9.18
    NAWM 109: Fryderyk Chopin, Nocturne in E-flat Major, Op. 9, No. 2
        (1830–31)
        CD 9.19 (Concise 3.52)

9. In what ways does Field embellish the melodic line in his Nocturne in A Major (NAWM 108)? How do his melodies resemble the style of opera?

10. How does Chopin embellish the melodic line of his Nocturne in E-flat Major (NAWM 109)? How is it like operatic singing? How is it like Field's nocturne?

11. What elements of style, sound, and texture distinguish Chopin's Nocturne from Schumann's *Phantasiestücke* (NAWM 107) and from earlier keyboard styles? Describe Chopin's style, based on this example.

---

12. Who was Nicolò Paganini? What was his significance for Liszt's career?

Music to Study
  NAWM 110: Franz Liszt, *Trois études de concert* (Three Concert Études),
     for piano (1849), excerpt: No. 3, *Un sospiro* (A Sigh)
  CD 9.20–24 (Concise 3.53–57)

13. What technical problem for the player is the focus of Liszt's étude *Un sospiro* (NAWM 110)? How is it addressed at the outset? How does the texture change over the course of the piece, to raise new problems for the performer?

14. What elements of style, sound, and texture distinguish Liszt's étude from Chopin's Nocturne (NAWM 109), from Schumann's *Phantasiestücke* (NAWM 107), and from earlier keyboard styles? Describe Liszt's approach to the piano, based on this example.

Chamber Music (CHWM 415–19)

15. Which Schubert chamber works borrow material from his songs, and how is that material used?

16. What is *developing variation*? How does Brahms use it in the first movement of his Piano Quintet in F Minor, Op. 34 (excerpted in CHWM, p. 418). How does it compare to Liszt's thematic transformation? (For Liszt, see Chapter 16, question 13.)

Vocal Music: The Lied (CHWM 419–23, NAWM 111–14)

17. What is a *ballad*? Why did ballads call for greater variety and expressivity from composers? What effect did this have on the piano accompaniments to art songs?

Music to Study
> **NAWM 111:** Franz Schubert, *Gretchen am Spinnrade* (Gretchen at the Spinning Wheel), D. 118, lied (1814)
> > CD 9.25–29 (Concise 3.58–62)
>
> **NAWM 112:** Franz Schubert, *Winterreise* (Winter's Journey), D. 911, song cycle (1827), excerpt: *Der Lindenbaum* (The Linden Tree), lied
> > CD 9.30–33
>
> **NAWM 113:** Robert Schumann, *Dichterliebe* (A Poet's Love), Op. 48, song cycle (1840), excerpts
> > 113a: *Im wunderschönen Monat Mai*   CD 9.34
> > 113b: *Ich grolle nicht*   CD 9.35

18. Schubert's *Gretchen am Spinnrade* (NAWM 111) sets a scene from Goethe's *Faust* in which Gretchen sits spinning thread while thinking of Faust. How is the spinning wheel depicted in this song? Why is this an effective device for depicting the spinning wheel?

    How does this device also capture Gretchen's mood?

    Where does the wheel suddenly stop, and then gradually start again? What does this suggest about Gretchen's feelings at this point?

19. Diagram the form of this song. How does Schubert use changes in melody, harmony, and key to portray Gretchen's changing emotions?

20. In *Der Lindenbaum* (NAWM 112), how does Schubert use figuration in the piano and contrasts between major and minor to suggest the images and meaning of the poem?

21. The text of *Im wunderschönen Monat Mai* (NAWM 113a) speaks of new love. How does Schumann's music imply, through melody and harmony, that this love is unrequited—as yet all "longing and desire" and no fulfillment? How are the opening piano prelude and closing postlude crucial in conveying this meaning?

22. What is the key of this song? Where does the tonic chord appear? What is unusual about the beginning and ending harmonies?

23. How does Schumann alter the poetry in his setting of *Ich grolle nicht* (NAWM 113b)?

24. In what way is Schumann's setting ironic, with the emotional tone of the music contradicting what the words claim?

25. Briefly trace the career of Clara Wieck Schumann.

Music to Study
   NAWM 114: Clara Wieck Schumann, *Geheimes Flüstern hier und dort,* Op. 23, No. 3, lied (1853)
   CD 9.36

26. In Clara Schumann's song *Geheimes Flüstern hier und dort* (NAWM 114), how does the figuration in the piano capture the imagery in the poem?

   Where is there metric conflict between piano and voice, or melody and accompaniment? How does this convey the poetic imagery?

   In what other ways does the music suit the poetry?

TERMS TO KNOW

lied (nineteenth-century)
character piece
mazurka
polonaise
tempo rubato
nocturne

ballade (for piano)
étude
developing variation
ballad
song cycle

NAMES TO KNOW

Wanderer Fantasy
Lieder ohne Worte (Songs
  without Words)
Robert Schumann
Neue Zeitschrift für Musik
Phantasiestücke
Fryderyk Chopin
John Field

Nicolò Paganini
George Sand
Gretchen am Spinnrade
Die schöne Müllerin
Winterreise
Dichterliebe
Clara Wieck Schumann

REVIEW QUESTIONS

1. Add the composers and major works discussed in this chapter to the time-line you made for Chapter 16.

2. Trace the history of piano music in the nineteenth century. Include in your discussion the changed character of the piano and the genres composers used, as well as describing the styles and works of the most prominent composers for the instrument.

3. What are the distinctive features of chamber music in the nineteenth century?

4. Describe the German lied as composed by Schubert and the Schumanns.

OPERA, MUSIC DRAMA, AND CHURCH MUSIC IN THE NINETEENTH CENTURY

18

CHAPTER OBJECTIVES

After you complete the reading, study of the music, and study questions for this chapter, you should be able to

1. trace the history of opera in France, Italy, and Germany in the nineteenth century and distinguish between the characteristics of each national tradition;
2. define and use terminology associated with nineteenth-century opera;
3. name the most significant composers in each nation and describe the style and approach of each of them;
4. describe characteristic excerpts from operas by Rossini, Bellini, Verdi, Weber, and Wagner; and
5. describe some of the varieties of choral music in the nineteenth century and name some important composers of choral music.

CHAPTER OUTLINE

Prelude (CHWM 425–26)

Nineteenth-century Paris was a center for opera. *Grand opera* combined spectacle and Romantic elements and appealed to a wide audience. Opera was the leading genre in Italy. German Romantic opera joined traits of the Singspiel and grand opera with Romantic literature, and Richard Wagner devised the new form he called *music drama*. Religious choral music varied from revivals of older styles to monumental works intended only for concert performance.

I. French Grand (and Not-So-Grand) Opera (CHWM 426–32)

1. Meyerbeer

Grand opera was established by the librettist *Eugène Scribe* (1791–1861) and the composer *Giacomo Meyerbeer* (1791–1864) with *Robert le diable* (Robert the Devil, 1831) and *Les Huguenots* (1836).

Etude: *Les Huguenots,* Closing Scenes of Act II
Les Huguenots dramatizes the sixteenth-century religious wars in France. Typical of grand opera are massed choruses and strong contrasts of mood and sonority.

2. Other grand operas
In grand opera, structure and style in the music convey grandeur as well as the plot. Grand opera remained influential into the twentieth century.

3. Opéra comique
Opéra comique used spoken dialogue rather than recitative and featured a smaller cast and simpler music than grand opera. Its plots were comic or romantic rather than historical.

4. Opéra bouffe
After the 1851 declaration of the Second Empire under Napoleon III, the satiric genre of *opéra bouffe* emerged with *Jacques Offenbach* (1819–1880). His comic style influenced the later operettas of Gilbert and Sullivan in England and of Johann Strauss and others in Vienna.

5. Lyric opera
Lyric opera lies between comic and grand opera in scale, with romantic plots and a focus on melody.

6. Gounod's *Faust*
The most famous lyric opera is *Faust* (1859) by *Charles Gounod* (1818–1893).

7. Berlioz
Berlioz's dramatic works do not fit traditional categories.

8. *La Damnation de Faust*
Berlioz's *La Damnation de Faust* (1846) is a series of scenes for concert rather than stage performance.

9. *Les Troyens*
Les Troyens (The Trojans, 1856–58) is Berlioz's operatic masterpiece, a Romantic contribution to the tradition of Lully, Rameau, and Gluck.

10. Bizet's *Carmen*
Carmen (1875) by *Georges Bizet* was classed as an opéra comique because it had spoken dialogue, but is a serious drama that reflects *exoticism* and a late-nineteenth-century taste for *realism.*

Window: The Musical Attraction of "The Other" (CHWM 428–29)

Western Europeans have at times been strongly attracted by the exotic "otherness" of foreign cultures. In order to portray the exotic in music, composers used timbres, rhythms, and melodic gestures they associated with other nations, or simply used unusual sounds to lend a sense of strangeness to the music. Foreign lands and peoples evoked in this way include American Indians for Rameau, Turkey for Mozart, Gypsies for Schubert, Spain in Bizet's *Carmen,* and Egypt in Verdi's *Aida.*

II. Italian Opera (CHWM 432–34, NAWM 117–18)

1. Rossini
Gioachino Rossini (1792–1868) was the most successful Italian opera composer of the early nineteenth century.

2. Comic operas
Rossini is best known today for his comic operas, such as *Il barbiere di Siviglia* (The Barber of Seville, 1816).

3. Scene structure
Instead of consigning the plot to dry recitative interspersed between arias, Rossini and his librettists made the action more continuous. They developed a new pattern for scenes, typically including orchestral introduction, *scena* ("scene," in accompanied recitative), *primo tempo* ("first movement," a slow, cantabile song), *tempo di mezzo* ("middle movement"), and *cabaletta* (a lively and brilliant solo). The primo tempo and cabaletta together comprise the aria, called *cavatina* if it marks the character's entrance.

4. Rossini's style
Rossini's style emphasizes shapely, ornamented melody over spare accompaniment. He often combined repetition of an idea with a crescendo to build excitement. He moved to Paris in 1824, wrote some operas in French, and then wrote smaller vocal and piano works. **Music: NAWM 117**

5. Bellini
Vincenzo Bellini (1801–1835) wrote ten serious operas in a refined style. His melodic style influenced Chopin's nocturnes. **Music: NAWM 118**

6. Donizetti
Gaetano Donizetti (1797–1848) composed about seventy operas in a style attuned to the public taste.

III. Giuseppe Verdi (1813–1901) (CHWM 434–38, NAWM 119)

Giuseppe Verdi (1813–1901) was the major figure in Italian opera after Donizetti. He continued the Italian operatic tradition and was a strong nationalist in both political and musical terms. Like those of his Italian predecessors, his operas focus on human drama conveyed through song.

1. Early operas
Verdi's career divides into three periods. The first culminates in 1853 (the year of *La traviata*) and focuses on stories of personal tragedy.

2. *La traviata*
La traviata exhibits many Verdi traits, including a flexible, declamatory style of song that differed from earlier arias. **Music: NAWM 119**

3. Second-period operas
After 1853 Verdi wrote fewer operas, as he experimented with Parisian grand opera, daring harmonies, comic roles, and other new resources. This period culminates in *Aida* (1871).

4. Reminiscence motives

Several operas use *reminiscence motives,* melodies recalled in more than one scene, which provide both musical and dramatic unity.

5. Late operas

After a long hiatus, Verdi wrote two late operas on plays by Shakespeare, *Otello* and *Falstaff.*

6. *Otello*

In *Otello* (1887), Verdi responded to intervening developments in German and French opera by making the music more continuous and by using several unifying motives.

Etude: *Otello,* Act IV

In Verdi's *Otello,* the conclusion of the drama unfolds without pause, contrasting lyrical aria with dialogue and interludes to carry the action.

7. *Falstaff*

Verdi's last opera, *Falstaff* (1893), takes comic opera to a new level, particularly the ensemble.

IV. German Romantic Opera (CHWM 438–39, NAWM 120)

Carl Maria von Weber (1786–1826) established the tradition of German Romantic opera with *Der Freischütz* (1821), whose humble characters, supernatural events, wilderness setting, and use of folklike style are typical.

1. *Der Freischütz*

The famous Wolf's Glen scene uses *melodrama* (spoken dialogue over music), startling chromatic harmony, and unusual orchestral effects to create an eerie scene. **Music: NAWM 120**

V. Richard Wagner (1813–1883) and the Music Drama (CHWM 439–46, NAWM 121)

Richard Wagner was the most important German opera composer.

1. *Der fliegende Holländer*

Wagner's *Der fliegende Holländer* (The Flying Dutchman, 1843) set the pattern for his operas with a libretto by the composer himself, a plot based on legend, the use of recurring themes, and the hero's redemption through the loving sacrifice of the heroine.

Etude: Wagner Reception, Nationalism, and the Jews

Wagner's legacy is marred by his anti-Semitism, as expressed in his notorious essay *Das Judentum in der Musik* (Judaism in Music, 1850), and by his later appropriation by the Nazi regime.

2. *Lohengrin*

Lohengrin (1850) uses a new declamatory vocal style. It is more continuous, with less division into numbers, more use of recurring themes, and the association of keys with characters.

3. Essays and librettos
The 1848 Revolution forced Wagner into exile in Switzerland, where he wrote essays on his musical theories.

4. *Der Ring des Nibelungen*
In exile, Wagner also wrote the librettos to his cycle of four music dramas, *Der Ring des Nibelungen* (The Ring of the Nibelungs), whose music he completed over two decades (1853–74). His other music dramas include *Tristan und Isolde* (1857–59), *Die Meistersinger von Nürnberg* (The Mastersingers of Nuremberg, 1862–67), and *Parsifal* (1882).

Etude: *The Ring of the Nibelungs*: A Brief Overview
The four music dramas of *The Ring of the Nibelungs* are linked by a continuous story, common characters, and shared motives.

5. *Gesamtkunstwerk*
Wagner's notion of music drama links drama and music in the service of a single dramatic idea. Together with scenery, staging, and action, they comprise a *Gesamtkunstwerk* (total artwork). Vocal lines are only part of a complete texture in which the orchestra plays a leading role, and music is continuous throughout an act rather than being broken into separate numbers, despite echoes of earlier types such as recitative, aria, and scene.

6. The *Leitmotif*
In Wagner's music dramas, a person, thing, or idea may be associated with a motive called a *Leitmotif*. By recalling and developing these motives, Wagner creates unity and and makes the music itself the locus of dramatic action.   **Music: NAWM 121**

7. Endless melody
Wagner sought to create an endless melody, a "musical prose" in place of the "poetic" four-square phrases of other composers.

8. Wagner's influence
The complex chromatic chords, constant modulation, and evasion of resolutions that characterize Wagner's harmony in *Tristan und Isolde* created a novel, ambiguous approach to tonality. His concept of opera as a combination of many arts and his notion of continuous music strongly influenced later composers.

VI. Church Music (CHWM 446–49, NAWM 115–16)

1. Berlioz
Some Romantic composers wrote large works on liturgical texts, intended for special occasions or performance in concert rather than in church. Berlioz's *Requiem* (1837) and *Te Deum* (1855) are dramatic symphonies for voices and large orchestras, with impressive instrumental effects.

2. Liszt
Several of Liszt's works are on a similarly large scale.

3. Cecilian movement

The Cecilian movement, named after St. Cecilia, the patron saint of music, worked within the Catholic church to revive the style of Palestrina and restore Gregorian chant to purer form.

4. Bruckner

Anton Bruckner (1824–1896) was a church organist. His Masses share qualities and some themes with his symphonies, and his motets show the influence of the Cecilian movement.   **Music: NAWM 115**

5. Rossini

Rossini's *Stabat Mater* (1832, rev. 1841), on the other hand, adapts the style of his operas to a sacred subject.

6. Verdi

Verdi's *Requiem* (1874) blends his operatic style with powerful choruses.

7. The Romantic oratorio

Romantic oratorios extended the Handel tradition in many ways, including an emphasis on the chorus. Brahms's *Ein deutsches Requiem* (A German Requiem, 1868) uses Old Testament passages, rather than the liturgical Requiem text, and sets them with deep feeling and rich Romantic harmonies. **Music: NAWM 116**

STUDY QUESTIONS

French Grand (and Not-So-Grand) Opera (CHWM 426–32)

1. What is *grand opera*? In what ways does *Les Huguenots* exemplify the style?

    Who were the librettist and composer for *Les Huguenots*?

    librettist: _____   composer: _____

2. What is *opéra bouffe,* and when and why did it come into existence?

    Who was a major composer of *opéras bouffes*? _____

    Who were major composers of comic opera or operetta in England and Vienna?

    England: _____   Vienna: _____

3. What is *lyric opera*? How does it differ from grand opera and opéra bouffe?

Italian Opera (CHWM 432–34, NAWM 117–18)

4. Briefly trace Rossini's career.

Music to Study
> **NAWM 117:** Gioachino Rossini, *Il barbiere di Siviglia* (The Barber of Seville), opera (1816), Act II, Scene 5: Cavatina, *Una voce poco fa*
> CD 9.43–46
> **NAWM 118:** Vincenzo Bellini, *Norma,* opera (1831), Act I, Scene 4: Scena and Cavatina, *Casta Diva*
> CD 10.1–6

5. Diagram the form of Act II, Scene 5 from Rossini's *Il barbiere di Siviglia* (NAWM 117), including indications of instrumental and vocal sections and changes of tempo, style, and figuration. How does this compare to the typical structure of a solo scene in a Rossini opera? How do the changes of style, tempo, and figuration in the different sections correspond to and help to convey what Rosina is saying and feeling?

6. How does Rossini's style compare to the operatic styles of Pergolesi (NAWM 85), Hasse (NAWM 86), Gluck (NAWM 88), and Mozart (NAWM 100)?

7. Diagram the scene from *Norma* (NAWM 118), showing changes of tempo, performing forces, and type. How does this fit or depart from the standard pattern for a scene in Italian opera at this time? How do the contrasts between elements convey Norma's inner conflict?

8. Compare the melodic writing of Bellini's Andante section to that in the Andante section of Rossini's *Una voce poco fa* (NAWM 117). What differences and similarities do you see? What characteristics mark the styles of Rossini and Bellini in their slow arias?

9. Now compare both to the melodic writing in Chopin's Nocturne in E-flat Major (NAWM 109). What does Chopin's melodic style have in common with Rossini's? With Bellini's?

Giuseppe Verdi (1813–1901) (CHWM 434–38, NAWM 119)

10. In what ways was Verdi a nationalist composer? How was his name used as a nationalist emblem?

11. Describe the following periods of Verdi's career and the main features of each: (1) to 1853, (2) 1854–71, and (3) after 1871. Name and briefly describe at least one opera from each period, highlighting the aspects that are typical for his operas around that time.

Music to Study
    NAWM 119: Giuseppe Verdi, *La traviata* (The Fallen Woman), opera (1853), excerpt from Act III: Scena and Duet
    CD 10.7–10 (Concise 3.63–66)

12. Compare the dialogue in the opening part (mm. 1–34) of this scene from Verdi's *La traviata* (NAWM 119) to the dialogue in recitative in the excerpt from Mozart's *Don Giovanni* in NAWM 100. What procedures does Verdi use to convey the sense of a spontaneous dialogue, without resorting to recitative? What does the orchestral backing provide?

13. How does Verdi use various musical forces, textures, and types to further the drama in this scene? How does this compare with the textures and types used in the excerpts from Rossini's *Il barbiere di Siviglia* (NAWM 117) and Bellini's *Norma* (NAWM 118)? (Note that the final cabaletta of the Verdi is omitted from the excerpt in NAWM.)

14. In the Andante section of the scene, *Parigi, o cara,* how does Verdi's melodic style compare to that of the slow arias in the excerpts from Rossini and Bellini (NAWM 117–18, and see question 8 above)?

German Romantic Opera (CHWM 438–39, NAWM 120)

Music to Study
> **NAWM 120:** Carl Maria von Weber, *Der Freischütz* (The Free Shot), opera (1821), Act II, Finale (Wolf's Glen Scene)
> CD 10.11–21

15. What is *melodrama*? How is it used in the Wolf's Glen scene from Weber's *Der Freischütz* (NAWM 120)? Why do you think it might be more effective here than recitative?

16. What supernatural events happen in the Wolf's Glen scene? For each one, how does Weber depict it in the music? How does he use tritones, diminished or augmented harmonies, orchestration, sudden dynamic change, or other effects to create a feeling of the supernatural or spooky? (Note: In examining the harmony, remember that the clarinets in A sound a minor third lower than written; the horns in D a minor seventh lower than written; and the trumpets in D a whole step higher than written.)

Richard Wagner and the Music Drama (CHWM 439–46, NAWM 121)

17. Who wrote the librettos for Wagner's operas? _____

18. What does *Gesamtkunstwerk* mean? What is its importance for Wagner?

19. Why did Wagner attack "Judaism in music"? How have his anti-Semitic views interacted with wider German culture and history? How have they affected his reputation?

Music to Study
> **NAWM 121:** Richard Wagner, *Tristan und Isolde* (1857–59), excerpt from
> Act I, Scene 5
> CD 10.22–30 (Concise 4.1–9)

20. How do text, action, scenery, and music reinforce each other in this scene
from *Tristan und Isolde* (NAWM 121)? How is this like, and how is it different from, the scene from Verdi's *La traviata* in NAWM 119?

21. In the section from m. 132 to m. 188, how do the singers' melodies relate to
the melodies in the orchestra? Where does the musical continuity lie, with the
singers or with the orchestra? How does this compare to the excerpts from
operas by Rossini, Bellini, and Verdi in NAWM 117–19?

22. How do Wagner's vocal melodies here and throughout the scene compare to
those of Rossini, Bellini, and Verdi in NAWM 117–19? Include observations
on phrasing and overall shape as well as on vocal embellishment. What are
the main characteristics of Wagner's vocal style?

23. What is a *Leitmotif*? Where do leitmotifs appear in this scene from *Tristan und Isolde,* and how are they used? (Note: Several appeared earlier, in the overture, and will recur in Acts II and III.)

24. How does the harmonic language used for the sailors (e.g., at mm. 196–203, "Hail! King Mark, hail!") differ from that used for Tristan and Isolde after they have drunk the love potion? Why is this contrast appropriate, and how does it heighten the drama?

25. What aspects of Wagner's music were especially influential on later composers?

Church Music (CHWM 446–49, NAWM 115–16)

26. How do Berlioz's *Requiem* and *Te Deum* differ from traditional church music of the previous hundred years?

27. What was the *Cecilian movement,* and what were its goals?

Music to Study
> **NAWM 115:** Anton Bruckner, *Virga Jesse,* motet (1885)
>   CD 9.37
> **NAWM 116:** Johannes Brahms, *Ein deutsches Requiem* (A German Requiem), Op. 45 (1868), No. 4: *Wie lieblich sind deine Wohnungen*
>   CD 9.38–42

28. How does Bruckner evoke or suggest sixteenth-century polyphony in his motet *Virga Jesse* (NAWM 115)?

29. What elements in the music make clear that this could not have been written earlier than the nineteenth century?

30. What traits in the fourth movement of Brahms's *German Requiem* (NAWM 116) are reminiscent of Baroque music? What contrapuntal devices are used?

    What elements in this movement are typical of nineteenth-century music, or of Brahms in particular?

    How do these Baroque and Romantic style traits help to depict the text and convey the emotions suggested in the text?

TERMS TO KNOW

grand opera
music drama
opéra comique
opéra bouffe
lyric opera
exoticism
realism
scena
primo tempo

tempo di mezzo
cabaletta
cavatina
reminiscence motive
melodrama
Gesamtkunstwerk
Leitmotif
the Cecilian movement

NAMES TO KNOW

Names Related to French Opera

Eugène Scribe
Giacomo Meyerbeer
Robert le diable
Les Huguenots
Jacques Offenbach
Charles Gounod

Faust
La Damnation de Faust
Les Troyens
Georges Bizet
Carmen

Names Related to Italian Opera

Gioachino Rossini
Il barbiere di Siviglia (The
   Barber of Seville)
Vincenzo Bellini
Gaetano Donizetti

Giuseppe Verdi
La traviata
Aida
Otello
Falstaff

Names Related to German Opera and Music Drama

Carl Maria von Weber
Der Freischütz
Richard Wagner
Der fliegende Holländer (The
   Flying Dutchman)
Lohengrin
Das Judentum in der Musik
   (Judaism in Music)

Der Ring des Nibelungen (The
   Ring of the Nibelungs)
Tristan und Isolde
Die Meistersinger von Nürnberg
   (The Mastersingers of
   Nuremberg)
Parsifal

Names Related to Church Music

Berlioz: *Requiem, Te Deum*
Anton Bruckner
Rossini: *Stabat Mater*

Verdi: *Requiem*
Ein deutsches Requiem (A German
   Requiem)

REVIEW QUESTIONS

1. Add the composers and major works discussed in this chapter to the time-line you made for Chapter 16.

2. What types of opera were written for production in Paris in the nineteenth century? Trace the emergence of the new types of opera, name a significant composer and opera for each type, and briefly describe what makes each type distinctive.

3. Describe the operas and operatic styles of Rossini, Bellini, and Verdi, noting the similarities and differences among them. Use examples from NAWM 117–19 to illustrate your points.

4. Trace the development of Verdi's operas through his three periods. What changed, and what remained constant?

5. How does the German Romantic opera of Weber and early Wagner differ from Italian and French opera in the first half of the nineteenth century? Use examples from the works excerpted in NAWM or described in CHWM to support your answer.

6. Describe the mature style of Wagner in his music dramas, using the scene from *Tristan und Isolde* in NAWM 121 as an example. At the end of your essay, explain the elements of this style that were particularly influential on later composers.

7. Choose two composers of choral music in the nineteenth century (such as Berlioz and Bruckner) and contrast their approaches. As part of your answer, describe at least one work by each composer.

EUROPEAN MUSIC FROM THE 1870s TO WORLD WAR I

CHAPTER OBJECTIVES

After you complete the reading, study of the music, and study questions for this chapter, you should be able to

1. name some of the most prominent European composers active in the late nineteenth and early twentieth centuries, characterize their styles, and describe some of their music;
2. describe the varieties of musical nationalism that were prominent at this time; and
3. define and describe impressionism and related trends in music of this period.

CHAPTER OUTLINE

Prelude (CHWM 450)

After Wagner, the search for an individual voice led composers in many different directions, undermining the shared conventions of the Classic and Romantic eras, including tonality. Nationalism prompted composers in Russia and eastern Europe to forge independent idioms, and new currents developed in France and Italy.

I. The German Tradition (CHWM 451–62, NAWM 122–24)

A. *Hugo Wolf*

1. Songs

Hugo Wolf (1860–1903) brought to his 250 lieder Wagner's harmony and ideal of fusing voice and instrument. Wolf chose fine poets and sought equality between words and music. The musical continuity is often in the piano, while the voice has a speechlike arioso.   **Music: NAWM 122**

B. *Gustav Mahler*

1. Career
Gustav Mahler (1860–1911) made a career as a conductor, directing the Vienna Opera (1897–1907) and the New York Philharmonic (1909–11).

2. Works
Mahler completed nine symphonies and five song cycles with orchestra.

3. Instrumentation of symphonies
Mahler's symphonies are long and often programmatic. He used a large orchestra but frequently created delicate effects with unusual instruments and combinations.

4. Programmatic content of symphonies
Mahler's symphonies usually lack explicit programs but suggest extra-musical ideas through quotations from his own songs, the use of pictorial details, and the sequence of movements with strong emotional content.

5. Use of voices
Four of Mahler's symphonies include voices, whose text makes the content clear.

6. Tonal organization of symphonies
Four Mahler symphonies begin and end in different keys.

Etude: Mahler's Fourth Symphony
Mahler included a greater diversity of elements and styles than did earlier symphonists, seeking to "construct a world" in all its variety, as in his *Fourth Symphony.*

7. Songs with orchestral accompaniment
The orchestral song cycle *Kindertotenlieder* (Songs of Dead Children, 1901–4) uses the large orchestra and chromatic harmony of Wagner in a spare, haunting style.   **Music: NAWM 123**

8. *Das Lied von der Erde*
Das Lied von der Erde (The Song of the Earth, 1908), on poems translated from Chinese, alternates between ecstasy and resignation.

C. *Richard Strauss*

Richard Strauss (1864–1949) is renowned for his symphonic poems, most written before 1900, and operas, most written after 1900. Like Mahler, he was well known as a conductor.

1. Types of symphonic programs
Symphonic poems may have a philosophical program, suggesting general ideas and emotions, or a descriptive one, relating specific events.

2. Symphonic poems
Strauss wrote symphonic poems of both types.

3. *Also sprach Zarathustra*
Strauss's *Also sprach Zarathustra* (So Spoke Zoroaster, 1896) is of the philosophical type, after a prose-poem by Friedrich Nietzsche, and represents images and ideas through musical symbols.

4. *Till Eulenspiegel*

In *Till Eulenspiegels lustige Streiche* (Till Eulenspiegel's Merry Pranks, 1895), Strauss uses the transformation of motives with extra-musical ties to convey the plot and a rondo-like form to suggest a series of adventures.

5. *Don Quixote*

In *Don Quixote* (1897), Strauss uses variations to suggest the changes that are experienced by the two main characters, Don Quixote and Sancho Panza.   **Music: NAWM 124**

6. Operas

Strauss changed to opera after the turn of the century, treating unprecedented subjects and intense emotions. These stimulated him to use more complex and dissonant harmony, which in turn influenced the growth of musical expressionism and the dissolution of tonality.

7. *Salome*

Strauss found new fame as an opera composer with *Salome* (1905), whose decadent subject he captured with heightened dissonance and contrast.

Etude: Strauss's *Elektra*

Elektra (1908) uses sharp, apparently unresolved dissonance contrasted with diatonic passages to tell the tragic story, along with leitmotifs and the association of certain keys with characters.

8. *Der Rosenkavalier*

Der Rosenkavalier (The Rose-Bearing Cavalier, 1911) has a lighter setting and plot and is thus less dissonant and more melodious.

II. National Trends (CHWM 462–70, NAWM 125–26)

Eighteenth-century composers often used styles of other nations or mixed styles. The nineteenth century saw a growing *nationalism*. In culture, this was marked by an esteem for the national language, literature, and folklore and a yearning for political unification or independence.

1. Folklore

Many composers of art music used folk or folklike melodies or rhythms. Some sought an exotic flavor within a cosmopolitan style. But other composers used native materials to achieve a nationalist idiom in music. Those in Russia, eastern Europe, England, France, and the United States especially sought a national style.

A. *Russia*

1. Glinka

Mikhail Glinka (1804–1857) was the first Russian composer to be recognized for a distinctively Russian style, notably in his operas.

2. Tchaikovsky

Piotr Il'yich Tchaikovsky (1840–1893) was more a cosmopolitan than a nationalist, but chose Russian subjects for his operas.

3. The Mighty Handful

The Mighty Handful (or Mighty Five) was a group of five composers who sought a fresh Russian style founded on folk music, folk polyphony, and modal and exotic scales. The group included Alexander Borodin, César Cui, Mily Balakirev, *Modest Musorgsky* (1839–1881), and *Nikolay Rimsky-Korsakov* (1844–1908.)

4. Musorgsky

Musorgsky was the most original of the Five. His vocal melodies follow Russian speech accents closely and imitate Russian folksong, and his harmony is innovative.   **Music: NAWM 125**

5. *Boris Godunov*

In his opera *Boris Godunov* (premiered 1874), Musorgsky's music depicts physical gestures realistically and reveals the psychology of the characters.

6. Rimsky-Korsakov

Rimsky-Korsakov was one of the Five but later developed a broader, still nationalist idiom. He taught at the St. Petersburg Conservatory and was a master of orchestration. His principal works are symphonic poems and operas, which often render human characters in a diatonic, modal style and supernatural characters and events in a chromatic, fanciful style marked by *whole-tone* and *octatonic scales* (respectively, scales made up of all whole tones or whole and half steps in strict alternation).

7. Rakhmaninov

Sergei Rakhmaninov (1873–1943), a virtuoso pianist, wrote passionate, melodious piano concertos and symphonic works in a style that was not deliberately nationalist.

8. Skryabin

Alexander Skryabin (1872–1915) wrote mostly for the piano, beginning in a style derived from Chopin and evolving to an individual idiom that was no longer tonal but used a complex chord or collection of notes as a reference point akin to a tonic chord. He sought a synthesis of the arts and intended his orchestral work *Prometheus* (1910) to be performed with changing colored lights.   **Music: NAWM 126**

B. *National Trends in Other Countries*

1. Bohemia

Bedřich Smetana (1824–1884) and Antonin Dvořák, the main nineteenth-century Czech (or Bohemian) composers, chose national subjects for program music and operas. *Leoš Janáček* 1854–1928) collected folk music and based his style on Moravian speech and song.

2. Norway

Edvard Grieg (1843–1907) was a nationalist who incorporated Norwegian national traits particularly in his short piano pieces and vocal works.

3. Finland

Finnish composer *Jean Sibelius* (1865–1957) drew programs and song texts from the literature of Finland. He does not use or imitate folksongs. He is known for symphonies, symphonic poems, and the Violin Concerto.

4. England

Edward Elgar (1857–1934) wrote in a style derived from Brahms and Wagner rather than from English folksong.

5. Spain

Spanish nationalism was sparked by the operas of *Felipe Pedrell* (1841–1922) and piano music of *Isaac Albeniz* (1860–1909). The major Spanish composer of the early twentieth century was *Manuel de Falla* (1876–1946), who used rhythms and melodic turns from Spanish popular music.

III. New Currents in France (CHWM 470–80, NAWM 127–29)

The *National Society for French Music* (founded 1871) performed music of living French composers and revived French music of the sixteenth through eighteenth centuries, helping to strengthen an independent French musical tradition. Three traditions coexisted in French music after 1871: a cosmopolitan tradition around Franck, a French tradition around Camille Saint-Saëns and Fauré, and a new style developed by Debussy.

1. Cosmopolitan tradition, Franck

César Franck (1822–1890) worked in instrumental genres and oratorio, enriching a restrained, traditional idiom with counterpoint and cyclic form.

2. French tradition

French music from Couperin to Gounod is typified by emotional reserve, lyricism, economy, refinement, and interest in well-ordered form rather than self-expression.

3. Fauré

Gabriel Fauré (1845–1924) worked as an organist, taught composition at the Paris Conservatoire, and became its director. He wrote songs, piano pieces, and chamber works marked by lyrical melodies and lack of virtuosic display.

4. Fauré's songs

Fauré's songs (or *mélodies*) are typical of his style. His harmony tends not to drive toward a resolution, but instead suggests repose. His students include Ravel and *Nadia Boulanger* (1887–1979), who taught many later composers.   **Music: NAWM 127**

5. Debussy

Claude Debussy (1862–1918) had a major influence on twentieth-century music. He blended traits of French music, Wagner, and Musorgsky.

6. Debussy's *Nocturnes*

Debussy often evokes a mood indirectly and without intense emotion. The orchestral sketch *Nuages* (Clouds), from *Nocturnes* (1899), draws on Musorgsky and Javanese music. Although his music usually has a tonal center, the harmony is often coloristic and the strong pull to resolution is missing, creating a sense of movement without direction and of pleasure without urgency.   **Music: NAWM 128**

7. Debussy's orchestration
Debussy's orchestration features a great variety of sounds and colors.

8. Debussy's piano music
Debussy's piano music shows similar traits, with many sparkling effects.

9. *Pelléas et Mélisande*
In his opera *Pelléas et Mélisande* (1902), Debussy's modal and subdued music perfectly suits the symbolist text.

10. Debussy's influence
Debussy's harmonic practice and use of the orchestra influenced most major composers of the early and middle twentieth century.

11. Satie
Erik Satie (1865–1925) consistently opposed sentimentality, from his early, deliberately simple works to his later piano pieces marked by parody, wit, surreal titles, and satirical commentary printed in the score.

12. Ravel
Maurice Ravel (1875–1937) looked back to earlier French tradition. His music features clean phrasing, clear forms, and functional harmonies.

13. *Le Tombeau de Couperin*
In *Le Tombeau de Couperin* (Memorial for Couperin, for piano 1917, orchestrated 1919), Ravel used classical dance forms and colorful orchestration. Some works were impressionist, others more classical or derived from music from other traditions.   **Music: NAWM 129**

Window: Impressionism (CHWM 476–77)

Debussy's style, called *impressionism* by analogy with the impressionist painters, suggests a mood or atmosphere rather than expressing the deep emotions of Romanticism.

IV. Italian Opera (CHWM 480–82)

1. Verismo
One trend in Italian opera in the late nineteenth century is *verismo* (realism or naturalism), which sought a realistic depiction of everyday people in extreme dramatic situations.

2. Puccini
Giacomo Puccini (1858–1924) was an eclectic composer who combined realism and exoticism with intense emotion through a style focused on melody over spare but harmonically enriched accompaniment.

STUDY QUESTIONS

The German Tradition (CHWM 451–62, NAWM 122–24)

1. What texts did Wolf choose for his songs, and what was his approach to the relationship of music and poetry?

Music to Study
   NAWM 122: Hugo Wolf, *Kennst du das Land,* Lied (1888)
      CD 10.31–38

2. Compare Wolf's vocal style in *Kennst du das Land* (NAWM 122) to that of Schubert's lieder (NAWM 111–12) and to that of Wagner's *Tristan und Isolde* (NAWM 121). What are the similarities and differences in each comparison? Which earlier composer does Wolf's style resemble most?

3. How does the piano part in Wolf's song compare to the piano parts in Schubert's lieder? What aspects of Wagner's operatic style does it incorporate?

Music to Study
   NAWM 123: Gustav Mahler, *Kindertotenlieder,* song cycle with orchestra
      (1901–4), No. 1: *Nun will die Sonn' so hell aufgeh'n*
   CD 10.39–40 (Concise 4.10–11)

4. Mahler's setting of *Nun will die Sonn' so hell aufgeh'n* (NAWM 123) high-
   lights the irony in the poem. In the poem, the tragedy that has befallen the
   speaker—the death of his child during the night—is ignored by the sun,
   which rises as if nothing bad has happened. Mahler heightens the irony by
   mismatching sad, lonely music to the bright, warm images in the first line of
   the poem, and bright, warm music to the sadness of the second line. Later
   repetition or reworking of these contrasting musical ideas is also ironic.

   a. How is the effect of sadness and loneliness achieved in the music for the
   first line? How does the contour of the vocal line negate the poetic image of
   a rising sun?

   b. How does the music of the second line suggest the rising sun and the
   warming earth?

   c. How does the varied repetition of this opening section in mm. 22–40 continue or expand upon the ironic setting of the first two lines of the poem?

   d. How does the music in mm. 40–63 work against the apparently comfort-
   ing message of the text?

   e. What indication is there in the music at the end of the song that the protagonist utters the final line, "Blessed be the joyous light of the world," with
   irony rather than with sincerity?

5. How does Mahler use the orchestra in this song? How is it different from Wagner's use of the orchestra in the excerpt from *Tristan und Isolde* (NAWM 121)?

6. Describe the characteristics of Mahler's symphonies that distinguish them from other nineteenth-century symphonies. How are these characteristics exemplified in the Fourth Symphony, as excerpted and discussed in CHWM, pp. 454–56? How does Mahler suggest a varied world in this work?

7. What two kinds of program did Richard Strauss use in his symphonic poems? Which does he use in *Don Quixote* (NAWM 124)?

Music to Study
   NAWM 124: Richard Strauss, *Don Quixote,* symphonic poem (1897), excerpts: Themes and Variations 1 and 2
   CD 10.41–46 (Concise 4.12–17)

8. How does Strauss depict Don Quixote and Sancho Panza in the themes of his *Don Quixote* (NAWM 124)? What musical devices does he use to depict their personalities?

9. How are these themes treated and varied in the first two variations?

10. Based on the descriptions of *Salome, Elektra,* and *Der Rosenkavalier* in CHWM, pp. 459–61, what is distinctive about each of these operas?

National Trends (CHWM 462–70, NAWM 125–26)

11. What was the role of Glinka in the creation of a Russian national music?

Music to Study
> **NAWM 125:** Modest Musorgsky, *Bez solntsa* (Sunless), song cycle (1874), No. 3, *Okonchen prazdnyi* (The idle, noisy day is over)
> CD 11.1–2

12. What is unusual about the harmony in Musorgsky's *Okonchen prazdnyi* (NAWM 125)? Describe some unusual progressions.

13. How does the vocal line in Musorgsky's song compare to that of the other nineteenth-century songs you have studied, by Schubert, Robert Schumann, Clara Schumann, and Hugo Wolf (NAWM 111–14 and 122)?

14. Briefly describe the styles and contributions of Rimsky-Korsakov and Rakhmaninov.

Music to Study
> **NAWM 126:** Alexander Skryabin, *Vers la flamme* (Toward the flame), poem for piano, Op. 72 (1914)
> CD 11.3–5

15. *Vers la flamme* (NAWM 126) is not tonal in a traditional sense. What kinds of chords does Skryabin use? How does he create a sense of tonal motion? What chord progressions (or root progressions) does he use most frequently?

16. What is the relationship between the opening passage of the piece and the closing passage (mm. 107–37) in terms of theme, rhythm, and harmony? How is a sense achieved of ending on a kind of tonic chord?

17. Describe the rhythm of this piece. Does it suggest a strong forward motion, or a static hovering? How is the effect achieved?

18. Name nationalist composers active in Czech regions, Norway, Finland, and Spain in the late nineteenth and early twentieth centuries and briefly describe what made their music nationalist.

New Currents in France (CHWM 470–80, NAWM 127–29)

19. What was the National Society for French Music? When was it founded, what did it do, and what was its importance?

Music to Study
   NAWM 127: Gabriel Fauré, *La bonne chanson* (The Good Song), Op. 61, song cycle (1891), No. 6, *Avant que tu ne t'en ailles*
   CD 11.6–10

20. What are the characteristics of Fauré's melodic and harmonic style, and how are they exemplified in *Avant que tu ne t'en ailles* (NAWM 127)?

Music to Study

    NAWM 128: Claude Debussy, *Trois Nocturnes,* tone poem suite (1899), No. 1: *Nuages* (Clouds)
    CD 11.11–16 (Concise 4.18–23)

21. How does Debussy use harmony in *Nuages* (NAWM 128) to create a sense of movement without direction, like clouds?

22. The motive in the English horn (here notated C–B–A–G♯–F♯ and sounding a fifth lower) is never played by another instrument, while the English horn never plays anything else. It is never transposed, and it is changed only by omitting notes until all that remains is B–A–F♯ (as notated). How does this treatment of a motive differ from motivic development as practiced in the nineteenth century? If motivic development suggests a drama or story, with the motives as characters, in what ways does Debussy's approach suggest a visual impression, rather than a plot?

23. How does the section at mm. 64–79 imitate a Javanese gamelan?

24. How does Debussy use the orchestra? How does this reinforce the sense of a visual impression moving without direction, rather than a drama with conflict and resolution? Take Strauss's use of the orchestra in *Don Quixote* (NAWM 124) as a point of comparison.

25. Briefly describe Satie's musical aesthetic and style.

Music to Study
>   **NAWM 129:** Maurice Ravel, *Le Tombeau de Couperin,* suite (1917, orches-
>   trated 1919), excerpt: Menuet (fourth movement)
>   CD 11.17–22

26. What does Ravel's minuet from *Le Tombeau de Couperin* (NAWM 129) have
    in common with eighteenth-century music? (If you have Volume 1 of
    NAWM, try comparing it to Couperin's suite in NAWM 73.)

27. Compare Ravel's minuet to Debussy's *Nuages* (NAWM 128). How are they
    similar? What is most different? Consider aspects of form, melody, harmony,
    and orchestration.

Italian Opera (CHWM 480–82)

28. What is *verismo*? What are some notable examples of it?

TERMS TO KNOW

nationalism

whole-tone scale

octatonic scale

mélodie

impressionism

verismo

NAMES TO KNOW

Names Related to the German Tradition

Hugo Wolf

Gustav Mahler

Mahler's Fourth Symphony

Kindertotenlieder (Songs of Dead Children)

Das Lied von der Erde (The Song of the Earth)

Richard Strauss

Also sprach Zarathustra

Till Eulenspiegels lustige Streiche (Till Eulenspiegel's Merry Pranks)

Don Quixote

Salome

Elektra

Der Rosenkavalier

Names Related to Nationalism in Eastern and Northern Europe and Spain

Mikhail Glinka

Piotr Il'yich Tchaikovsky

The Mighty Handful

Modest Musorgsky

Boris Godunov

Nikolay Rimsky–Korsakov

Sergei Rakhmaninov

Alexander Skryabin

Prometheus

Bedřich Smetana

Leoš Janáček

Edvard Grieg

Jean Sibelius

Edward Elgar

Felipe Pedrell

Isaac Albéniz

Manuel de Falla

Names Related to French and Italian Music

National Society for French Music

César Franck

Gabriel Fauré

Nadia Boulanger

Claude Debussy

Nocturnes

Pelléas et Mélisande

Erik Satie

Maurice Ravel

Le Tombeau de Couperin

Giacomo Puccini

REVIEW QUESTIONS

1. Add the composers and major works from the nineteenth century discussed in this chapter to the time-line you made for Chapter 16. Make a new time-line for the entire twentieth century, and place on it the twentieth-century composers and major works discussed here. Leave plenty of space, as you will be adding to it in Chapters 20–22. (Some composers, such as Strauss, will appear on both time-lines.)

2. How did Wolf, Mahler, and Strauss respond to the German Romantic tradition from Beethoven through Wagner? What elements did they continue in their music, what aspects did they further intensify or develop, and what did they introduce that was new and individual?

3. What is nationalism, and how is it manifest in music of the nineteenth and early twentieth centuries?

4. Beethoven's music conveys a sense of drama and forward motion toward a goal, as in the first movement of his *Eroica* Symphony (NAWM 103). Some of the music studied in this chapter conveys a different sense, of harmonic and rhythmic stasis, or of movement that is not directed toward a goal. Compare the works you have studied by Musorgsky, Skryabin, Fauré, and Debussy (NAWM 125–28) with Beethoven and with each other, seeking to show what musical techniques these later composers use to avoid tension, negate forward momentum, and create a musical experience of being present in the moment, rather than striving toward a goal.

5. For any of the following pairs of composers, compare and contrast their musical styles and aesthetics, showing what they have in common as composers from the same region or nation and what is individual about each: Mahler and Strauss; Musorgsky and Skryabin; Debussy and Ravel.

THE EUROPEAN
MAINSTREAM
IN THE
TWENTIETH CENTURY

20

CHAPTER OBJECTIVES

After you complete the reading, study of the music, and study questions for this chapter, you should be able to

1. identify some of the factors that have led to a diversity of style and technique in the twentieth century that is greater than in any previous era;
2. name some of the most significant composers active after World War I in Hungary, Russia, England, Germany, and France and describe what makes their music individual;
3. describe the synthesis of folk and classical elements in the music of Bartók;
4. describe the music of Shostakovich and his circumstances under the Soviet regime; and
5. summarize the careers and describe the musical styles of Hindemith and Stravinsky.

CHAPTER OUTLINE

Prelude (CHWM 483–86)

After World War I, the division of the former Austro-Hungarian Empire and the rise of totalitarian regimes in Russia, Italy, Germany, and Spain reduced cultural interaction between nations and led to a growing diversity in musical trends. Some composers abandoned common-practice tonality or thematic development. Folk and traditional music from Eastern Europe and Asia suggested new possibilities in rhythm and pitch organization. Recordings, radio, and television broadened audiences for popular and art music around the world. Composers of film music and of *Gebrauchsmusik* (music for use) for schools and amateurs sought more accessible idioms. *Neo-Classic music* evoked forms and styles of the eighteenth century. In some times and places, government control limited what composers could do; elsewhere, composers went beyond what audiences would accept. The diversity of music in the twentieth century is unprecedented, as composers have sought individual paths even within wider trends.

I. Ethnic Contexts (CHWM 486–90, NAWM 130)

New recording technologies aided the collection and study of the music of traditional peoples. Rather than changing this music to fit art music, as had been done in the previous century, composers used it to create new styles.

1. Bartók
Béla Bartók (1881–1945) collected and published folk tunes from his native Hungary, Romania, and elsewhere. Besides arranging or borrowing folk tunes in his music, he synthesized a personal style that united folk and art music. He was also a pianist and a piano teacher, and his *Mikrokosmos* (1926–37) is a series of graded piano pieces that encapsulates his style.

2. Bartók's early works
Bartók combined influences from late Romanticism, impressionism, and folk music to achieve an individual style.

3. Bartók's late works
Bartók's late works are his best known. He worked in traditional forms, creating a distinguished series of string quartets, sonatas, and concertos.

4. Bartók's style
From the Western tradition, Bartók took imitative and fugal techniques, sonata and other forms, and thematic development; from eastern Europe, modal scales, irregular meters, and certain types of melody.

5. Bartók's harmony
Bartók often uses harmonic seconds and fourths, drawn in part from the character of his melodies.

6. Bartók's tonal organization
Most of his music has a tonal center, but this is established in novel ways.

Etude: Bartók's *Music for Strings, Percussion, and Celesta*
Music for Strings, Percussion, and Celesta (1936) has a tonal center on A, with a secondary center a tritone away. The middle movements also feature a tritone relationship, between C and F♯. The piece shows Bartók's fondness for symmetry and his incorporation of elements of folk style.
Music: NAWM 130

7. Kodály
Zoltán Kodály (1882–1967) collected Hungarian folk tunes and developed a strongly nationalist style. He was well known as a music educator.

II. The Soviet Orbit (CHWM 491–94, NAWM 131–32)

In the Soviet Union, authorities encouraged nationalism, but several composers cultivated international styles.

1. Prokofiev
Sergey Prokofiev (1891–1953) left his native Russia after the 1917 Revolution, toured as a pianist, and composed on commission. He returned to

the Soviet Union in 1934 and wrote some of his most popular music there. Soviet authorities demanded that composers adhere to the concept of *socialist realism* and attacked Prokofiev for *formalism*.

2. Shostakovich

Dmitri Shostakovich (1906–1985) was the most prominent composer to spend his entire career under the Soviet state, which supported him yet sought to control him. His opera *Lady Macbeth of Mtsensk* (premiered 1934) was a success until it was condemned by the official newspaper *Pravda* in 1936. **Music: NAWM 131**

Etude: Shostakovich's Fifth Symphony

The Fifth Symphony shows Shostakovich's blending of Russian influences with international ones, especially Mahler.

3. Post-Soviet music

The relaxation of state control in the 1970s allowed younger composers to learn more about music in the West, and exchanges have intensified since the 1991 dissolution of the Soviet Union.

4. Schnittke

Alfred Schnittke (1934–1998) often incorporated existing music or alluded to Baroque and popular styles to produce music that is *polystylistic*.

5. Gubaidulina

Sofia Gubaidulina (b. 1931) writes music with a spiritual dimension, often inspired by Christian themes. **Music: NAWM 132**

III. England (CHWM 494–96)

1. Vaughan Williams

Ralph Vaughan Williams (1872–1958) drew on English folksong, hymnody, and earlier English composers, as well as German Baroque and recent French music. He wrote in a mixed tonal and modal style. (His first name is pronounced "Rafe," and his last name is "Vaughan Williams," not "Williams.")

2. Britten

Benjamin Britten (1913–1976), the most important English composer of the century, is known for his choral works and operas.

3. *Peter Grimes*

Mixing diatonic tonality with modal and chromatic effects and orchestral color, Britten's music uses simple means to convey deep human emotions, as in his opera *Peter Grimes* (1945) and his choral *War Requiem* (1962). **Music: NAWM 133**

IV. Germany (CHWM 497–500)

Nazi policies in the 1930s, especially the persecution of Jews, hindered music in Germany and led many musicians to leave.

1. Hindemith

Paul Hindemith (1895–1963) was important as a composer and teacher. Concerned about the growing gulf between composers and the public, in the late 1920s he began to compose *Gebrauchsmusik* in an accessible style.

2. *Mathis der Maler*

Hindemith's opera *Mathis der Maler* (Matthias the Painter, 1934-35) examines the role of the artist in a time of political turmoil.

3. Weill

Kurt Weill (1900–1950) composed operas on librettos by Bertolt Brecht.

Etude: Weill's *Mahagonny*

In *The Rise and Fall of the City of Mahagonny* (1927–31), Brecht and Weill sought to promote a social ideology. Weill used an easily understood musical language that parodied American popular music.

4. *Die Dreigroschenoper*

Brecht and Weill's most famous collaboration was *Die Dreigroschenoper* (The Threepenny Opera, 1928), adapted from John Gay's *The Beggar's Opera*. After the Nazis rose to power in 1933, Weill emigrated to the United States and had a second career writing Broadway musicals.

V. Neo-Classicism in France (CHWM 500–502)

Composers in the first half of the twentieth century often imitated styles and genres from earlier periods. Music that referred to eighteenth-century models was frequently called *neo-Classic*. When the reference is to the early eighteenth century, some writers now prefer the term neo-Baroque.

1. Honegger

Arthur Honegger (1892–1955) is best known for his opera-oratorio *King David* (1921).

2. Milhaud

Prolific in almost every genre, *Darius Milhaud* (1892–1974) absorbed a variety of influences, from earlier French composers to Brazilian music, ragtime, and blues.

3. Milhaud's polytonality

Milhaud frequently used *polytonality,* in which two or more streams of music, each implying a different key, are superimposed.

4. Poulenc

Francis Poulenc (1899–1963) wrote in an engaging style influenced by French popular song and eighteenth-century French composers.

VI. Stravinsky (CHWM 502–13, NAWM 134)

1. Career

Igor Stravinsky (1882–1971) was born and trained in Russia, lived and worked in Paris and Switzerland, and moved to the United States in 1940. He took part in most major compositional trends during his lifetime. He made his reputation with three early ballets commissioned by Sergei Diaghilev for the Russian Ballet in Paris.

2. Early works

All three ballets feature plots from Russian culture and use Russian folk melodies. *The Firebird* (1910) continues the exoticism and colorful orchestration of Rimsky-Korsakov, Stravinsky's teacher.

Etude: Stravinsky's *Petrushka*

Some of Stravinsky's distinctive stylistic traits emerge in the second ballet, *Petrushka* (1911), including independent superimposed layers of sound, blocks of sound that alternate without transitions, repetitive melodies and rhythms over static harmony; and octatonic and polytonal sonorities.

3. *Le Sacre du printemps*

Le Sacre du printemps (The Rite of Spring, 1913) adds to those elements new orchestral effects, heightened dissonance, and rhythm whose changing meters and unexpected accents negate regular meter and emphasize instead a basic pulse, suggesting a musical primitivism. *Le Sacre* precipitated a riot at its premiere, but all three ballets have since become Stravinsky's most popular works. **Music: NAWM 134**

4. 1913–23

Partly due to economic necessity, Stravinsky's works during and just after World War I are for smaller ensembles.

5. Stravinsky's neo-Classicism

From the 1920s to 1951, Stravinsky adopted a neo-Classic approach that abandoned the Russian tunes and extra-musical concerns of his earlier works and sought to create abstract, objective music based on historical models. This was inaugurated by his reworkings of eighteenth-century music in the ballet *Pulcinella* (1919) and continued in a series of works that evoked earlier styles, particularly the Classic era, yet continued to show the personal characteristics exemplified in *Le Sacre du printemps*.

Etude: *The Rake's Progress*

Stravinsky's opera *The Rake's Progress* (1951) is based on engravings by William Hogarth and modeled after eighteenth-century opera.

6. *Symphony of Psalms*

In the *Symphony of Psalms* (1930), Stravinsky set psalms in Latin for chorus and orchestra. In works of the 1950s and 1960s, Stravinsky adapted the serial techniques of Schoenberg and Webern.

Window: Nijinsky's Lost Ballet (CHWM 510–11)

Vaslav Nijinsky (1888–1950) was the Russian dancer and choreographer who created the dance for Stravinsky's *Le Sacre du printemps*. The dance was not filmed, but a reconstruction was made in the 1980s by choreographer Robert Joffrey and danced by his company, the Joffrey Ballet.

STUDY QUESTIONS

Prelude (CHWM 483–86)

1. What were some of the factors that led to the diversity of musical aesthetics, styles, and procedures in the twentieth century?

Ethnic Contexts (CHWM 486–90, NAWM 130)

2. What were Bartók's activities in music, in addition to composing?

Music to Study
   NAWM 130: Béla Bartók, *Music for Strings, Percussion, and Celesta*, suite (1936), third movement: Adagio
   CD 11.23–28 (Concise 4.24–29)

3. In the Adagio movement of *Music for Strings, Percussion, and Celesta* (NAWM 130), how does Bartók use mirrors, retrogrades, and palindromes? (A palindrome is its own retrograde, as in the palindrome about Napoleon, "Able was I ere I saw Elba.")

4. What elements of East European folk music are used in this movement?

---

5. This movement also uses techniques derived from Western art music, in addition to the use of traditional orchestral instruments and a complex arch form. Find instances of the following:

imitation and canon _____

ostinato _____

inversion of melodic material _____

rhythmic diminution of material _____

6. Bartók's synthesis of the folk and art music traditions creates something new within the realm of the orchestral repertory. List the ways in which this movement offers new sounds and ideas, in comparison with twentieth-century symphonic music. (You may use NAWM 103, 105, and 124 as points of comparison.)

The Soviet Orbit (CHWM 491–94, NAWM 131–32)

7. As used by Soviet authorities, what is *socialist realism*? What is *formalism*? How did Prokofiev and Shostakovich attempt to conform to the demand for socialist realism?

Music to Study
> **NAWM 131:** Dmitri Shostakovich, *Lady Macbeth of Mtsensk,* opera (1932), Act IV, Scene 9, excerpt
> CD 11.29–33
> **NAWM 132:** Sofia Gubaidulina, *Rejoice!* Sonata for violin and violoncello (1981), fifth movement, "Listen to the still small voice within"
> CD 11.34–37 (Concise 4.30–33)

8. What characteristics of Shostakovich's *Lady Macbeth of Mtsensk* displeased the Soviet authorities? Once you translate the negative words of the *Pravda* article (quoted in NAWM, pp. 695–96) into neutral or positive ones, which of these traits, if any, appear in the excerpt in NAWM 131?

9. Describe the main elements of Shostakovich's style in this excerpt. How does it compare to the operatic style of Wagner (see NAWM 121) and Verdi (see NAWM 119)? How does it differ from Bartók's style in *Music for Strings, Percussion, and Celesta* (NAWM 130), written around the same time?

10. What spiritual lesson does Sofia Gubaidulina seek to convey in the movement from *Rejoice!* (NAWM 132)? How is it conveyed in the music?

11. How does Gubaidulina use repetition, variation, and contrast in this movement? How is this like traditional eighteenth- and nineteenh-century procedures, and how is it different?

England (CHWM 494–96)

12. Briefly describe the music of Vaughan Williams. How does his music contrast with that of Bartók (NAWM 130) in its relation to tonality and diatonicism? In what other ways is his music similar to Bartók's?

Music to Study
NAWM 133: Benjamin Britten, *Peter Grimes,* opera (1945), excerpt from Act III, Scene 2: *To hell with all your mercy!*
CD 11.38–40

13. In the concluding scene of *Peter Grimes* (NAWM 133), how does Britten portray Grimes's madness through musical means? (Note that the passage at mm. 22–33 is a reminiscence of an earlier, more hopeful scene, but now trails off at the end.)

14. What musical elements (including motives, chords, keys or collections of pitches, timbres, and so on) are associated with the townspeople (the chorus) and with the sea (the figuration in the orchestra)? How does Britten create the effect of events happening simultaneously, but remaining separate from one another?

Germany (CHWM 497–500)

15. Briefly summarize Hindemith's career. How does his music relate to the past? How did he address the gulf between composers and audiences?

16. What were Kurt Weill's "two careers"? What were his musical aims? Describe his musical style, and explain how it suited his aims and the types of music he composed.

Neo-Classicism in France (CHWM 500–502)

17. If a work is *neo-Classic,* what are some characteristics one might expect to find in it?

18. Describe the music and musical style of Milhaud.

Stravinsky (CHWM 502–13, NAWM 134)

Music to Study
> **NAWM 134:** Igor Stravinsky, *Le Sacre du printemps* (The Rite of Spring),
> ballet (1913), excerpt from Part I: *Danse des adolescentes* (Dance
> of the Adolescent Girls)
> CD 11.41–44 (Concise 4.34–37)

19. For each of the following traits of Stravinsky's style, find two passages that
exemplify it in *Danse des adolescentes* (NAWM 134). Indicate each passage
by measure numbers and describe it briefly.

ostinatos

repetitive melodies over static harmony

blocks of sound that succeed each other without transitions

independent layers of sound that are superimposed on one another

unexpected accents that negate regular meter and emphasize pulsation

novel orchestral effects

Note: Here is a guide to some of Stravinsky's orchestral markings:
- In m. 1 he asks the strings to play each beat with a down-bow instead of
bowing up and down; this will create a forceful, detached effect.
- "Con sord." in m. 18 means "with mute," which on the trumpet yields
a thin, metallic sound.
- "Flttzg." on the chromatic scales in the winds in mm. 27–31 means
fluttertonguing, which creates a sort of buzzy effect.
- The cellos in mm. 78–81 have a harmonic glissando, an effect
Stravinsky invented; bowing the C string while moving the finger rapidly
along it without touching the string to the fingerboard creates this effect by
allowing only certain overtones to sound.
- "Col legno" (m. 82) means to hit the string with the stick of the bow.

20. Within this essentially static texture of repeating figuration and almost constant pulsation, how does Stravinsky achieve variety?

21. How does Stravinsky create the effect of building intensity toward the end of the excerpt?

22. Summarize Stravinsky's career, including where he lived, his major compositions, and the main elements of his style in each period.

23. In the excerpts from Stravinsky's *Symphony of Psalms* and *The Rake's Progress* shown in Examples 20.12 and 20.13 in CHWM, pp. 509 and 512, what elements recall Classic or Baroque music? Which of the characteristics of Stravinsky's style listed above in question 20 do you find in one or more of these excerpts?

TERMS TO KNOW

Gebrauchsmusik
neo-Classic music
socialist realism

formalism
polystylistic music
polytonality

NAMES TO KNOW

Béla Bartók
Mikrokosmos
Music for Strings, Percussion,
  and Celesta
Zoltán Kodály
Sergey Prokofiev
Dmitri Shostakovich
Lady Macbeth of Mtsensk
Alfred Schnittke
Sofia Gubaidulina
Ralph Vaughan Williams
Benjamin Britten
Peter Grimes
War Requiem
Paul Hindemith
Mathis der Maler
Kurt Weill

The Rise and Fall of the City of
  Mahagonny
Die Dreigroschenoper (The
  Threepenny Opera)
Arthur Honegger
Darius Milhaud
Francis Poulenc
Igor Stravinsky
The Fire Bird
Petrushka
Le Sacre du printemps (The Rite
  of Spring)
Pulcinella
Symphony of Psalms
The Rake's Progress
Vaslav Nijinsky

REVIEW QUESTIONS

1. Add the composers and major works discussed in this chapter to the time-line you made for the twentieth century in Chapter 19.

2. Write an essay in which you summarize the major trends in European music between about 1915 and 1950 (excepting the atonal and twelve-tone music of Schoenberg and his associates, treated in Chapter 21).

3. How does Bartók achieve an individual style within the Western art music tradition by integrating traditional procedures with elements abstracted from East European folk music? Describe how this synthesis works in *Music for Strings, Percussion, and Celesta.*

4. Compare the music of Shostakovich and Gubaidulina, using the excerpts in NAWM 131–32 as examples. What was each trying to achieve in these works, and what musical procedures or traditions did each find useful in achieving these aims? What did Soviet authorities ask of composers in the Soviet Union, and how did Shostakovich and Gubaidulina relate to the Soviet state?

5. Trace the career of Igor Stravinsky, naming major pieces and describing the changes in his style. What distinctive characteristics of his music, established in *Petrushka* and *Le Sacre du printemps,* continued throughout his career, and how are these traits embodied in his neo-Classical music?

ATONALITY, SERIALISM, AND RECENT DEVELOPMENTS IN TWENTIETH-CENTURY EUROPE

21

CHAPTER OBJECTIVES

After you complete the reading, study of the music, and study questions for this chapter, you should be able to

1. describe the music and innovations of Schoenberg, Berg, and Webern;
2. describe in simple terms how twelve-tone music works and analyze a brief passage;
3. describe the style of Messiaen and some of his characteristic devices; and
4. define expressionism, total serialism, electronic music, musique concrète, and indeterminacy, and name and describe at least one work representing each trend.

CHAPTER OUTLINE

Prelude (CHWM 515–16)

The twentieth century saw a continuing pursuit of new resources, among them atonality, serialism, electronic technology, and indeterminacy.

I. Schoenberg and His Followers (CHWM 516–27, NAWM 135–38)

1. Schoenberg's career
Arnold Schoenberg (1874–1951) was born in Vienna, was largely self-taught, and in turn attracted devoted students. He fled Nazi Germany in 1933 and settled in the United States. His career can be divided into four periods: tonal (to 1908), atonal (1908–23), serial (1923–36), and diverse in style (1936–51).

2. First period
Schoenberg first composed in a Romantic style derived from Wagner, Mahler, and Strauss and favored large, often programmatic works.

3. Second period

About 1905, Schoenberg turned to smaller forms and a more concentrated language with complex rhythms and counterpoint.

4. Atonality

Around 1908, Schoenberg began to write music that was *atonal,* meaning that it avoided any sense of a tonal center (whether through traditional tonal harmony or any new way of establishing a central pitch). Instead of treating each pitch and chord in terms of its function within a key and requiring dissonant notes and chords to resolve, all notes were equal and all sonorities possible; Schoenberg called this *"the emancipation of the dissonance"* (since dissonance was freed of its need to resolve to consonance).

5. *Pierrot lunaire*

Pierrot lunaire (Moonstruck Pierrot, 1912) for female voice and chamber ensemble is Schoenberg's best-known atonal piece.

6. *Sprechstimme*

In *Pierrot lunaire,* the voice uses *Sprechstimme* (speech-voice or speech-song), voicing only approximate pitches. By distorting speech and song, the technique expresses extreme feelings, making the work *expressionist.*

Etude: *Pierrot Lunaire*

Without tonality, Schoenberg creates unity in *Pierrot lunaire* through canons, motives, and reliance on the text.   **Music: NAWM 135**

7. Third period: Twelve-tone method

Seeking a way to compose unified longer works without a tonal center and without depending on a text, Schoenberg by 1923 devised the *twelve-tone method.* The twelve chromatic notes are ordered in a *row* or *series.* Tones from the row (or from a segment of it, such as the first three or four notes) may be sounded in succession as a melody or simultaneously as a chord, in any octave and rhythm. (The order of notes in the row is not arbitrary, but is based on the melodic motives and chords the composer plans to use in the piece, which are embedded in the row.) The row may be used in its original (*prime*) form, in *inversion* (upside down), in *retrograde* (backward), in *retrograde inversion* (upside down and backward), and in any transposition of these four forms. Each row statement includes all twelve notes (but different statements can appear simultaneously). Schoenberg wrote many twelve-tone works, most of them in standard forms.

Etude: Schoenberg's *Variations for Orchestra*

The *Variations for Orchestra* (1927–28) show Schoenberg's blending of traditional and twelve-tone methods.   **Music: NAWM 136**

8. Fourth period

Most of Schoenberg's late music is twelve-tone, but some works are tonal or blend aspects of tonal and atonal or twelve-tone music.

9. *Moses und Aron*

In Schoenberg's unfinished twelve-tone opera *Moses und Aron* (1930–32), Moses speaks in Sprechstimme, symbolizing his inability to convey his vision of God.

10. Alban Berg

Alban Berg (1885–1935) was Schoenberg's student and adopted many of his techniques, but infused his music with warmth of feeling and with sounds borrowed from tonal music.

11. *Wozzeck*

Berg's expressionist opera *Wozzeck* (1917–21) is atonal (*not* twelve-tone). It uses leitmotifs and continuous music (as did Wagner) and casts each scene as a traditional form, such as suite or passacaglia. The use of tonal effects and familiar types of music helped Berg to convey strong emotions in a language listeners could understand.   **Music: NAWM 137**

Etude: *Wozzeck,* Act III, Scene 3

This scene is an invention on a rhythm. Announced at the outset in the piano, it pervades the entire texture and symbolizes Wozzeck's obsession.

12. Anton Webern

Anton Webern (1883–1945) also studied with Schoenberg and adopted his atonal and twelve-tone methods. But Webern's works are usually spare in texture, often canonic, and without tonal implications.

13. Webern's instrumentation

Webern's melodies may change timbre as well as pitch, as a single line passes from one instrument to others in turn. He often uses unusual instrumental colors and special effects.

14. Webern's brevity

Webern's works are usually brief, some extremely brief.

15. Webern's three periods

Like Schoenberg, Webern first wrote tonal music, then adopted atonality and finally the twelve-tone method.   **Music: NAWM 138**

16. Webern's influence

Webern achieved little recognition in his lifetime but significantly influenced composers after World War II.

Window: Expressionism (CHWM 524–25)

Expressionism in art and music portrayed extreme inner feelings such as anxiety, fear, and despair through extreme means. In music, this included heightened dissonance, fragmented and angular melodies, and distortion of past conventions.

II. After Webern (CHWM 528–30, NAWM 139)

1. Darmstadt movement

After World War II, Stravinsky and others took up the twelve-tone system. The young composers associated with the *Darmstadt* summer composition courses, notably *Pierre Boulez* (b. 1925) and Karlheinz Stockhausen, looked to Webern as a model.

2. Total serialism

By 1950, composers began to apply the serial procedures of twelve-tone music to aspects other than pitch, such as duration and dynamics, resulting in *total serialism.*

3. Boulez

Boulez practiced total serialism, then moved beyond it to a more flexible language in works such as *Le Marteau sans maître* (The Hammer without a Master, 1954).

4. Messiaen

Olivier Messiaen (1908–1992) was an organist, composer, and teacher. His music often has religious subjects.

5. *Méditations sur la mystère de la Sainte Trinité*

In *Méditations sur la mystère de la Sainte Trinité* (Meditations on the Mystery of the Holy Trinity, 1969), Messiaen juxtaposes a variety of motives with symbolic meanings, including bird songs. **Music: NAWM 139**

6. Messiaen's style

Messiaen devised his own musical system, incorporating modal and octatonic scales, repeated rhythmic series (related to medieval isorhythm and the music theory of India), durational patterns that are the same forward and backward, and other devices.

III. Recent Developments (CHWM 530–39)

1. New timbres

Throughout the century, composers introduced new sounds into music, using instruments in unconventional ways or new instruments. *Edgard Varèse* (1883–1965) wrote music that used many novel timbres and juxtaposed contrasting masses of sound.

2. *Musique concrète*

Electronically produced or altered sounds came into use after World War II. *Musique concrète* used recorded sounds that were manipulated through tape and electronic procedures.

3. Electronic resources

Electronic music used electronically generated sound.

4. Diminished role of performers

Unlike music for live performers, music on tape allowed composers total control and an unlimited range of sounds.

5. New technology

At first, electronic music generated and altered sounds with oscillators and used tape and mixers to manipulate them.

6. Synthesizers

Composition of electronic music was facilitated by the development of *synthesizers.* Since the invention of portable synthesizers, and especially since the rise of portable computers and the MIDI interface, it has become possible to create electronic music in real time, rather than solely on tape, and combinations of electronic music with live performers are frequent.

7. Influence of electronic music
Electronic music in turn suggested new sounds for traditional instruments and voices.

8. Spatial effects
Electronic music also renewed interest in the spatial effects of locating performers or sound sources in different places around a performing space. Varèse's *Poème électronique* was a tape piece played at the 1958 World's Fair through 425 loudspeakers while colored lights and slides were projected on the walls, giving a sense of sounds moving through space.

9. The pitch continuum
Partly influenced by electronic music, composers increasingly used the entire continuum of pitch, not only the discrete tones of the chromatic scale.

10. Penderecki
Threnody for the Victims of Hiroshima for string orchestra (1960) by *Krzysztof Penderecki* (b. 1933) uses traditional instruments to play glissandos, extremely high notes, and bands of pitch within which every quarter-tone is played simultaneously.

11. Ligeti
György Ligeti (b. 1923) also used traditional instruments to achieve quasi-electronic effects in *Atmosphères* for orchestra (1961).

12. Composer/performer interaction
Throughout the history of notated music, performers have made choices or filled in what is not specified in the notation. In the twentieth century, some composers tried to exercise greater control through detailed indications in the score.

13. Indeterminacy
Others have explored *indeterminacy,* in which certain aspects of the music, such as the order of events, are not determined by the composer.

14. Stockhausen
Karlheinz Stockhausen (b. 1928) used indeterminacy in several pieces. Some works use fragments of existing music.

15. Lutosławski
Witold Lutosławski (1913–1994) used indeterminacy to allow individual players to play at varying speeds or create a cadenza-like elaboration on a figure within controlled boundaries.

16. New notation
Indeterminacy has brought new systems of notation.

17. New concept of composition
Indeterminacy has also introduced a new concept of a composition as the sum of its possible performances.

STUDY QUESTIONS

Schoenberg and His Followers (CHWM 516–27, NAWM 135–38)

1. What is *atonal* music? What did Schoenberg mean by *"the emancipation of the dissonance"*?

Music to Study

NAWM 135: Arnold Schoenberg, *Pierrot lunaire,* Op. 21, song cycle for female speech-song voice and chamber ensemble (1912), excerpts

135a: No. 8, *Nacht* (Night)   CD 11.45–46
135b: No. 13, *Enthauptung* (Decapitation)
                                  CD 11.47–50

NAWM 136: Arnold Schoenberg, *Variationen für Orchester* [Variations for Orchestra], Op. 31 (1926–28), excerpts

136a: Theme   CD 11.51 (Concise 4.38)
139b: Variation VI
136b: Variation VI   CD 11.52 (Concise 4.39)

(Note: The *Variations for Orchestra* score is at sounding pitch. Transposing instruments like clarinet and horn are written as they *sound,* and not according to the former practice of writing them in the score as they are notated for the player. Notice also that in the first excerpt the cello is in tenor clef, in which the second line from the top is middle C.)

2. What is *Sprechstimme*? How is it notated, and how is it performed?

How is Sprechstimme used in the two numbers from *Pierrot lunaire* in NAWM 135? Where is it *not* used by the voice?

---

3. What musical gestures does Schoenberg use to express or illustrate the text in these two songs?

4. What is *expressionism*? What characteristics of these two songs mark them as expressionist works?

5. In the theme of Schoenberg's *Variations for Orchestra* (NAWM 136a), the main melodic line is in the cello, later joined by Violin I (marked in the score "I. Gg," for Geige). Just considering these melodies, what rhythmic and melodic motives does he introduce, and how are these motives varied as the melodies unfold?

6. In what sense is Variation VI (NAWM 136b) a variation of the theme? What stays the same, and what is changed?

7. As shown in Example 21.1 in CHWM, p. 520 (also in NAWM, p. 755), the first half of the theme (NAWM 136a, mm. 34–45) presents the row in the cello, in two forms: first the untransposed prime form (P–0, meaning prime transposed up zero semitones), and then the retrograde inversion transposed up nine semitones (RI–9). These are accompanied by chords drawn from I–9 (the inversion transposed up nine semitones) and R–0 (the untransposed retrograde), respectively. With the first half of the theme as an example, the following questions will help you figure out what happens in the second half of the theme (mm. 46–57).

a. What form of the row appears in the cello in mm. 46–50? _____\
(Hint: See the diagram of row forms in Example 21.1.)

b. What form of the row is used for the accompanying chords? _____\
(Hint: Look at the three-note chord in m. 46. Which form of the row as shown in Example 21.1 begins with those three notes, in some order?)

c. Measures 46–47 include all twelve tones of the chromatic scale, six in the melody, and the other six in the accompaniment. What is the relationship between these two forms of the row that makes this possible? (Hint: Look at the row chart in Example 21.1, and compare the first six notes and last six notes in each row to the same groupings in the other row.)

d. What form of the row appears in Violin I (I. Gg) in mm. 51–57? What row form appears in the accompanying chords in the winds and horn?

    in Violin I _____   in winds and horn   _____

What is the relationship between these two rows? (Hint: See part c. above.)

e. A new transposition of the prime form of the row appears in the cello in mm. 52–57. By how many semitones up is it transposed, in comparison to P–0? If P–0 is the prime form transposed up zero semitones, what would you call this form of the row?

    number of semitones by which it is transposed up: _____name: _____

The point of Schoenberg's twelve-tone music is neither to be the musical equivalent of crossword puzzles nor to create completely arbitrary music, but to create logical, unified music based on motives that are developed and accompanied by harmonies derived from them. In that respect, twelve-tone pieces continue the nineteenth-century tradition of thematic development.

Music to Study
  NAWM 137: Alban Berg, *Wozzeck,* Op. 7, opera (1917–21), Act III, Scene 3
    CD 11.53–55 (Concise 4.40–42)
  NAWM 138: Anton Webern, *Symphonie* [Symphony], Op. 21, for nine solo
      instruments (1928), Ruhig schreitend (first movement)
    CD 11.56–60

(Note: The Webern Symphony score is written at sounding pitch.)

8. What characteristics of Act III, Scene 3, from Berg's *Wozzeck* (NAWM 137) mark it as an expressionist work?

9. Berg called this scene "Invention on a Rhythm." The rhythmic idea is presented in the right hand of the piano at the beginning of the scene (mm. 122–25) and immediately repeated. Wozzeck then states it in augmentation and with a new melody (mm. 130–36). (The attacks are in the same rhythm, even though one note is sustained through what was originally a rest.) List below the appearances of this rhythm in mm. 138–54, by the measure in which each statement begins and the instrument(s) or voice that carry it.

Measure	Instrument(s) or Voice		Measure	Instrument(s) or Voice
1. _____	_____		6. _____	_____
2. _____	_____		7. _____	_____
3. _____	_____		8. _____	_____
4. _____	_____		9. _____	_____
5. _____	_____		10. _____	_____

How does the constant reiteration of this rhythm convey the dramatic situation?

10. Where does Berg imitate a polka? A folk song? How does he suggest these types of tonal music, despite using an atonal language?

11. Which characteristics of Webern's style, as described in CHWM, p. 527, are evident in the first movement of his Symphony (NAWM 138)?

12. The opening section of this movement is a double canon. The leading voice of the first canon begins in Horn 2, passes to the clarinet, and continues in the cello (see the example in NAWM, p. 782). The canonic answer is in inversion and begins in Horn 1. In what instruments does the answer continue?

After Webern (CHWM 528–30, NAWM 139)

13. What is *total serialism*?

Music to Study
  NAWM 139: Olivier Messiaen, *Méditations sur le mystère de la Sainte Trinité*
       (Meditations on the Mystery of the Holy Trinity) for organ (1969),
       Vif (fourth movement)
    CD 12.1–5 (Concise 4.43–47)

14. The fourth movement of Messiaen's *Méditations sur le mystère de la Sainte Trinité* (NAWM 139) features numerous birdsongs that are labeled in the score. What birdsongs are used, and where do they appear? How does Messiaen imitate these birdsongs on the organ?

15. How does Messiaen use his musical material? What happens to it over the course of the movement? How is it repeated or varied?

16. Describe Messiaen's use of rhythm. Is there a regular meter? Is there a sense of momentum toward a goal?

17. How do the musical material, the form, and the treatment of rhythm suggest mystical contemplation?

Recent Developments (CHWM 530–39)

18. What have been some important developments in electronic and tape music since 1945?

19. How did Penderecki and Ligeti use traditional instruments to create novel sounds and textures in *Threnody for the Victims of Hiroshima* and *Atmosphères*?

20. What is *indeterminacy*? How has it been used in composition? Name two European composers who have used it, and describe a piece by each.

TERMS TO KNOW

atonal music, atonality
"the emancipation of the
　dissonance"
Sprechstimme
twelve-tone method
row, series
prime, inversion, retrograde,
　retrograde inversion

expressionism
total serialism
musique concrète
electronic music
synthesizer
indeterminacy

NAMES TO KNOW

Arnold Schoenberg
Pierrot lunaire
Schoenberg: Variations for
　Orchestra
Moses und Aron
Alban Berg
Wozzeck
Anton Webern
Darmstadt
Pierre Boulez
Le Marteau sans maître

Olivier Messiaen
Edgard Varèse
Poème électronique
Krzysztof Penderecki
*Threnody for the Victims of
　Hiroshima*
György Ligeti
Atmosphères
Karlheinz Stockhausen
Witold Lutosławski

REVIEW QUESTIONS

1. Add the composers and major works discussed in this chapter to the time-line you made for the twentieth century in Chapter 19.

2. Compare the atonal music of Schoenberg's *Pierrot lunaire* (NAWM 135) to the music you know by Wagner, Wolf, Mahler, and Strauss (NAWM 121–24). How does Schoenberg continue the late-Romantic German tradition, and what does he introduce that is new?

3. How does Schoenberg's twelve-tone music, as exemplified in the *Variations for Orchestra* (NAWM 136), continue and extend nineteenth-century procedures?

4. How does Berg's music resemble that of Schoenberg, and how does it differ? How does it compare to the music you know by Wagner, Mahler, and Strauss?

5. How does Webern's twelve-tone music differ from that of Schoenberg?

6. List the predominant characteristics of Messiaen's style and explain how they are exemplified in the organ work in NAWM 139.

7. What are some of the trends in European art music since 1945? Describe an example of each trend.

THE AMERICAN TWENTIETH CENTURY

22

CHAPTER OBJECTIVES

After you complete the reading, study of the music, and study questions for this chapter, you should be able to

1. summarize the historical background for art music in the United States;
2. outline the history of vernacular music in the United States from ragtime to rock; and
3. name the most significant composers of and trends in art music in the United States during the twentieth century, explain what is individual about each one, and describe pieces by some of the major composers of the century.

CHAPTER OUTLINE

Prelude (CHWM 540–41)

The United States became the center for new music in the classical tradition after World War II. American music grew out of the European tradition, as European composers emigrated to or visited the United States and as many Americans studied with Nadia Boulanger in Paris or with other European teachers at summer festivals. But American music also drew from its many ethnic and popular traditions.

I. Music in the North American Colonies (CHWM 542–46)

New England colonists sang psalms, and singing schools were established in the eighteenth century to teach singing in parts from notation.

1. William Billings
William Billings (1746–1800) wrote psalms, hymns, anthems, and canons. Most of his hymns were simple four-part harmonizations, but many were *fuging tunes,* which include a middle section in free imitation. Billings did not follow the rules of "correct" counterpoint, but allowed parallel fifths and octaves and often used chords without thirds.

2. Immigration and its influences
Other immigrants brought their musical cultures.

3. Moravians
The Moravians, German-speaking Protestants from Czech and Slovak regions, encouraged music in church, including arias and motets. German immigrants were prominent as music teachers, and American composers often studied in Germany.

4. Lowell Mason
Lowell Mason (1792–1872), trained by a German immigrant, introduced music into the public school curriculum and sought to replace the music of Billings and others with hymns harmonized in the "correct" European style. Many of his hymns are still in hymnals. The Yankee tunes remained in use in the South. The folk tradition of African-American *spirituals* was popularized after the Civil War by the *Fisk Jubilee Singers.*

5. Brass and wind bands
In the nineteenth century, almost every town and city had an amateur *wind* or *brass band,* and in the twentieth century almost every high school and college had a wind band. The nineteenth-century repertory included marches, dances, song arrangements, and solo display pieces.

6. Sousa
John Philip Sousa (1854–1932) wrote more than one hundred marches. Brass bands and dance orchestras played an important role in African-American social life and provided training for black musicians.

II. Vernacular Styles (CHWM 546–52)

1. Ragtime
Ragtime developed from American and African traditions. A typical *rag,* such as *Maple Leaf Rag* (1899) by *Scott Joplin* (1868–1917), uses march form in duple meter and presents a syncopated melody over a steady bass.

2. Blues
Black laments evolved in the early twentieth century into a style called *blues.* Blues songs have a text in rhymed couplets, the first line repeated, and use *blue notes,* lowering the third, seventh, or fifth degree of the major scale.

Etude: Form of the Blues
The standard blues form has a twelve-bar harmonic framework, often with improvised instrumental "breaks" between lines of the song.

3. Jazz
Jazz is a form of group or solo improvisation over a blues or popular tune, developed by black musicians and imitated by white bands by 1915.

4. Improvisation
A leading band was *King Oliver's Creole Jazz Band,* which used the typical instrumentation of cornet, clarinet, trombone, piano, banjo, and drums. The band practiced the New Orleans style of group improvisation.

5. Big bands

The popularity of jazz brought larger performing spaces, leading in the 1920s to *big bands,* which had trumpets, trombones, saxophones, and clarinets in sections, and a *rhythm section* of string bass, piano, guitar, and drums.

6. Arrangers

Big bands performed from an arrangement, or *chart,* which still provided some opportunities for improvised solos. This style is also called *swing,* from the swinging uneven rhythms.

7. Bebop

Bebop (or *bop*) of the 1940s and 1950s used smaller groups, more improvisation, and new techniques, some borrowed from modern classical music, to create a serious art music in the jazz tradition.

8. Modern jazz

Bebop and its successors demanded knowledgeable, attentive listeners.

9. Country music

Country-and-western or *country music* blended the Anglo-American folk tradition of the Appalachian and Ozark Mountain regions with cowboy music and some jazz elements. Singers accompanied themselves on guitar or were backed by a band featuring violins and guitars.

10. Rhythm-and-blues

Rhythm-and-blues was a black urban blues-based style with an unrelenting rhythm emphasizing the offbeats and often using electric guitar and bass.

11. Rock-and-roll

Rock-and-roll or *rock* emerged in the mid-1950s from a blending of white country and black rhythm-and-blues styles. (Like those two styles, it was promoted and virtually created by the recording industry and radio.) *Elvis Presley* (1935–1977) in the 1950s and *The Beatles* in the 1960s were both enormously popular.

12. Musical comedy

The *Broadway musical* (or *musical comedy*) is the main genre of musical theater in the United States. Many popular songs by Jerome Kern, Irving Berlin, and *George Gershwin* (1898–1937) were written for Broadway shows. Gershwin also wrote music that combines popular with classical traditions, such as his blend of jazz with the Romantic piano concerto in *Rhapsody in Blue* (1924) and his folk opera *Porgy and Bess* (1935).

III. Foundations for an American Art Music (CHWM 552–60, NAWM 140–44)

New England was a center for art music in the late nineteenth and early twentieth centuries. *Amy Cheney Beach* (1867–1944) wrote songs, chamber music, and orchestral music in a style influenced by Brahms and late-Romantic chromatic harmony. **Music: NAWM 140**

1. Ives

Charles Ives (1874–1954) had a strong background in music but made his living in insurance while writing highly original works.

2. Ives's works

Ives's works include symphonies, symphonic poems, chamber music, and art songs. Although most of his music was not published or performed until years after he wrote it, he anticipated many radical developments of his time.

3. Ives's style

Ives blended elements of the American vernacular and European art music traditions. He often used existing music, especially American tunes, as a basis for his own, reworking borrowed material in a variety of ways and with various meanings. **Music: NAWM 141**

4. Ives's influence

Ives's independence of mind, experimentation, innovations, multilayered textures, and use of popular materials inspired many younger composers.

5. Ruggles

Carl Ruggles (1876–1971) wrote atonal, very original works, of which the best known is *Sun-Treader* (1926–31).

6. Cowell

Henry Cowell (1897–1965) was a Californian and looked to both America and Asia for inspiration.

7. Cowell's special piano effects

Cowell explored new effects on the piano, including strumming or playing directly on the strings.

8. Cowell's tone clusters

Cowell is best known for introducing *tone clusters,* collections of notes separated by seconds. His later music uses folk and non-Western elements. Cowell was also a promoter and publisher of new music.

9. Crawford Seeger

Ruth Crawford Seeger (1901–1953) composed in a modern atonal style, creating a series of very individual works, before changing her interests to transcribing and arranging American folksongs. **Music: NAWM 142**

10. Varèse

Edgard Varèse (discussed in Chapter 21) was born in France and moved to New York in 1915.

11. Varèse's style

Rather than using themes, harmony, or conventional rhythm, Varèse's works use pitch, duration, dynamics, and timbre (including percussion) to create *sound masses* that move and interact in musical space.

Etude: Varèse, *Intégrales*

Intégrales (1925) illustrates Varèse's juxtaposition of elements.

12. Copland

Aaron Copland (1900–1990) studied in France with Nadia Boulanger.

13. Copland's early works

His early works use jazz elements and dissonance. In the mid-1930s he turned to a more popular style of simple textures, diatonic writing, and folk tunes, as in *Appalachian Spring* (1944). **Music: NAWM 143**

14. Copland's later works

His later works encompass a range of styles but retain his individual stamp. In the 1950s, his music became more abstract, and he adopted some twelve-tone methods.

15. Copland's style and influence

Copland's music tends to have a tonal center and sounds new without complexity. He influenced many younger American composers.

16. Harris

Roy Harris (1898–1979) is best known for symphonic music that evokes the American West through modal themes and open textures.

17. Virgil Thomson

Critic and composer *Virgil Thomson* (1896–1989) studied with Boulanger but emulated the playful simplicity of Satie. His two operas on texts by Gertrude Stein, *Four Saints in Three Acts* (1928) and *The Mother of Us All* (1947), draw on the styles of American hymns, songs, and dance music.

18. Still

William Grant Still (1895–1978) combined European forms and genres with African-American elements in the *Afro-American Symphony* (1931). **Music: NAWM 144**

19. Price

Florence Price (1888–1953) incorporated African-American elements in her Piano Concerto and First Symphony.

20. National *vs.* cosmopolitan elements

Many American composers in the first half of the century wrote music that was more cosmopolitan than nationalist.

IV. Since 1945 (CHWM 560–77, NAWM 145–50)

A. *Abstract Idioms*

1. Sessions

Roger Sessions (1896–1985) wrote dissonant, complex music in an individual style based on continuous development.

2. Carter

Elliott Carter (b. 1908) is noted for innovations in rhythm and form.

3. Metric modulation

Carter often uses *metric modulation,* in which the meter and tempo change in such a way that a fraction of the beat in the old meter becomes the beat in the new meter (for example, a dotted eighth in 4/4 becomes a quarter note in 4/4 at a proportionally faster tempo). Inspired by Ives's layered textures, Carter often gives each instrument a different rhythmic and melodic character to create a counterpoint of thoroughly independent lines, as in his String Quartet No. 2 (1959).   **Music: NAWM 145**

4. The post-Webern vogue
Webern influenced composers in the universities who sought an objective approach free from Americanism and the influence of popular music.

5. Babbitt
Milton Babbitt (b. 1916) extended twelve-tone music in new directions and was the first to apply serial principles to duration and other parameters.

Etude: The University as Patron
In the United States and Canada, composers of music in the classical tradition have been supported in the twentieth and twenty-first centuries largely through university teaching positions. This has isolated composers from the public and has sometimes encouraged avant-garde experimentation, but it has also been the major way younger composers have been trained. Important universities for composers have included Yale (where Hindemith taught), UCLA (Schoenberg), and Princeton (Sessions and Babbitt).

B. *New Sounds and Textures*

1. Nancarrow
Conlon Nancarrow (1912–1997) used player-piano rolls to create pieces whose complex and rapid rhythms were beyond human performers.

2. Partch
Harry Partch (1901–1974) rejected equal temperament, formulated a scale of forty-three unequal steps using only the pure harmonic ratios of just intonation, and built new instruments that used this scale. His works typically use these instruments to accompany dancing and singing.

3. Johnston
Ben Johnston (b. 1926) applies just intonation to traditional instruments, such as piano or string quartet.

4. Crumb
George Crumb (b. 1929) draws new sounds from traditional instruments to create emotionally powerful music in an eclectic style, as in *Black Angels* (1970) for amplified string quartet.   **Music: NAWM 146**

5. Electronic music
Lacking performers, electronic music is less often played in concert than heard in recording. But several composers have combined live performers with electronic music, as in Babbitt's moving *Philomel* (1964) for soprano and tape.   **Music: NAWM 147**

6. Druckman
Jacob Druckman wrote a series of dialogues between live performers and electronic tape.

7. Influence of jazz
Many twentieth-century composers have used jazz elements in classical works, and in the 1950s some sought to merge the two streams.

8. Schuller and "third stream" music
Gunther Schuller (b. 1925) combined jazz and classical elements in music he called *third stream*. **Music: NAWM 148**

9. Babbitt, *All Set*
Other composers have mixed jazz and classical music in other ways. Babbitt's *All Set* is a total serial work for jazz ensemble. University-trained jazz pianist *Anthony Davis* (b. 1951) juxtaposed jazz and classical styles in his opera *X: The Life and Times of Malcolm X* (1984).

10. John Cage and indeterminacy
John Cage (1912–1992) used *indeterminacy,* in which some aspect of the music is left undetermined by the composer, to encourage listeners to hear sounds as sounds in themselves, not as means by which a composer communicates a feeling or idea.

11. Cage's *4'33"*
One aspect of indeterminacy is shown in Cage's *4'33"* (1952), in which the performer sits silently and the music is the ambient sounds one hears during the duration of the piece.

12. Cage's interest in Chinese thought
In other works, Cage used *chance,* in which some aspect of the music is determined, not by the composer's will or intentions, but by chance operations. For example, the pitches in *Music of Changes* (1951) were determined by the Chinese *I Ching* (Book of Changes). (Indeterminacy and chance are often confused, but they are quite distinct. If something is determined by chance operations, it is not indeterminate.)

13. Earle Brown
Other composers also used indeterminacy. Earle Brown's *Available Forms I* and *II* (1961 and 1962) allows the conductor to choose the order in which segments of music are played.

14. Influence of Asia
Asian music exercised a growing influence on American music after 1960, stimulating simpler styles focusing on melody, rhythm, and repetition.

15. Minimalism
The approach called *minimalism* uses a deliberately restricted set of notes or sounds and a large amount of repetition.

16. Reich
Steve Reich (b. 1936) has used small repeated units that begin in unison and gradually move out of phase with each other.

Etude: Reich's *Violin Phase* (1979)
Reich's *Violin Phase* (1967, rev. 1979) involves a short pattern of notes repeated many times and played out of phase with itself.

17. Glass
Philip Glass (b. 1937) has written operas and works for his own ensemble using a very repetitive style.

18. Adams
John Adams (b. 1947) has written piano music, orchestral music, and operas using repeated ideas that evolve and shift in alignment with each other.   **Music: NAWM 149**

C. *The Mainstream*

Many American composers continue to write music that is accessible to a wide public. They do not share a style or aesthetic, but their music tends to avoid extremes and to include a sense of a tonal center.

1. Barber
Samuel Barber (1910–1981) is noted especially for his operas and songs, marked by intense lyricism.

2. Rorem
Ned Rorem (b. 1923) has written hundreds of songs that singers esteem for their sensitive setting of English poetry.

3. Menotti
Gian Carlo Menotti (b. 1911) wrote operas on his own librettos based on modern life, in a style influenced by Puccini.

4. Tower
Joan Tower (b. 1938) draws on a wide variety of approaches.

5. Zwilich
Ellen Taaffe Zwilich (b. 1939) was the first woman to win the Pulitzer Prize in music. Her *Concerto Grosso 1985,* written for the 300th anniversary of Handel's birth, incorporates music from one of his sonatas and other sounds and procedures of Baroque music.   **Music: NAWM 150**

6. Post-modern styles
Recent post-modernist architects have incorporated elements of earlier styles into their designs, and so do a number of recent composers. *Post-modernism* views styles of all eras and cultures as equally available for use.

7. Rochberg
George Rochberg (b. 1918) revisits and deconstructs the style of J. S. Bach in *Nach Bach* (After or According to Bach, 1966).

Etude: Rochberg and Bach Compared
In *Nach Bach,* Rochberg uses similar gestures to Bach, but a different harmonic language.

8. Del Tredici
David Del Tredici (b. 1937) has written several works based on parts of *Alice's Adventures in Wonderland* and *Through the Looking Glass,* using a style derived from Wagner and Strauss in order to communicate with an audience.

Postlude (CHWM 578)

Four characteristics that have defined Western music since the Middle Ages have been challenged in the twentieth century. Composition has been augmented in some music by controlled improvisation. In some pieces, notation is less a set of directions than a starting point for creativity. Principles of order have been challenged by indeterminacy and are not always perceptible in serial music. Polyphony and harmony continue in novel forms. "Serious" music has found only a small audience, and radical experimentation a still smaller one. Recent composers have sought ways to please a broader public, often by incorporating ideas from popular music, non-Western music, or music of the past.

STUDY QUESTIONS

Prelude (CHWM 540–41)

1. What were some of the ways in which twentieth-century European composers interacted with and influenced American composers of art music?

Traditional Music (CHWM 542–46)

2. When did William Billings live? What kinds of music did he write?

3. What were Lowell Mason's contributions to music in the United States?

4. What was the importance of brass and wind bands in the United States? What was their repertory? What was their significance for African Americans?

Vernacular Styles (CHWM 546–52)

5. What is *ragtime*? From what traditions did it derive?

6. Describe the style and form of the *blues*.

7. Briefly trace the evolution of *jazz* from early jazz through big bands to modern jazz.

8. Describe the characteristics of *country music*. From what traditions did it derive?

9. Describe the origins and style of *rhythm-and-blues*.

10. Describe the origins and style of *rock-and-roll*.

Foundations for an American Art Music (CHWM 552–60, NAWM 140–44)

Music to Study
   NAWM 140: Amy Cheney Beach, Quintet for Piano and Strings in F-sharp
        Minor, Op. 67 (1908), Allegro agitato (third movement)
     12.6–10

11. Diagram or describe the form of the finale of Beach's Piano Quintet
    (NAWM 140). How does it relate to standard forms of nineteenth-century
    European instrumental music?

12. Describe the melodic material and figuration. What elements and character-
    istics reveal the influence of Brahms? What traits suggest other influences or
    Beach's individual voice?

---

13. What are some prominent characteristics of Charles Ives's music? What was
    his significance for American music?

Music to Study

   NAWM 141: Charles Ives, *"They Are There!": A War Song March,* for unison chorus and orchestra (adapted in 1942 from Ives's 1917 song *He Is There!*)

   CD 12.11–13 (Concise 4.48–50)

Most of Ives's mature works are in European genres and use modernist techniques to evoke nineteenth-century America. *They Are There!* (NAWM 141) is unusual, for it uses the verse-chorus format and ragtime-like melodic style of a Tin Pan Alley tune. But it illustrates several traits of Ives's music.

   Tin Pan Alley composers often quoted existing tunes. Ives intensifies this practice, quoting or paraphrasing fragments of the following tunes. Most are Civil War songs, used here to link what Ives considered the idealism of the fight to end slavery with the cause of fighting tyranny in World War I and II.

Measures	Parts	Tune
1–2	brass, piano, clarinets	*Country Band March,* by Ives
8–9	voices, trumpets, violin 1 & 2	*Country Band March*
12–14	voices, trumpets, violin 1 & 2	*Marching through Georgia*
18–19	voices, trumpets, violin 1	*Tenting on the Old Camp Ground*
19–21	voices, trumpets, violin 1	*Columbia, the Gem of the Ocean*
20–23	trombones	*The Battle Hymn of the Republic*
21–22	winds	*Dixie*
23	winds	*Marching through Georgia*
23–25	voices, trumpets, trombones, violin 1	*Tramp, Tramp, Tramp*
24	winds	*Yankee Doodle*
25–26	winds	*Marching through Georgia*
27–30	voices, trumpet 1, viola 1	*Columbia, the Gem of the Ocean*
29–30	winds	*Maryland, My Maryland*
31–35	winds	*La Marseillaise*
32–33	voices, brass, viola 1	*Columbia, the Gem of the Ocean*
34–38	voices and brass	*Tenting on the Old Camp Ground*
40–44	voices and brass	*Tenting on the Old Camp Ground*
43–47	winds	*The Battle Cry of Freedom*
44–48	voices, trumpet 1, violin 1	*The Battle Cry of Freedom*
48–50	winds and brass	*The Star-Spangled Banner*
51–53	flutes and trumpets	*Reveille* (bugle call)

14. In the voice part throughout and the upper winds from m. 21 to the end, how does Ives join these fragments of tunes into a coherent melody?

15. Ives harmonizes his vocal melody with the expected tonal harmonies, in most cases. But he also adds many elements that one would not expect to find in a Tin Pan Alley song, or in a traditional tonal work. What are some of these added elements? How do these added elements affect your experience of the work? In your opinion, how do they affect the work's meaning?

16. Ives often superimposed layers of music, each with its own rhythm, melodic or harmonic character, and instrumental timbre. In mm. 28–29, what rhythmically independent layers are sounding simultaneously? For each layer, name the instruments or voices that are performing it and describe its rhythmic and melodic character.

17. What new musical resources did Henry Cowell introduce in his piano music? For each one, name at least one piece that uses it.

Music to Study
>   **NAWM 142:** Ruth Crawford Seeger, Violin Sonata (1926), Buoyant (second movement)
>   CD 12.14–16

(Note: In this work, accidentals apply only to the note to which they are affixed. For example, the fifth note of the piece is A-natural, not A-flat.)

18. The second movement of Ruth Crawford Seeger's Violin Sonata (NAWM 142) is built on a bass ostinato. How is this figure treated during this movement? Where is it repeated, where and how is it varied, and where (if ever) does it not appear?

19. How is the theme introduced by the violin varied and developed over the course of the movement?

---

20. Describe the music of Edgard Varèse. What resources does he use, and how does he deploy them? How does the excerpt from *Intégrales* in CHWM, p. 530, Example 22.3, illustrate his approach? (Note: In addition to pp. 554–56, Varèse is also discussed in CHWM on pp. 530 and 532 in Chapter 21.)

21. Outline Aaron Copland's career, indicating distinctive aspects of his style in each period.

Music to Study
> **NAWM 143a:** *'Tis the Gift to Ge Simple,* Shaker hymn
>   not on recordings
> **NAWM 143b:** Aaron Copland, *Appalachian Spring,* ballet (1944), excerpt, including variations on *'Tis the Gift to Be Simple*
>   CD 12.17–24 (second part of excerpt on Concise 4.51–55)

22. How does Copland vary the Shaker tune *'Tis the Gift to Be Simple* in the excerpt from *Appalachian Spring* in NAWM 143b?

23. What kinds of harmonies does Copland use in this excerpt?

---

24. Name two operas by Virgil Thomson on librettos by Gertrude Stein.

_____   _____

What are the characteristics of Thomson's music for these operas? How are they exemplified in the passage in Example 22.4 in CHWM, p. 558?

Music to Study
> **NAWM 144:** William Grant Still, *Afro-American Symphony* (1931), Animato
> (third movement)
> CD 12.25–27 (Concise 4.56–58)

25. William Grant Still's *Afro-American Symphony* unites the symphonic and African-American traditions. What elements from the symphonic tradition does he use in the third movement (NAWM 144)? What elements does it draw from African-American traditions (including spirituals, ragtime, blues, and jazz)? Refer back to pp. 544–49 in CHWM for a discussion of these types of music. (Two elements not mentioned there, both from jazz, are the trumpets with Harmon mutes starting at m. 58 and the wire brush used to play the drum starting at m. 69.)

Since 1945 (CHWM 560–77, NAWM 147–52)

Music to Study
> **NAWM 145:** Elliott Carter, String Quartet No. 2 (1959), Introduction and
> Allegro fantastico
> CD 12.28–30

26. What are some of the ways in which Elliott Carter gives each of the four instruments a distinctive rhythmic and melodic character in his String Quartet No. 2 (NAWM 145)?

27. What has been the role of North American colleges and universities in supporting composition of new music? How does this differ from the situation in Europe?

Music to Study

NAWM 146: George Crumb, *Black Angels: Thirteen Images from the Dark Land,* for electric string quartet (1970), excerpts

146a:	Image 4. *Devil-Music*	CD 12.31
146b:	Image 5. *Danse macabre*	CD 12.32
146c:	Image 6. *Pavana lachrymae*	CD 12.33
146d:	Image 7. *Threnody II: Black Angels!*	CD 12.34
146e:	Image 8. *Sarabanda de la muerte oscura*	CD 12.35
146f:	Image 9. *Lost Bells*	CD 12.36

NAWM 147: Milton Babbitt, *Philomel,* for soprano, recorded soprano, and synthesized sound (1964), opening section
CD 12.37–41 (Concise 4.59–63)

28. What new playing techniques for string instruments does George Crumb use in these six movements from *Black Angels* (NAWM 146)? (Hint: Check the footnotes that explain how to perform certain effects; these footnotes sometimes appear on a different page.) What additional instruments and sounds does he call for, beyond the four instruments of the string quartet? List all the new playing techniques, instruments, and other sounds you can find. For each one, put down one or a few words that describe how the device sounds and what emotional effect it conveys.

29. Crumb quotes or refers to earlier music several times. *Danse macabre* (NAWM 146b) refers to the piece of the same name by Camille Saint-Saëns and—like Saint-Saëns—quotes the famous chant *Dies irae* from the Gregorian Mass for the Dead. *Pavana lachrymae* (NAWM 146c) uses the title of a William Byrd keyboard transcription of a John Dowland song (see NAWM 44 and 46), but Crumb instead quotes Schubert's song *Death and the Maiden,* which Schubert himself used in a string quartet. *Sarabanda de la muerte oscura* (NAWM 146e) presents a sarabande that is apparently not borrowed but written in fifteenth-century style, with double-leading tone cadences, a Landini cadence, and appropriate ornamentation. What is the effect of these references to earlier music within the context of Crumb's music? In your opinion, what might these references mean?

30. How does Milton Babbitt use the singer, taped vocal sounds, and electronic sounds in *Philomel* (NAWM 147)? What is each component like? How do they relate? And how do they work together to suggest the story and the feelings of Philomel?

Music to Study
   NAWM 148: Gunther Schuller, *Seven Studies on Themes of Paul Klee* for
          orchestra (1959), excerpts
      148a: 3. *Kleiner blauer Teufel* (Little Blue Devil)
                                        CD 12.42–43
      148b: 5. *Arabische Stadt* (Arab Village)   CD 12.44–46

31. What is *third stream*? How is it exemplified in *Kleiner blauer Teufel,* the third
     movement of Gunther Schuller's *Seven Studies on Themes of Paul Klee*
     (NAWM 148a)?

32. How does Schuller evoke Arab music in *Arabische Stadt,* the fifth movement
     of his *Seven Studies on Themes of Paul Klee* (NAWM 148b)?

33. Why did John Cage use indeterminacy and chance operations in his music?
     How did he use them?

Music to Study
> **NAWM 149:** John Adams, *Phrygian Gates,* for piano (1977–78), opening
> section
> CD 12.47–52 (Concise 4.64–69)
> **NAWM 150:** Ellen Taaffe Zwilich, *Concerto Grosso 1985* (1985), excerpts
> Presto (fourth movement)   CD 12.53
> Maestoso (fifth movement)   CD 12.54

34. How does John Adams use repetition in *Phrygian Gates* (NAWM 149)? How
    does he vary the material?

35. In Adams's terminology, what is a "gate"? Where do gates occur? What
    changes at each one? And how do they relate to the work's title?

36. What is *minimalism*? In what sense is this work minimalist? In what sense is it
    complex?

37. How can you follow this music? In your opinion, what should you listen for?

38. What does *Phrygian Gates* have in common with a piece by Beethoven (such as NAWM 101, 103, or 104) or any other nineteenth-century composer, and what is different?

39. How does Ellen Taaffe Zwilich evoke the sounds and procedures of Baroque music in the last two movements of her *Concerto Grosso 1985* (NAWM 150)?

40. What other means does Zwilich use to create a piece that is immediately accessible to a listener, yet fresh and individual?

Postlude (CHWM 578)

41. How have the four characteristics that have defined Western music since the Middle Ages (composition, notation, principles of order, and polyphony) been challenged or changed since the beginning of the twentieth century?

TERMS TO KNOW

Terms Related to American Music before 1900 and to Vernacular Music

fuging tunes
spirituals
wind band, brass band
ragtime
rag
blues
blue notes
jazz
big band
rhythm section

chart
swing
bebop (bop)
country music (country-and-western music)
rhythm-and-blues
rock (rock-and-roll)
Broadway musical (musical comedy)

Terms Related to Twentieth-Century American Art Music

tone clusters
sound masses
metric modulation
third stream

indeterminacy
chance
minimalism
post-modernism

NAMES TO KNOW

Names Related to American Music before 1900 and to Vernacular Music

William Billings
Lowell Mason
Fisk Jubilee Singers
John Philip Sousa
Scott Joplin
Maple Leaf Rag

King Oliver's Creole Jazz Band
Elvis Presley
The Beatles
George Gershwin
Rhapsody in Blue
Porgy and Bess

Names Related to American Art Music 1900–1945

Amy Cheney Beach
Charles Ives
Carl Ruggles
Sun-Treader
Henry Cowell
Ruth Crawford Seeger
Intégrales
Aaron Copland

Appalachian Spring
Roy Harris
Virgil Thomson
Four Saints in Three Acts
The Mother of Us All
William Grant Still
Afro-American Symphony
Florence Price

Names Related to American Art Music Since 1945

Roger Sessions
Elliott Carter
Milton Babbitt
Conlon Nancarrow
Harry Partch
Ben Johnston
George Crumb
Black Angels
Philomel
Jacob Druckman
Gunther Schuller
Anthony Davis
X: The Life and Times of Malcolm X
John Cage

4'33"
Music of Changes
Steve Reich
Violin Phase
Philip Glass
John Adams
Samuel Barber
Ned Rorem
Gian Carlo Menotti
Joan Tower
Ellen Taaffe Zwilich
Concerto Grosso 1985
George Rochberg
Nach Bach
David Del Tredici

REVIEW QUESTIONS

1. Add the composers and major works discussed in this chapter to the time-line you made for the twentieth century in Chapter 19, or to the earlier time-lines you made for Chapters 13 and 16, as appropriate.

2. Summarize the eighteenth- and nineteenth-century historical background for music in the United States.

3. What were the major forms of popular music in the United States between the 1890s and the 1960s? Describe each kind, and explain how each relates to the others in historical succession.

4. Trace the course of American art music in the first half of the twentieth century, naming the most important composers and describing their music.

5. What are some of the main trends in American art music since World War II? Define each trend, and describe at least one composer and piece associated with each.

6. Write a brief essay in which you defend or reject the position Milton Babbitt articulates in his statement on p. 564 of CHWM. Whichever position you take, use examples from at least two twentieth-century works in NAWM to support your point of view about the relationship between a composer and his or her listeners.

7. Of the eight pieces in NAWM composed since 1950 (NAWM 132, 139, and 145–50), which one or two do you like the best? Which one or two do you like the least? Write an essay in which you explain what is especially good about the piece(s) you like and what is unappealing about the piece(s) you like less, as if you were writing a review or trying to persuade a friend about which CD to purchase. Explain what it is you find most valuable in music and how your judgments are based on those values.